Sudan

THE BRADT TRAVEL GUIDE

D1337403

PUBLISHER'S FOREWORD

The first Bradt travel guide was written in 1974 by George and Hilary Bradt on a river barge floating down a tributary of the Amazon, and was followed by *Backpacker's Africa* in 1977. In the 1980s and '90s the focus shifted away from hiking to broader-based guides covering new destinations – usually the first to be published on those places. In the 21st century Bradt continues to publish these ground-breaking guides, along with guides to established holiday destinations, incorporating in-depth information on culture and natural history alongside the nuts and bolts of where to stay and what to see.

*

The manuscript for this book arrived when Sudan was headline news every day and we were anguishing about whether we were right to publish a guide to a country whose government seemed unable or unwilling to stop an attempted genocide. But the first paragraph of Paul's introduction swept me back to 1976, when I too crossed the Ethiopian border into Sudan. I can remember it so vividly; we had had a tough time in Ethiopia – arrested at dawn and given 24 hours to leave the country, hassled by slogan-chanting kids, bitten by fleas – so our guard was up when we entered this new country. Our first impression was of cleanliness. The simple village of Gallabat at the border was spotless, and the coal-black men were dressed in dazzling white robes. When one of these dignified gentlemen approached us to ask if we needed help, we were cautious. Offers of help rarely came without strings attached.

We wrote in *Backpacker's Africa*, published in 1977: 'The Sudanese are mysterious, beautiful and hospitable. Anyone asking directions in the Sudan evokes their traditional laws of hospitality, which means a cup of tea or a cooling drink, at the very least. They'll really bend over backwards to see that you're looked after. If they can't answer your questions they'll find someone who can, and their helpfulness is entirely without expectation of reward. We certainly never saw the like of it anywhere else on the continent.' How wonderful to read Paul's comment: 'Indeed, it's not uncommon for trans-Africa travellers to commend Sudan as their favourite country in the whole continent.' So it hasn't changed!

Hilary Bradt

23 High Street, Chalfont St Peter, Bucks SL9 9QE, England
Tel: 01753 893444   Fax: 01753 892333
Email: info@bradtguides.com   www.bradtguides.com

Sudan

THE BRADT TRAVEL GUIDE

Paul Clammer

Bradt Travel Guides Ltd, UK

The Globe Pequot Press Inc, USA

First published February 2005
Reprinted August 2005

Bradt Travel Guides Ltd
23 High Street, Chalfont St Peter, Bucks SL9 9QE, England
Published in the USA by The Globe Pequot Press Inc,
246 Goose Lane, PO Box 480, Guilford, Connecticut 06437-0480

British Library Cataloguing in Publication Data
A catalogue record for this book is available from the British Library

ISBN-10: 1 84162 114 5
ISBN-13: 978 1 84162 114 2

Photographs
Cover Mariantonietta Peru (A Beja tribesman in the Red Sea Hills, eastern Sudan)
Text Paul Clammer (PC), Mariantonietta Peru (MP)

Illustrations Carole Vincer, Annabel Milne
Maps Matt Honour

Typeset from the author's disc by Wakewing, High Wycombe
Printed and bound in Italy by Legoprint SpA, Trento

Author

Paul Clammer is a freelance travel writer. He has travelled widely throughout the Islamic world, and worked as a trekking and tour guide in Morocco, Turkey and Pakistan. He first visited Sudan while following the Nile from its source in Ethiopia to the sea, and immediately fell in love with the country and the hospitality of its people. Paul also runs www.kabulcaravan.com, a website dedicated to independent travel in Afghanistan. He currently lives in Wiltshire, England.

Contents

Acknowledgements

No guidebook was ever written by just one person alone, so it's a pleasure to be able to thank those who made producing this book easier than it would otherwise have been.

First, thanks must go to Tricia Hayne at Bradt, whose throwaway remark that it would be good to have a guide to Sudan brought this project into being. Her support has been invaluable in helping to put this book in your hands. Large thanks should also go to Maurizio Levi of the Italian Tourism Company.

In Sudan, my biggest thanks go to Waleed Arafat for his friendship and help in a dozen ways, from helping ferret out embassy phone numbers to his comic asides on how just about every major figure in history was actually Nubian. *Shukran*, Waleed. Thanks also to Midhat Mahir for his hospitality and boundless energy. Saleh Omar Sadiq at the National Museum kindly helped arrange archaeological permits (thanks also to Abdur Rahman Ali). In Karima, Maura Castagno was a gracious host on New Year's Eve and Paulo Campodell'Orto kindly let me tag along on a trip to the Fourth Cataract. Bruce Wannell was equally generous with his time and provided an introduction to the Traditional Music Archive. Roger Dean was enlightening on gum arabic. In Port Sudan, thanks to Steve Coverdale of Emperor Divers for the background on scuba diving. Helpful travellers included Peter Bennett, Peter Strong, Andrew Shawyer, Anke Röhl, Maddy Leslie and Willemien Den Oudsten. Georg Shmelz was ever helpful with book lists. Simon Boa should be mentioned as a fine travelling companion on my first trip to Sudan.

Particular thanks must also go to Derek Welsby of the British Museum, who answered many questions on Kushite history – any mistakes are entirely my own. Suleiman Musa Rahhal of Nuba Vision and Nanne op t'Ende provided similar insights into Nuba culture.

The book has benefited from several fine contributions from others: thanks to Natalie McComb for her piece on rafting through South Sudan, Ulli Rubasch who wrote about motorbikes, and Rob Cassibo for his bicycle piece. Thanks also to David Else for his information on Jebel Marra – when I signed up I hadn't realised that David had written Bradt's *No Frills Guide to Sudan* back in 1984! Thanks also to Philip Marsden for kind permission to reprint an extract from his travel story *The Nubian Desert*.

Finally, thanks and love to Jo for her support in too many ways to mention and apologies for being away over Christmas – sleeping in a generator shed somewhere between Wadi Halfa and Abri on Christmas Eve definitely felt like second best!

Introduction

On my first trip to Sudan I was having trouble with money. I'd just arrived overland from Ethiopia and was still learning the currency. Taking a minibus into the centre of Khartoum I couldn't find out how much the fare was. The Sudanese have a peculiar habit of referring to their dinars as pounds, and dropping or adding zeroes to a sum with reckless abandon. Was the fare 25, 250 or 2,500? I couldn't figure it out. I was still struggling when we arrived at my stop, only for someone to lean forward and tell me in impeccable English, 'Do not worry. I have paid your fare for you.'

My benefactor was a tall Dinka man called Simon. Insisting he couldn't take my money, that I was a guest, he volunteered to help me find my hotel. It had been recommended by another traveller and proved a devil to track down. It wasn't even signed in English. After half an hour in which Simon asked half of Khartoum for directions, we finally made it. While I checked in I asked Simon if we could go to a café, so I could buy him a drink for his generosity. Suddenly he became shy and insisted he had things to do, so he took his leave. Welcome to Sudan.

Many visitors recount similar experiences. Long hidden from the world and better known for civil war, famine and its radical Islamic government, Sudan presents a much warmer face to those who make a trip there. On top of the gracious welcome, Sudan is a culturally rich country. Over a hundred languages are spoken by dozens of different tribes, from the Nubians along the Nile and the nomadic Beja of the east to the Nuba from the centre of the country and the proud Nuer and Shilluk from the south. Sudan is as diverse as Africa itself.

For many people, Sudan's history is best known for the story of Gordon of Khartoum, who was overwhelmed by the hordes of the Mahdi. Less often told is the story of Sudan's ancient past. The Kingdom of Kush dealt with the pharaohs of Egypt and emperors of Rome as an independent power and left behind an array of archaeological sites to reward the modern visitor. Ruined temples can be visited without a tourist bus for miles and the country has more pyramids than Egypt.

The lack of a guidebook to Sudan has long been frustrating. Many travellers who are in Sudan are there as part of a larger trip across Africa, and the overwhelming impression they have of the country before arriving is that of a big sandy place to be transited as quickly as possible, en route to the better-known attractions of Egypt or Ethiopia. At best, people might know a little about some pyramids north of Khartoum but that's about it. The magic of

Sudan is that once they arrive they are immediately taken in by its easy going nature and the welcome they receive from the Sudanese people. Indeed, it's not uncommon for trans-Africa travellers to commend Sudan as their favourite country in the whole continent.

This has been both an exciting and frustrating time to produce a guidebook to Sudan. There is cause for genuine optimism concerning the peace process between the government and SPLM/A rebels in the South. Many Southerners I met on my research trip would tell me of their plans to return home and their prospects for the future, even thrusting a copy of one of the peace protocols into my hand on one bus trip so I could understand their feelings. The South is on the brink of a momentous change and that can only be a good thing for Sudan.

And yet, on the verge of a historic settlement in the South, the Sudanese government suddenly seems set on blowing the peace elsewhere. Dark clouds are forming in the west of the country, as a nascent rebellion in Darfur looks set to turn into the worst ethnic cleansing that Africa has seen since Rwanda. Each day as I was writing this guide, the news from Darfur seemed to get worse, and as the book went to press a successful resolution to the Darfur crisis had still to be reached.

Sudan is known for its bureaucracy, but visas are becoming easier to obtain, and once you're there, the abolishing of travel permits for North Sudan – the area of most interest to first-time visitors – has simplified travelling considerably. The riches of the ancient Kingdom of Kush are becoming better known, as are the marine wonders along the Red Sea. The travelling can sometimes be a bit rugged but the rewards are immense. I hope that you will be as taken with Sudan as I have been.

FEEDBACK REQUEST

At Bradt Travel Guides, we're well aware that a guidebook starts to go out of date on the day it is published – and that you, our readers, are out there in the field doing research of your own. You'll find out before us when a fine new family-run hotel opens or a favourite restaurant changes hands and goes down hill. Why not tell us about your experiences so that we can ensure forthcoming editions are as accurate as possible? We'll be sure to reply personally. You can write to us at Bradt Travel Guides, 23 High St, Chalfont St Peter, Bucks SL9 9QE or send us an email to info@bradtguides.com.

Part One

General Information

SUDAN AT A GLANCE

Name Republic of Sudan

Location Northeastern Africa, facing the Red Sea. Borders with Egypt, Eritrea, Ethiopia, Kenya, Uganda, Democratic Republic of Congo, Central African Republic, Chad and Libya

Size 2,505,810km^2

Climate North: arid desert and *sahel* (semi-arid grassland), rains from July to September. South: tropical, rains from April to November.

Time GMT +2

International telephone code +249

Currency Sudanese Dinar (SD). US$1 = 260SD (approx)

Electricity 220V (50 cycles AC), round two-pin plugs

Population 38 million (2003 estimate)

Population growth per year 2.7%

Capital Khartoum

Language Arabic (official), Dinka and other local languages, English

Religion Islam (70%), traditional religions (20%), Christianity (5%)

Ethnic Groups Arab (39%), Black (52%, including Dinka, Nuer, Shilluk and Azande), Beja (6%), Nubian (3%).

Flag Three horizontal bands of red, white and black, faced with a green triangle.

Economy Oil, agriculture (cotton, sugar, sorghum, millet and sesame), livestock (sheep and camels), gum arabic

The Land and its People

INTRODUCTION

Sudan is vast. The largest country in Africa, it covers 8% of the continent's surface. The Sudanese often describe their country as the whole of Africa in one country. It's easy to understand why – Sudan ranges from desert in the north to tropical forest in the south, the whole bisected by one of the greatest rivers in the world. It has – or had – a range of wildlife to rival East Africa. Sudan is also one of the most ethnically diverse countries in Africa, with nearly twenty major tribes and five times that many languages spoken. Straddling the fault line between the Islamic world and sub-Saharan Africa – the Arabs called the country *bilad as-sudan*, or 'land of the blacks' – it is superlative in every sense.

CLIMATE

Sudan is a tropical country with a climate divided roughly into a rainy and dry season, although given its size, the temperature and amount of rainfall depend greatly on location. The country becomes increasingly dry proceeding north. Since the country is largely flat, with no major mountain ranges to break up weather patterns, the seasons are governed by two prevailing winds – dry northeasterly winds from the Arabian Peninsula and wet southwesterly winds from the Congo Basin.

For the first three months of the year, the Arabian winds predominate, cooling the north. In April the weather system from the Congo moves into Sudan. This carries a phenomenal amount of rain, which moves north in a wide band. Its arrival in Khartoum in July is presaged by the *haboub*, summer afternoon dust storms that can cut visibility to zero. The rains persist in Khartoum until September, but only reach as far north as Atbara until August, which receives only a few short showers. Regions beyond this are continually arid. In contrast, the far south of Sudan receives rain for up to nine months of the year – the closer to the equator, the longer the wet season.

Countrywide, temperatures average around 30°C throughout the year but rise and fall with the rains. Khartoum is at its hottest at the onset of the rains in July, with temperatures reaching 45°C or higher. Temperatures can exceed this in Port Sudan, with summer heat of over 50°C not unknown – the same applies to the far desert north. Winter temperatures drop considerably. Daytime temperatures in December fluctuate around 30°C, with nights quite cool. Wadi Halfa, near the Egyptian border, and Darfur usually have night-

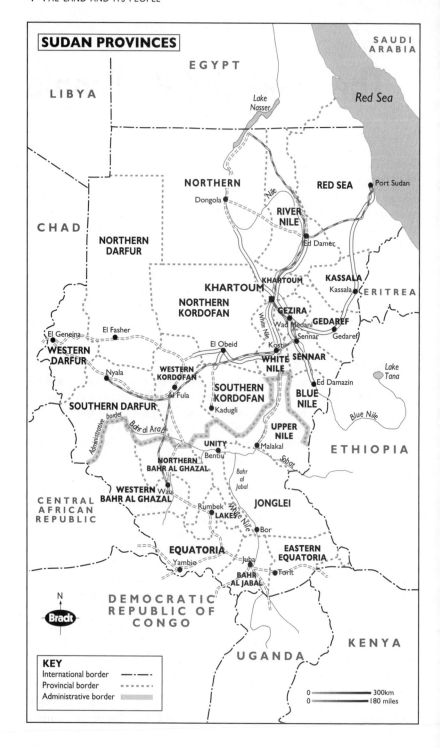

time temperatures in single figures at this time. South Sudan is more consistently hot throughout the year.

GEOGRAPHY

Sudan is divided into four main geographical regions, roughly corresponding to the cardinal points.

The north is desert, a mix of sand and gravel stretching out either side of the Nile that receives little or no rainfall. In the west is the Libyan Desert, part of the Sahara proper. To the east is the Nubian Desert, the most barren land in the country and entirely devoid of oases.

West Sudan is semi-desert, with rolling sand dunes and light grassland that rise to the highlands of Darfur. There are no permanent rivers, only seasonal watercourses that spring into life with the summer rains.

East Sudan is dry grassland, ideal for supporting large numbers of pastoral nomads. The Gash Delta near Kassala acts as a seasonal drain for the region and produces rich grazing. The Red Sea Hills separate the coastal plain from the rest of Sudan; the rising Ethiopian plateau naturally demarcates the eastern border.

South Sudan is made up of a huge clay plain that extends into the centre of the country, with Khartoum at its apex. The White Nile crosses this, getting lost in the slow waters of the Sudd swamp. Heading upstream, the land rises into the Ironstone Plateau and the Nile-Congo watershed that forms the country's southern borders.

In the main, Sudan is as flat as it is large, but there are some notable mountainous areas. The highest peak in the country is Mt Kinyeti (3,187m) in the Immatong Mountains that rise in the far southeast along the Ugandan border and that are covered with lush tropical forest. In the west is the Marra Plateau in Darfur, a broad area above the plains averaging 900m above sea level but reaching 2,600m around the collapsed volcanic crater of Jebel Marra. The area's height results in a Mediterranean climate that's ideal for farming. The Red Sea Hills are a barren spine of low mountains cutting the coastal plain off from the rest of Sudan; lifestyles here are necessarily marginal. Finally, there are two large areas where isolated hills rise unexpectedly from the plains: the bare granite Taka Mountains around Kassala, and the more fertile Nuba Mountains in southern Kordofan.

The Nile

Sudan's dominant geographical feature is the Nile. In the words of one history of the country, 'it is the great melody that recurs throughout the whole opera.' The Nile in Sudan is two rivers, the White and the Blue Niles, which meet at Khartoum before making slow progress north to the sea. Travellers in North Sudan will spend much of their time following the river and the narrow strip of fertile land on either bank that holds back the desert.

Over 80% of the Nile's water is provided by the Blue Nile, which rises near Lake Tana in the Ethiopian Highlands. The level of the river fluctuates with the season, reaching its rushing height in July and August. The Blue Nile is dark with rich alluvial silt – the fertile earth that allowed ancient Egypt to grow and prosper.

During the winter, the Blue Nile's volume decreases considerably and the flow of the river is maintained by the slower waters of the White Nile. The ultimate source of the White Nile was a mystery for centuries. The matter wasn't settled until the 1860s when a series of expeditions by John Hanning Speke, James Grant and later Henry Morton Stanley fully explored Africa's Great Lakes Region. The rains that fall on the Mountains of the Moon and drain Uganda, Rwanda and Burundi into Lake Victoria provide the waters of the White Nile. The river traverses Uganda before entering Sudan at Nimule, where it is known as the Bahr al-Jabal.

The reason for the problems in tracing the source of Nile becomes apparent as the river flows north. It soon enters the Sudd, a labyrinth of waterways and papyrus that make up a swamp the size of Belgium. The name means 'barrier' in Arabic, and it proved so formidable that explorers searching for the source chose to start their journeys in Zanzibar and cross East Africa rather than tackle the swamp. 'The fabulous Styx must be a sweet rippling brook compared to this horrible creation,' despaired Samuel Baker, the governor general of Equatoria in the 1870s.

The White Nile loses over half of its waters to evaporation in the Sudd, but is replenished by the Sobat River from western Ethiopia as it nears Malakal. After this, the Nile only receives one more tributary, the seasonal Atbara River to the north of Khartoum, before turning south in a great loop and finally flowing north into Egypt.

The Nile has been dammed in several places. Egypt's Aswan High Dam is the most famous, but Sudan has also built several dams. The Roseires Dam on the Blue Nile provides most of the country's electricity, supplemented by a dam at Jebel Aulia on the White Nile just south of the capital. A huge new dam at Merowe near the Fourth Cataract is currently being constructed to meet Sudan's energy needs, but will displace thousands of families living along the river.

WILDLIFE

The visitor of a hundred years ago would have been astounded by the variety of Sudan's wildlife. The great plains of the South rivalled anything that East Africa had to offer: huge herds of elephant, white rhino, lion, cheetahs and a profusion of antelope species. West Sudan, wetter than it is now, supported giraffe, addax and oryx and pastoral tribes everywhere defended their herds against lions. In the eastern hills, Nubian ibex and barbary sheep were plentiful. The situation today is rather different. Changing weather patterns have led to the almost total loss of game in the west, with the remainder of the trophy antelope wiped out by hunting. Sudan's national parks have been despoiled by war. Only in the deep swamps of the Sudd is wildlife still flourishing: the white-eared kob and Nile lechwe survive in vast numbers (possibly up to a million animals in the case of the former). The true extent of Sudan's surviving wildlife populations remains unknown.

THE JONGLEI CANAL

Most modern maps of Sudan show a man-made waterway cutting a diversion through the White Nile between Malakal and Bor, but the Jonglei Canal currently only exists on paper.

A canal through southern Sudan was first mooted by the British in 1901, who wanted to harness the waters of the Nile lost to evaporation in the great marshes of the Sudd, and increase irrigation projects in northern Sudan and Egypt. The project didn't get under way until 70 years later, when it was resurrected as part of Nimeiri's 'Breadbasket' scheme. A 360km canal was planned that would take 25 million cubic metres of upper Nile water per day for downstream use, and that would be excavated with the biggest mechanical digger in the world.

There was no consultation with the local population, and little analysis done on the environmental impact of diverting such quantities of water away from one the world's largest wetlands. Whilst it was claimed that the canal would allow the introduction of mechanised agriculture, pilot projects were quickly shelved. Instead, it was clear that the canal would severely disrupt the nomadic pastoralism of groups such as the Dinka, with the loss of their dry-season pasture, and would create a physical barrier to the free movement of livestock and wildlife. Southern groups protested that the canal was another example of the North exploiting the South's resources without compensation.

When civil war broke out again in 1983, work on the Jonglei Canal, by then three-quarters complete, was shelved. The huge digger was blown up by the SPLA a year later. The abandoned canal trench has had 20 years to be reclaimed by the earth; it is unclear whether future governments will want to attempt its resurrection.

National parks

Sudan has four national parks – Dinder, Nimule, Southern and Sanganeb Marine Park – along with around a dozen game reserves. Sanganeb, a recent creation, is in a good position to be managed well and receive sustained tourism. The others paint a less optimistic picture. Even government tourist information seems more concerned with the prospects of hunting wildlife rather than observing it. A recent report produced by the United Nations Environment Programme makes for depressing reading.

Nimule National Park is on the Ugandan border, a mix of woodland and open savannah. Its population of northern white rhino was poached to extinction after independence during the first civil war. The last wildlife survey here was carried out in 1987 and recorded around 1,000 elephants as well as healthy populations of hippo, Ugandan kob, waterbuck, warthog and grey duiker, along with vervet monkeys and baboons. Bird species included the crowned crane, fish eagle, secretary bird, kori bustard and many smaller species.

DINDER NATIONAL PARK

Sudan's largest national park, Dinder, runs the length of the Sudan–Ethiopia border, from Gallabat to the Roseires Dam, an area of over 10,000km². Years of neglect and civil war have left it in a very sorry state.

Dinder is a mix of savannah and acacia forest, criss-crossed by the Rahad and Dinder rivers. The rainy season causes floods from June to October, leaving behind large waterholes called *mayas* that attract wildlife.

Dinder used to have a thriving large mammal population. No survey has been undertaken to reveal the current state of the wildlife. The most populous large mammal is probably the common baboon. Spotted hyenas are still found in some numbers, and it is possible that there may be remnant populations of lion and leopard. Antelope are represented mainly by bushbuck, reedbuck and waterbuck. Sommering's gazelle are probably extinct in Dinder, and the population of tiang is on the verge. Giraffes were last seen in the park in 1985, but the elephant and black rhino are long gone.

Bird watchers have a better time of it in Dinder. The rivers and *mayas* have good birdlife, including several species of egret, heron and ibis, yellow-billed and marabou storks, white pelicans, and many geese and ducks.

Since 1989 park forces (run from Juba) have been unable to visit the park, which is now controlled by the SPLA. Animals are regularly poached outside the park boundaries, including elephants which villagers target for damaging crops. The fact that SPLA troops have been heavily implicated in ivory poaching in nearby Garamba National Park in the Democratic Republic of Congo does not augur well for the wildlife remaining inside the park. Conservation efforts have been virtually non-existent and it is hoped that the peace process may bring about some protection for whatever wildlife remains, although even UNEP suggest there is 'little future' for many of Nimule's large mammal species.

THE PEOPLE

There are 19 major ethnic groups in Sudan, divided into over 500 subgroups and speaking over a hundred languages. Understanding the many ethnic groups is key to understanding Sudan, and close examination gives the lie to the commonly held image of a country neatly divided into Arab (or Muslim) and Black (non-Muslim) halves in the north and south. Sudan's official language and lingua franca is Arabic. The peace deal with the SPLM/A may lead to recognition of English as a second official language, which is traditionally the language of government in the South. The most widely spoken local languages are Dinka, Beja and Nubian.

Arabs

Around 40% of the population identify themselves as Arab and speak Arabic as their mother tongue. Although the term Arab refers to tribes descended from a common ancestor, the label is as much cultural as it is lineal.

The main pressure on Dinder has been from the movement of people displaced by the civil war. Land has been cleared on both sides of the park boundary for cultivation, with trees being felled for fuel and to harvest wild honey. The abundance of small arms has resulted in poaching on a huge scale.

A programme led by the United Nations Development Programme (UNDP) and the Sudanese Environmental Conservation Society (SECS) is trying to rectify the situation. The park infrastructure, in a state of collapse, is now slowly being rebuilt. A permanent camp for the park service has been built and will eventually provide as accommodation for tourists. The lack of good roads makes 4WD vehicles useless in the rainy season, so staff get around mainly by tractor or camel, making patrols difficult.

Attempts are also being made to encourage locals to make sustainable use of the park's resources rather than to wantonly exploit them. To this end, tree nurseries for firewood have been started, some fishing is now permitted and beekeeping projects have been funded. Education programmes raise awareness and also help to increase literacy.

There are currently no tourist facilities in Dinder.

There are two main Arab tribes in Sudan, the Jaalayin and Juhayna, who can roughly be categorised as sedentary and nomadic respectively. The Jaalayin are agriculturalists mainly living along the Nile, from Dongola to south of Khartoum. The Juhayna have two major divisions: the Kabbabish are camel herders in the west, while the Baggara Arabs are found mainly in southern Kordofan and Darfur, raising cattle along the borders with the non-Muslim areas of southern Sudan.

The mixing of nationalities and tribes in Sudan has left the physical definition of Arab loose in the extreme. Pale-skinned Arabs, such as those from the Gulf or Levant, are extremely rare, and most Sudanese Arabs are very dark and often have distinctly African features. A few Arab lineages in Sudan can claim to be *ashraf* – descendants of the Prophet Mohammed.

Beja

The second largest Muslim group are the Beja, semi-nomads who live along the Red Sea coast and from Kassala to the Atbara River. An ancient people known to the Romans, the Beja adopted Islam early. Although they're traditionally herders of camels and sheep, drought has led many to settle and take up agriculture, but they are still as proud and independent as their ancestors, and suspicious of most forms of government. Famed warriors, the Beja have fought everyone from the Kushites to the British.

Nubians

The Nubians are the third most populous Muslim people in Sudan. They live along the Nile, around the Third Cataract and up into southern Egypt. They have their own language and a strong cultural identity dating back to their pre-Islamic Christian and Kushite heritage. Nubian culture was heavily disrupted by the construction of the Aswan Dam in the 1960s and the flooding of much of their homeland. Thousands of Nubians were resettled on the Atbara River near Kassala, and today there are as many Nubians living in Khartoum as in Nubia itself.

Other Muslim peoples

The Fellata are descended from West African migrants, mostly Hausa and Fulani who travelled through the country en route to Mecca and were encouraged to settle and farm in Sudan. This migration was particularly encouraged during the Condominium to expand Sudan's agricultural sector. Around a million Fellata live in Sudan, with many settled in the rich agricultural areas of Gezira.

In Darfur, the dominant ethnic groups are the Fur and Masalit, both tribes black African farmers. The Fur are the old rulers of Darfur's sultanate and were known for their skill with horses. The Masalit are also found across the border in Chad. Both have been the target of the great upheavals wracking Darfur since 2003.

Dinka

The Dinka are the largest non-Arab ethnic group in Sudan, with Dinka being spoken as a first language by around a tenth of the population. They are Nilotic pastoralists who live on either side of the White Nile and across Bahr al-Ghazal. Cattle are central to Dinka culture, with each man identifying with and adorning his prize ox. Cattle are also sacrificed in Dinka religious ceremonies. Traditional Dinka culture follows the flooding and receding of Nile waters and the creation of pasture, with family groups living in seasonal homesteads. The Dinka dominate the SPLM/A rebel movement.

Nuer

The pastoralist Nuer are the traditional rivals of the Dinka. They're spread across the Upper Nile region and share much of the same lifestyle. Cows, for example, are similarly esteemed in Nuer culture. The reason for the old enmity between the two peoples is their shared creation myth. God had two sons, Nuer and Dinka. God promised the Dinka son his old cow, and gave his young calf to the Nuer son. One night, the Dinka son imitated the Nuer's voice and tricked God into giving him the young calf. On discovering the deceit, God told his Nuer son to avenge him and raid the Dinka's cattle forever more.

Shilluk

Another Nilotic group, the Shilluk, live around the western bank of the White Nile north of the Sobat River. They're primarily farmers and fishermen. This sedentary lifestyle has led to permanent settlements and a centralised political economy far removed from the loose tribal structures of the Dinka and Nuer.

A king, or *reth*, acts as the representative of the tribe's semi-mythical founder, Nyikang, and still wields considerable political influence.

Equatorians

The Azande, living in the southern quarter of the country, are the largest Equatorian tribe in Sudan. Their language belongs to the Niger-Congo family. They are an agricultural hierarchical society headed by a king. They were the first people to take advantage of British education policies, and were early supporters of the Anyanya rebels in the first civil war.

Smaller Equatorian tribes include the Bari and Mandari, who live around Juba.

Nuba

More than any other ethnic group, the Nuba illustrate the dichotomy between North and South Sudan, and Muslim/non-Muslim identities. They occupy the rich farming land in the Nuba Mountains of South Kordofan, straddling the divide between North and South Sudan. The Nuba are best known for their great love of wrestling and sorghum beer. Many Nuba are Muslim, while others are Christian or follow traditional beliefs.

RELIGION
Islam

Sudan is around 70% Muslim, with its adherents following the Sunni tradition. Islam first arrived in Sudan with the Arabs as part of their great expansion following the death of the Prophet Mohammed in the 7th century AD. Its advance was checked by the powerful Christian states of Nubia, and it took a further 600 years and the decline of Christianity for the religion to start spreading across the rest of the country. Islamisation was a slow process as the Arabs initially kept to their own nomadic traditions, instead of creating new political structures as they took control of the land. Rather, individual holy men or *faqis* took Islam away from the Nile to Gezira and the west of the country.

The rise of the Funj Kingdom at the start of the 16th century paved the way for the great spread of Islam across Sudan. The Funj were Muslim rulers, and the stability they brought attracted missionaries from the great centres of Cairo, Baghdad and Fes. These missionaries were full of the new ideas sweeping Islam at the time, particularly the new Sufi orders.

Sufism was to play, and continues to play, an important role in Sudan. Central to Sufism is the idea of a mystical path to reach God that's completely separate from the orthodox Muslim prayer ritual. Sufis divide themselves into orders or brotherhoods (*tariqa*) headed by a charismatic leader or *sheikh*. The commonest *tariqa* in Sudan is the Qadiriyah, founded in Baghdad in the 12th century and introduced to Sudan during the Funj period. The famous 'Whirling Dervishes' of Omdurman follow the Qadiriyah *tariqa*. Other *tariqa* include the Samaniyah and Tijaniyah.

Orthodox Islam has always looked askance at Sufism, even going so far as to proclaim its practices heretical. Sufis counter this by saying that they accept

SUDANESE MUSIC

Hole-in-the-wall shops selling the latest music cassettes are everywhere in Sudan's large towns. Much popular music you'll hear is influenced by Egyptian pop – heavy on string and synthesizers and overblown vocal performances in Arabic.

Sudan's own musical heritage is slightly different. It's overwhelmingly based on the pentatonic scale, making it more accessible to Western ears than a lot of Arabic music. Sudanese musicians have readily adopted saxophones, keyboards and electric guitars, leading to the 'jazz boom' of the 1960s and 70s. The al-aghani al-hadith (literally 'modern songs') fuse the best of traditional call-and-response chanting styles with Western and Arabic elements. Two of the best-known modern Sudanese artists are Abdel Gadir Salim (from the Nuba Moutains) and Abdel Aziz el-Mubarak (from Wad Medani) – both are worth checking out for their big-band styles. Nubian music is also particularly lively – exiled Mohammed Wardi is its most acclaimed performer. Straddling the country's northern border, the music of Egyptian Nubians, such as that played by Ali Hassan Kuban in Cairo, is also popular.

Traditional Sudanese music is hard to find, as it tends to be crowded out in music shops by more modern forms. The Traditional Music Archive at the University of Khartoum documents and records Sudan's ethnomusical heritage, runs a library of archived recordings and occasionally puts on live performances. Its sample video of local music is a mind-boggling panorama of Sudan's cultural diversity. Tapes of traditional music from across Sudan are for sale and the Archive is planning a series of CD releases in conjunction with the Smithsonian Institution. Part of the continent-wide Africa Culture Network based in Cape Town, the Traditional Music Archive can be found at the Institute of African and Asian Studies in the University of Khartoum (Sharia al-Jama'a; tel: 011 775820; fax 011 780295).

Sharia (the religious law set down in the Koran) as the basis for their beliefs, and that tariqa is a path that connects Sharia with Haqiqa, or the truth of God himself. Sufis also pray in the traditional Muslim manner.

An important indigenous Sudanese tariqa is the Khatmiyah, founded in the early 19th century in eastern Sudan. The Khatmiyah supported the Turco-Egyptians in the face of the rise of the Mahdi and later played a key role in the independence movement. They remain a potent political force today in the form of the Democratic Unionist Party.

The Mahdist movement found a radically different form of political expression through Islam. The Mahdi, Mohammed Ahmed, proclaimed himself not as a political leader, but as a representative of the Prophet Mohammed sent in anticipation of Judgement Day. His followers, the Ansar, suppressed the many tariqa, declaring them (and anyone who did not follow the Mahdi) to be infidels, and urged a return to traditional Islamic values. The Mahdi's followers continue to influence the political scene in modern Sudan through the Umma Party.

For most Sudanese Muslims, the teachings of the Koran are supplemented with older beliefs regarding the power of spirits and saints. In many rural areas, a *faqi* acts not only as a leader of prayers but as a healer, making amulets that contains verses from the Koran to protect wearers against disease or the 'evil eye'. A *faqi* or the leader of a *tariqa* may reach something approaching the Western concept of sainthood on death: his tomb is regarded as a source of blessedness (*baraka*) and people may pray there, regarding him as an intercessor with God.

The popularity of Sufism and the traditions of folk Islam go some way to explaining the relaxed nature that most Sudanese have towards their religion, and provide a reason for why radical movements like the Muslim Brotherhood and, more recently, the National Islamic Front, have only found a restricted constituency throughout the country at large despite significant political successes.

ZAR SPIRIT POSSESSION

The *zar* cult, a mixture of religious ritual and folk medicine, is thought to have pre-Islamic origins and was brought to Sudan by slaves from the Ethiopian hinterland in the mid-19th century. It is practised almost exclusively by women. At the heart of *zar* is the concept of spirit possession – women undergo the ceremony to appease or banish certain troublesome spirits that may be haunting them. *Zar* can also be used as a form of divination, with women seeking advice in the same way as those in the West seek guidance from horoscopes.

Led by a *sheikha*, the women in attendance beat drums and chant, aiming to create a heightened atmosphere in which the possessed women can be questioned and the spirit appeased or banished. Abandoned dancing is common, as are the hysterical symptoms associated with the spiritual release of the possessed. The rituals of *zar* have also been heavily influenced by Sudan's Sufi traditions, with the ecstatic nature of the ceremony mirroring the trance-like *dhikr* of Sufism.

The women-only nature of the ritual has led some anthropologists to suggest that one purpose of *zar* is to create an exclusively female environment outside accepted cultural norms. Those attending *zar* frequently do so in the hope of solving problems of sexual relations or social status (there are no inherent class distinctions when it comes to participation in *zar*). The music and dancing that accompanies the ritual allows women to express themselves in an exhibitionist manner that falls far outside the norms expected of women in a traditional Islamic society.

SLAVERY IN SUDAN

The slave trade has played an important part in Sudanese history and has had a dramatic influence on relations between the north and south of the country. Since Pharaonic times, the centralised states along the Nile have enriched themselves through human traffic. During the Funj Kingdom, Shendi was an important channel for slaves heading to the markets of Cairo. The Fur Sultanate also sent slaves to Egypt along the Forty Days Road, while domestic economies relied heavily on captured labour.

The acquisition of slaves was a major motivating factor for Mohammed Ali's invasion. Slaving corridors were opened along the White Nile and through Bahr al-Ghazal, and the influx of modern weaponry had a terrible effect. Europeans got in on the act too, raiding for slaves to support the burgeoning ivory trade. The infamous slaver Zubeir Pasha carved out a private empire for himself in the southwest, becoming a major political player. Although Khartoum's slave market was closed in 1854 the trade continued to grow. In Arab eyes, the terms 'black' and 'slave' became interchangeable.

Abolitionist pressure led to attempts to suppress the trade in Sudan. Patrols on the Nile intercepted slave cargoes, but the majority of slaves were transported through the lawless open spaces of Kordofan and Darfur. General Gordon led attempts to clamp down on this when he was appointed governor general of Sudan in 1877, but a lack of resources meant he was doomed to failure. Even Gordon recognised the Sudanese economy was founded on slavery, which made an immediate and total suppression impossible. Those slaves he was able to free he was unable to repatriate, so many returned to forced labour.

During the Condominium, the British had to grapple with the same problem, realising that a shortage of labour meant that only a gradual phasing-out of domestic slavery was feasible. The Closed Districts Ordinance barring Arabs from the South effectively stopped the trade, but small-scale raids were still recorded into the 1920s.

Slavery today

Through the civil war, slavery has returned to modern Sudan. Again, the main area for slave raids has been Bahr al-Ghazal and its borders with Southern Kordofan and Darfur. This is the hinterland between the Dinka tribes and the Baggara Arabs who have historically competed for pasture for their herds. The two have always raided each other's cattle, occasionally taking hostages for ransom. These hostages would often be put to work while in captivity.

Following the outbreak of civil war in 1983, traditional conflict resolution mechanisms disappeared. The Baggara in Kordofan and Darfur lost much livestock to drought in the 1980s and sought to restock their herds by raiding their neighbours'. At the same time, the government started arming the Baggara to act as proxy militias in their war against the South. The free hand given to these *murahilin* encouraged more violent raids. As well as taking cattle, the Baggara abducted women and children to be put to use tending herds and working their households. The captives would be given Arab names and converted to Islam. Although the government itself did not participate in such slavery, it was content to turn a blind eye to the practice. The *murahilin* were a potent weapon of terror against the SPLM/A-supporting Dinka

During the famine of 1988, some impoverished Dinka families also 'sold' their children into slavery, aiming to buy them back at a later date (an old form of debt bondage in the region). Such practices encouraged many Sudanese to deny the existence of slavery. Where the abductee was assimilated into the family of their captor and converted, there was a common perception that that person then ceased to be a victim and was now wholly part of the family.

In 1999, the government established the Committee for the Eradication of Abduction of Women and Children (CEAWC), supported by UNICEF and Save the Children, which has had some success in freeing captives and creating safe corridors for their return home. The authorities have judiciously continued avoiding the word 'slavery', preferring 'abduction' and 'kidnapping'.

Slave redemption

While the civil war often remained ignored in the West, the issue of slavery has had a much higher profile, particularly among many Christian groups keen to see the war as a simple clash of Islam and Christianity. In 1995 several foreign organisations began to 'redeem' slaves in Bahr al-Ghazal. Dinka communities had already been making ad hoc efforts to retrieve captives, with the Dinka Committee having some success in freeing slaves through contacts with Baggara tribes. Outside groups like Christian Solidarity International started making their own contacts, paying up to US$50 a head to middlemen to free slaves.

Such policies have been highly controversial. Human Rights Watch and Anti-Slavery International (who have been campaigning against slavery in Sudan since the days of Gordon) have heavily criticised slave redemption. While freeing some individuals, redemption failed to tackle the roots of the problem, namely the war. At the same time, redeemers could be seen as being complicit in slavery, driving up the price and encouraging more abductions. Local resolutions, such as halting raids in exchange for access to pasture, were undercut.

Redemption also created new business opportunities. In 2002 it was discovered that in some cases, children being bought back were not even captives, but were being 'sold' to redeemers to make a quick profit. Even SPLA officers participated, acting as middlemen and inflating the price by getting local children to pose as slaves. Despite this, many foreign groups have continued to fund redemptions. Slavery continues to be a chronic problem in Sudan. The ceasefire and peace deal should bring an end to the raids, but repatriation and reconciliation may take years.

While Islam took hold in the north of Sudan from Darfur to the Red Sea, the south remained a barrier to the Arabs. The Sudd proved impenetrable, and it wasn't until the mid-19th century that Arab traders entered the region in any numbers, and even then they were more interested in slavery than proselytising. British policies during the Condominium explicitly prevented the spread of Islam into the South by restricting the movement of Arab and other northern traders in the region. Following independence these restraints were removed.

Islamisation is a major source of conflict between the North and South. Nimeiri's declaration of *sharia* across the south was the spark that re-lit the war in 1983; President Bashir later called for a *jihad* (holy struggle) against the Southern rebels. Elsewhere, the Nuba have found their lack of Muslim credentials has led to fertile agricultural land being confiscated and given to Arab farmers. In contemporary Sudan, Islam is as much a political issue as a religion.

Christianity

Byzantine missionaries brought Christianity to Sudan in the 5th century AD. The Christian kingdoms of Nubia prospered for 600 years before giving way to Islam. Modern Sudanese Christians, who make up 5% of the population, are the product of Western missionary enterprises starting in the mid-19th century.

The Sudanese first saw the return of Christianity through the promotion of many Europeans to administrative positions during Turco-Egyptian rule. The presence of Christians in positions of power was frequently resented as an insult to Islam. The efforts of Samuel Baker and Charles Gordon to suppress slavery drew the most criticism and later gave encouragement to the Islamic revivalism of the Mahdi.

Under British rule, missionaries were encouraged to operate in southern Sudan. The South was divided into spheres of influence for the many Christian sects, who were allowed to open schools and churches. The missions had a larger impact on education than on rates of conversion to Christianity, but the sectarian divisions did little to help Southern integration on independence.

One of the most enduring of the Christian missions was the Catholic Verona Fathers, who first came to Sudan in 1854. Their head, Daniel Comboni, became the first Bishop of Central Africa. He died in Khartoum and was canonised 100 years later for his work. Missionaries were expelled from the South soon after independence.

Outwardly, Christianity appears to be in good health in Sudan. Churches are common and the Christian holy days are observed as public holidays (leading to the incongruous sight of Christmas trees and fake snow in the lobbies of upmarket Khartoum hotels). While ground-level relations between Christians and Muslims are generally good, the Islamic policies of successive governments tell a different story.

The Foreign Missionary Act passed in 1962 classified churches as foreign institutions rather than domestic ones, and has repeatedly been used to confiscate church land. Muslim converts to Christianity face the death penalty and priests and congregations alike are subject to harassment. The Sudanese Council of Churches and the Sudan Catholic Bishop's Conference have repeatedly spoken out against the discrimination of Christians, with both the Archbishop of Canterbury and the Pope making high-profile visits in the 1990s to raise these issues with the government. The status of Sudanese Christians has found resonance with evangelical lobbying groups in the USA and influenced the policies of the government there.

The greatest irony is that despite the Islamist policies of recent years conversions to Christianity have increased faster in this period than during nearly 60 years of British rule.

Traditional religions
A fifth of the Sudanese population subscribe to traditional African religions, overwhelmingly in the Nilotic south. These are often lumped together under the unhelpful umbrella of Animism, a term that says more about Western prejudices than any religious practices actually found in Sudan. Animism indicates a world view dominated by supernatural and primal spirits that order the world, and the worship of those spirits. In fact, while the South is religiously diverse, most ethnic groups have highly developed theistic beliefs.

While religions vary, there is an almost universal belief in a supreme creator or God. Concepts of an afterlife are less common; a more typical belief is that the world is divided into visible and invisible realms. The latter is populated by spirits, with those of ancestors often playing an important role in day-to-day life. Spirits are aspects of God and are used to explain the workings of the world rather than to directly alter it. The Nuer provide a good example of this.

The Nuer have no single word for the concept of God. The creator is often referred to as Kwoth, but this depends on the context in which he is addressed – ancestor (Gwandong), father (Gwara) or friend (Maadh). In the face of their creator, the Nuer consider themselves ants, and the bridge between the earth and the sky (where God is found) is too great to cross. Instead, God is manifested through spirits. Spirits of the sun, rain and of the Nuer's ancestors are particularly important – there is no belief in an afterlife. The Nuer use sacrifice as a central part of their relationship with God in rites of passage ceremonies and as appeasement for acts within the community. Cattle, being highly prized, are used in sacrifices. It should be stressed that sacrifices and prayers are made directly to God or the spirits he manifests himself as, since the Nuer do not believe in the inherent divinity of inanimate objects. God can also manifest himself through holy men, and prophets have played an important role in Nuer culture and history.

For the Dinka, the supreme creator is Jok, also a collective name for ancestral spirits. Among the Shilluk, the king (*reth*) is the direct representative of God.

 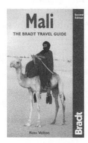  

History

The history of Sudan, the giant of Africa, is dominated by the interplay between its northern and southern halves. At different times the North, with its riverine culture along the Nile, has represented the interests of Pharaonic Egypt, the indigenous civilisation of Kush, and the Arab culture of Islam. The South, with its African heritage, has stood for the natural wealth of the continent, and has provided many of the resources that allowed the North to prosper. For centuries this North–South tension has provided the motor for cultural exchange, trade, exploitation and war – a fact that continues to overshadow the political scene in modern Sudan.

APPROACHES TO SUDANESE HISTORY
There is no good single-volume history of Sudan currently available. Part of the problem is that the history of Sudan has rarely been seen as a single narrative. The history of the Kushite kingdoms has long been overshadowed by the glories of Egypt's pharaohs and many treatments of this period have relegated Nubia merely to a colonial outpost of Egypt. In his 1920s tome *Cook's Handbook to Egypt and the Egyptian Sudan*, E A Wallis Budge, one of the fathers of modern Egyptology, seems to dismiss Kush as a degenerate form of Egyptian culture rather than having any intrinsic qualities of its own (reflecting the prejudices of the time, Sudanese history for him barely seems to start until the saintly Victorian figure of General Gordon is stabbed to death in Khartoum in 1885). The role of Christianity in early Sudan has also been largely overlooked.

Other histories have taken the arrival of Islam as the beginning of the Sudanese state. While understandable, this ignores the experience of the people of the South; it's almost as if they existed outside history until they were discovered by Arab traders, slavers and plucky European explorers. Sudanese politics has always tended to ignore the margins of the country, a fact reflected in the telling of its history. Unfortunately, this has often made it harder to untangle the complicated reality of the biggest problems afflicting Sudan since independence, namely the many civil wars that have raged almost continuously since 1956. The story of Sudan as told by a Dinka, Nuba or Fur would be very different from that told by an Arab in Khartoum.

Thankfully, this book is a travel guide and not a history textbook. I have attempted to create an accessible narrative for Sudan as a whole. Covering Sudan's post-independence history, the civil war and, more recently, the crisis in Darfur, has threatened to dominate this narrative completely, crowding out other important developments. To prevent this, the history presented below covers them as part of the wider Sudanese story; for more detailed information on the background and progress of these conflicts, you are directed to the relevant sections on South Sudan (*Chapter 14*) and Darfur (*Chapter 13*) later in the book.

ANCIENT SUDAN
Egypt and Kerma

Sudan's early history is tied to Egypt. The ancient Egyptians first knew Nubia – the land south of the First Cataract at Aswan – as Ta-Seti, or 'Land of the Bow', due to the fighting prowess of its inhabitants, and later christened it Kush, 'the wretched'. The pharaohs of the First Dynasty (around 2900–2500BC) led military expeditions into Nubia in search of slaves. Gold and copper were mined, and stone quarried and shipped north to Egypt. They left a string of forts along the Nile.

By the end of the Sixth Dynasty (2345–2181BC), Egyptian power had over-reached itself. Domestic turmoil led to the withdrawal of forces from Nubia and the first great flourishing of indigenous Nubian culture at Kerma, upstream of the Third Cataract. Kerma was a city-state that grew rich thanks to its location between the resources of the south and the markets of the north. Local arts, and in particular pottery and architecture, flourished. Kerma's influence eventually extended as far as Aswan.

As Kerma prospered, Egypt came under threat from its northern neighbours, the Hyksos. Kerma's rulers allied themselves with the Hyksos and drove north beyond the Egyptian fortresses of the Second Cataract. Such expansionist dreams came to nothing when the Egyptians eventually kicked out their invaders from Thebes and set about re-ordering their state into the New Kingdom around 1550BC.

New Kingdom Egypt had its eyes firmly set on its southern borders. Whereas previously they had been content to send occasional punitive expeditions to Kush to secure their trade routes, now the pharaohs wanted nothing less than complete conquest. The army of Thutmose I sacked Kerma at the start of the 15th century BC, and his son Thutmose III drove his men almost to the Fifth Cataract. Reliefs of conquered Nubians decorate the walls of Rameses II's great temple of Abu Simbel and even the boy-king Tutankhamun was buried wearing sandals with Nubians on his soles, to be trampled into eternity. Kush was now Egyptian territory. At Napata, a great temple to the god Amun was constructed at Jebel Barkal, in part as a symbol of Egyptian power. Kush was governed by a viceroy and local rulers had their children sent to the pharaoh's court to ensure loyalty. Egyptian culture was adopted by the Kushites in everything from religion to writing.

At the end of the New Kingdom (11th century BC), Egypt's power waned again and the viceroys of Kush became independent from their masters in Thebes, setting the stage for Nubia's resurgence.

The Kingdom of Kush

In around 780BC King Alara unified Upper Nubia. The worship of Amun was resurrected, centred on Napata at Jebel Barkal, provoking a renaissance of Egyptian culture in Kush. Alara's successor, Kashata, expanded into Lower Nubia and claimed the symbolic title of Pharaoh, setting the stage for the Nubian conquest of Egypt. He was followed by Piye (or Piankhy) who took control of Thebes and set up the 25th Dynasty – also known as the Nubian Dynasty.

The Kushite kings had all the zeal of recent converts. As the keepers of the Temple of Amun at Jebel Barkal they saw themselves as the true guardians of Egyptian religion and tradition, in contrast to the rulers of Thebes who had allowed their kingdom to decay. They revelled in Egypt's past, even going as far as bringing back the building of pyramids for incarcerating their kings. At death, their bodies were returned to be buried in their homeland at El Kurru and Nuri.

The greatest of the Kushite kings was Taharqa, who took the borders of Nubian control to the edges of Libya and Palestine and left many monuments to his rule. Unfortunately for Taharqa, his rise to power coincided with the Assyrian expansion from Babylon. The Assyrians swept into Egypt and kicked the Kushite back to Napata, where he died. Although his nephew briefly recaptured Thebes, the 25th Dynasty was at an end.

At this point the historical record becomes very hazy. The so-called Napatan Phase of Kushite history that started with the conquest of Egypt and a fevered copying of Egyptian culture ended with Kush spending the next 250 years as the whipping boy of a re-emergent Egypt. The kings of Nubia were reduced to a rump of power.

Meroe

In around the 3rd century BC, the royal cemeteries moved from Napata to Meroe. This marked a move away from such heavy dependence on Egyptian practices and prompted the development of a more indigenous culture. The move can be dated to the reign of King Arkamani. The priesthood held great power over the king, in so far as it was able to declare through divine interpretation that the monarch's reign had run its course and that he must take his own life to ensure a smooth succession. Unsurprisingly, Arkamani reacted rather badly to this, and abolished the tradition by killing the priests and moving his seat from Napata to Meroe.

The move ultimately prompted Kush to replace Egyptian hieroglyphics with a cursive Meroitic script of its own. Archaeologists have yet to decipher this, so our knowledge of Meroe at this time is greatly dependent on Greek and Roman sources.

One advantage of the move to Meroe was that it provided a wetter and more fertile environment. Sorghum, millet and barley production supported a large population and agriculture was made easier with iron tools. The area was rich in iron ore and it soon became a major production centre. (More recently it has been dubbed 'the Birmingham of Africa'.)

Little is known about the day-to-day running of the kingdom. The king was all-powerful and was supported by the priesthood. Queens appear to have ruled as much as kings, a fact that excited some classical writers who spoke of Meroe as being ruled exclusively by women. They continued the practice of burying royalty in pyramids.

The Kushite god Apedemak became pre-eminent in Meroe at this time, with many temples raised in dedication to him. Apedemak is associated with war; the archaeological record of the time gives evidence of almost constant warring on Meroe's frontiers. It is quite possible that the Kushites learned to train elephants to fight in battle to complement their famed archers.

Rome grabbed Egypt from the control of Anthony and Cleopatra in the first century BC, ending the rule of the Ptolemies. The new power to the north regarded Kush as a client state, a status the Kushites could not accept. As soon as Rome's attention was focused elsewhere, they sent an army to sack Aswan. Rome's reply was to sack Napata and establish a permanent garrison there. The occupation wasn't very successful and, constantly harried by the rebellious Kushites, the Romans eventually sued for peace. Borders were permanently established, and the two powers entered into a period of entente that would last 300 years. Kush returned to growing rich from the Nile trade. The stunning temples at Naqa date from this period of prosperity.

Emperor Nero sent an expedition through Kush to find the source of the Nile, and probably carried out a little spying on Kush in the process. The force managed to penetrate some way down the White Nile before getting lost in a tangle of marsh and papyrus – the Sudd.

From the 3rd century AD, Kush fell into decline. There has been speculation that the massive hills of iron slag that are found throughout the kingdom may point to some environmental catastrophe, as deforestation for charcoal and iron-smelting may have led to extensive erosion of topsoil. A loss of agricultural capability would certainly make collapse inevitable, but there is currently not enough evidence to state this categorically. More likely is that the decline was caused by a combination of several pressing factors.

The Roman Empire had entered its own period of decline. This would have had a knock-on effect on Meroe's economy, which had grown rich from trade along the Nile. At the same time new trade routes were also opening to link sub-Saharan Africa with the Red Sea. These were dominated by the powerful kingdom of Axum, in modern Ethiopia.

Axum has also been blamed for dealing Meroe its deathblow in a more direct way, with the Axumite king Ezana leading campaigns against it.

Ethiopian claims that the Axumites actually sacked Meroe are now discounted, but it seems likely that raids on the periphery of Meroe's territory from Axum as well as from the perennially troublesome desert tribes helped tip a declining civilisation over the edge. By the 5th century AD, missionaries from the north had introduced Christianity, and the days of the Kingdom of Kush were over.

MEDIEVAL SUDAN
Christian Nubia

At the fall of Kush, Nubia was occupied by the Nobatae (called the X-Group by archaeologists), who possibly originated in the deserts between Kordofan and Libya. They shared (and fought over) the land with the nomadic Blemmyes – ancestors of the Beja of modern Sudan. Both were driven into history by the newly Christian Romans, by both the sword and the proselytising of the missionaries.

Nubia became divided into three kingdoms: Nobatia, extending from the First to the Third Cataracts with its capital at Faras; Makuria, from the Third to the Sixth Cataract, centred on Old Dongola; and Alwa, stretching to the borders with Axum and with its capital at Soba on the Blue Nile. The kingdoms converted at a time of great upheaval in the church, with great debates about the divine and human nature of Christ.

In time, Makuria absorbed Nobatia to the north and adopted the Monophysite faith, asserting the single divine nature of Christ and accepting the primacy of the Coptic Church in Alexandria. The new kingdom had 13 provinces, each with its own bishop and cathedral.

The arrival of Christianity put Nubia back in touch with the Mediterranean world, providing a new flow of trade and ideas. Literacy was encouraged, at least among the clergy. The coffers of the state swelled and Nubia became a powerful military force once again.

The art and architecture of Nubia was heavily influenced by Byzantium – churches were fortress-like basilicas, with the insides entirely covered with frescoes that might easily have come from Constantinople. The cathedral at Faras was the most spectacular example. In keeping with the trends of the time, monasteries were commonly used as seats of learning and asceticism.

The Christian kings were representatives of Christ but do not appear to have held any special spiritual role. No paintings of kings have been found and their tombs remain undiscovered. In an echo of Meroe culture, the queen mother played a key role in arranging the succession of an heir. The latter was often the son of the monarch's sister. Competing nephews and other usurpers frequently made succession difficult and bloody.

Bishops appear to have been held in higher temporal and spiritual regard than the monarch and wielded considerable political power. Images of bishops appear frequently and they were buried in their robes in dedicated chambers, often with New Testament scenes painted on the tomb walls.

Also commonly depicted are the Eparchs. The Eparch was the head official or prefect of the state, a powerful figure responsible for maintaining political relations with the newly emerging Muslims to the north. Kings seem to have frequently turned their faces away from politics during this time and there are numerous accounts of monarchs giving up the throne to become priests.

The prosperity of Christian Nubia was soon threatened by the rise of a new religion in the east. Islam flourished following the death of the Prophet Mohammed in 632, quickly enveloping Egypt and cutting Nubia off from its parent church. The Arab armies didn't stop there, but marched on with an eye on the riches to the south. They met with heavy resistance. The Nubians lived up to their reputation as hardy warriors and despite the sacking of Old Dongola and destruction of its cathedral they fought the Arabs to a standstill.

With neither side able to gain the upper hand, a peace treaty or *baqt* was negotiated between the two sides. There was an annual exchange of gifts to cement relations, with Nubia offering slaves in return for crops. Trade relations were also established and a border was drawn up just south of Aswan. The Arabs had peace on their frontier and profited from the trade goods from Africa. Nubia retained its independence and placed a brake on the seemingly unstoppable expansion of Islam, but was isolated from the mainstream of Christianity, a factor that must have contributed to the kingdom's ultimate downfall. Religion became increasingly rarefied, with later churches seemingly designed for a clergy that was becoming increasingly isolated from the general populace.

The spread of Islam

The *baqt* lasted 600 years, with both parties profiting from the agreement. Nubia remained unafraid to send the occasional sortie into Egyptian territory in support of the Coptic patriarch. In return, Egyptian merchants bought land south of Wadi Halfa and moved in on gold and emerald mines east of Nubia. Arabs slowly began to penetrate the kingdom, putting slow but unstoppable pressure on the Christians. The Red Sea port of Suakin was established to take pilgrims to Mecca. Islam became increasingly accepted in Nubia.

The rise of the Mamelukes in Egypt in the 13th century marked the end for the Nubian kings. Over a period of 200 years they sent a series of military expeditions into an increasingly weakened and fragmenting Nubia. In 1275 they acted as kingmakers, placing their own nominee on the throne at Old Dongola. Intermarriage between Arabs and the Dongola elite brought about the final stage of conquest – in 1323 a Nubian convert to Islam was crowned king and the cathedral in Old Dongola was turned into a mosque.

Further south, the kingdom of Alwa was initially spared from the Arabs by its remoteness. It persisted in its Christian traditions for another 200 years but its isolation led to the eventual decay and corruption of its own religious rituals and in 1500 Alwa finally succumbed to Islam.

The Funj Kingdom

The Arabs weren't to have things entirely their own way. As Alwa slipped into the pages of history a new power was rising on the Blue Nile. In 1504 Amara Dunqas founded *as-Saltana as-Zarqa*, the Black Sultanate at Sennar, giving rise to the Funj Kingdom.

The origins of the Funj have yet to be unravelled. Some experts have placed them as cattle nomads from the Ethiopian border on the Blue Nile, others from further south along the White Nile. Two things, however, are clear: that they were non-Arab and non-Muslim. Within a hundred years they were expanding rapidly from their base, pushing the Arabs back to the Third Cataract and conquering territory along both arms of the Nile. Amara Dunqas, the first Funk or *mek*, was constantly on the move, building a loose federation of vassal states with power decentralised to local rulers.

The greatest of the Funj *meks* was Badi Abu Duqn, better known as Badi II. He pushed the Funj borders to their furthest extent, crossing the White Nile to conquer the hinterland between the river and the Nuba Mountains and bringing the Muslim Nuba Tegali Kingdom under his patronage. Badi II's forces also headed south and established a border with the increasing powerful Shilluk Kingdom. Sennar prospered, with its five-storey palace and market rich with goods from across Sudan.

Slavery was the cornerstone of Funj wealth and power. Badi II created an army of slave soldiers and carried out raids to increase its ranks. The powerful army allowed the *mek* to reduce his reliance on local governors for support but it would also lead to the downfall of the kingdom. Power eventually became so highly invested in the slave army that the *mek* could only rule with the support of his officers, who became kingmakers in their own right – Badi IV was little more than a figurehead, who was packed off into exile in 1762 by an army flushed with power.

The Funj converted to Islam quite soon into their reign. The stability provided by the state was ideal for allowing wandering *faqis* or holy men to cross Sudan, teaching Islamic law and bringing about a slow but steady conversion of the population. The *faqis* were more than just itinerant teachers and many became important power brokers; they were given tax exemptions and land by the *mek* and carryied considerable political sway.

The Funj were known to the Europeans. Germany sent missionaries to Sennar in the early 18th century. Among them was Theodoro Krump whose book *Palm Baum* remains one of the most important first-hand accounts of Sennar culture in existence. Sennar was also visited by later adventurers like the Scot James Bruce and Johann Ludwig Burckhardt, who visited the kingdom in its final years of decline.

At the turn of the 19th century the Funj Kingdom was a spent force. The *mek* was nothing more than a puppet in the endless power struggles between the army, local governors and powerful officials at court. All that was needed was a slight push to bring the whole edifice down.

Other Sudanese powers

The Funj weren't the only important regional powers in Sudan during this period. The Ottoman Empire had assimilated the Mamelukes in Egypt and held a firm grip on the trading port of Suakin, as well as on Lower Nubia.

In the far west of the country, the Muslim Fur were carving out a kingdom of their own in Darfur. At the same time that Badi II was expanding the borders of his territory, the horsemen of the Fur Sultanate were doing the same from the Marra Plateau. Also known as the Keira Dynasty, the Sultanate raided south into Bahr al-Ghazal with the Baggara Arabs in search of slaves, which were sent north to Egypt along the Forty Days Road caravan route. Sultan Abd al-Rahman even sent a tribute to Napoleon Bonaparte in 1799 when the French leader attempted to conquer Egypt. The Fur and the Funj repeatedly clashed over Kordofan, which remained a buffer zone between the two powers.

Neither were the Funj's southern borders totally safe. The Nilotic Shilluk tribe settled along the White Nile near Malakal under their king (*reth*) Nyikang in around 1490. Smaller tribes were assimilated, creating an energetic centralised kingdom that expanded west almost as far as the Nuba Mountains. Northern ambitions were halted by Badi II at Ilays, but the Shilluk remained a persistent problem for the Funj (explorer James Bruce suggested that the Funj were an offshoot of the original expansionist Shilluk, a theory that hasn't entirely been discounted). In 1684 the Shilluk raided and destroyed Islamic schools as far north as Khartoum and still held sway over Aba Island (near modern Kosti) in the early 19th century.

Other tribes were moving in from the south. The Dinka, a loose grouping of tribes, settled along the Nile plains in the 17th and 18th centuries, forcing the Shilluk and Funj into a partnership to halt the rise of these pastoralists. The Dinka expanded west into Bahr al-Ghazal and by 1820 had crossed the Sobat River, pushing the Shilluk Kingdom into the boundaries it holds today.

The northern migration of the Dinka was concurrent with the arrival in the far south of Sudan of the war-like Azande. Originally hailing from the modern Democratic Republic of Congo, they crossed the Congo-Nile watershed to occupy the high fertile grounds of Equatoria. The Azande identity was formed through conquest and the absorption of many smaller tribes, until they were the dominant tribal grouping in the area.

THE TURKIYAH
The Turco-Egyptian Conquest of 1821

As the Funj Kingdom was sliding into decay, events in Cairo were unfolding that would have a lasting impact on Sudan. Egypt had been in turmoil following Napoleon's ill-fated attempt to conquer the country. In the chaos that followed, the Ottoman Empire attempted to restore control by placing Mohammed Ali on the throne. Mohammed Ali, with his army of Albanian soldiers, hit Egypt like a storm. The rump of Mameluke power was kicked down the Nile to take refuge at Dongola, on the hinterland of Funj territory. Within a few years Mohammed Ali expanded his power base to rival even the sultans in Istanbul, to whom he still bore fealty. Damascus, Jerusalem and even the holy cities of Mecca and Medina soon came under his direct control.

Unable to rely permanently on his mercenary army, Mohammed Ali turned his gaze south. Sudan had long been a source of slaves, and he began to covet its great pool of human resources as a way to build up an army. In 1820 he sent letters to the Funj *mek* Badi VI to ask him to expel the Mamelukes at Dongola, who still had the potential to control the Nile trade. Badi VI was unable or unwilling to comply so Mohammed Ali drew up plans for invasion.

In early 1821 an army of 4,000 soldiers set off by boat up the Nile, led by Mohammed Ali's son, Ismail. The army was a mixed bag of Bedouins, Arabs from the Maghreb and trusty Albanians, along with a few European adventurers along for whatever pickings they could get. To the Sudanese the invaders were all the same – the Turks.

Ismail made fast progress. The Mamelukes were swiftly dispatched along with the Shaqiya Arabs, whose swords and lances were no match for the firearms of the invaders. The tribal leaders who surrendered were confirmed as local rulers on an oath of loyalty. In June Ismail reached Sennar. He was received by Badi VI, who surrendered power without a shot being fired. Having conquered the Funj, a separate column was sent to Kordofan to bring it under the rule of Ismail. The first stage of the Turkiyah – the colonial rule of Sudan from Cairo – was complete.

Abuse and exploitation

Mohammed Ali's plans for Sudan were clear: 'You are aware that the end of all our effort and this expense is to procure negroes,' he wrote in a letter to Ismail's successor. 'Please show zeal in carrying out our wishes in this capital matter.' While the conquest had been relatively bloodless, the Turco-Egyptian rule was harsh. Taxes were set at an oppressively high level, with the intention more to confiscate domestic slaves from defaulters rather than to generate a steady income. Early slave raids along the Blue Nile were less successful, but there was soon a steady supply of human cargo heading north to Egypt, where they formed the *jehadiya*, a well-trained army of black slaves.

The Arabs along the river revolted against this new regime. A rebellion spread along the Nile that took nearly four years to completely suppress. Only the appointment of the far-thinking Ali Khurshid Agha to the governorship saw an end to the uprising. Khurshid reduced taxes and brought Arab tribal leaders into the fold by granting amnesties and restoring confiscated land. The state monopoly on the slave trade was abolished, and with an influx of private merchants the new capital founded at Khartoum started to grow.

The boom was kick-started in 1839 by the opening of the White Nile to steamer navigation and the breaching of the great swamps of the Sudd. Within a year, the Turco-Egyptians had penetrated as far as Gondokoro, near the site of modern Juba. The consequences for the tribes of the region were disastrous. The Shilluk, Dinka, Nuer and Azande were all hit terribly by slavery. The penetration of their lands became known in the Nilotic languages as 'the time when the world was spoiled'. Further west, the Baggara Arabs moved south into Bahr al-Ghazal to mount raids in search of slaves.

The hunt for slaves went hand-in-hand with the ivory trade. Arab and European traders, collectively known as *jallaba,* bought off local tribes and encouraged them to raid others. Demand for ivory fuelled the demand for slaves, who were pressed into service as porters. Khartoum's slave market became one of the biggest in the world, and the slave trade becamse the mainstay of Sudan's economy. Although the European powers pressured Mohammed Ali to curtail this trade, his response was ineffective – Khartoum's market was closed but a larger one opened in the Shilluk Kingdom. The Nile river trade was suppressed but alternative slave routes were opened in Kordofan. By the time that Mohammed Ali died in 1848, Sudan was being plundered to its limits.

Attempts at reform

The Viennese-educated Khedive Ismail, Mohammed Ali's grandson, took the throne in Cairo in 1863. Ismail saw himself as a great reformer but had the same imperial notions as his grandfather, imagining himself ruling an empire stretching from the Mediterranean to Africa's Great Lakes. Ismail also recognised the damage that the slave trade was doing to Egypt's reputation and set about trying to suppress it with earnest. To meet these twin ambitions he turned to European adventurers to do his work in Sudan.

The first of these was the explorer Sir Samuel Baker. Baker had already travelled through much of Sudan, venturing up the White Nile with his wife Florence in an attempt to discover its source. In 1869 he was commissioned by Ismail to retrace his steps and lead an expeditionary force to extend Egypt's borders into central Africa. Baker forced a thousand armed men through the Sudd and set up his garrison at Gondokoro, creating the province of Equatoria. Local tribes such as the Bari didn't take kindly to finding themselves under Ismail's rule, and Baker's attempts at pacification were bloody in the extreme. His Christian faith didn't help matters as he was distrusted by his men, many of whom mutinied. Only in suppressing the slave trade on the White Nile did he have any success. Baker resigned in 1874, to be replaced by Charles 'Chinese' Gordon, a hero of British military campaigns in the Far East.

Bahr al-Ghazal continued to be the playground of the slavers, outside any governmental control. The slave trader Zubeir Pasha was so powerful here that he was the virtual ruler of the region – so much so that the Turkiyah ruler in Khartoum actually proclaimed him governor in 1873. Zubeir went on to conquer Darfur and overthrow the old Fur Sultanate, before later being disgraced in Cairo.

In 1877 Ismail made Gordon the governor-general of the whole of Sudan. As a devout Christian, Gordon was a popular choice with Ismail's European backers, but was less well received in Khartoum. His faith counted against him, he spoke little Arabic and his suppression of the slave markets won him few friends in a country where domestic slavery was the bedrock of Sudanese life. He partially brought Darfur and Bahr al-Ghazal to heel but made little lasting impact elsewhere. When Ismail fell from power in 1879, a disillusioned Gordon tendered his resignation.

The Mahdist rebellion 1881–85

With the end of Ismail's rule, Britain was now fully in charge in Egypt, colonial masters in all but name. They showed little interest in Sudan and Gordon was succeeded in Khartoum by two feckless governor-generals. They were ill equipped to deal with a new movement spreading from a small island on the White Nile, led by the charismatic holy man Mohammed Ahmed.

Hailing from a family of Dongolawi boat builders, Mohammed Ahmed was a devout and ascetic preacher. In 1881 he began to send out letters from his home on Aba Island proclaiming himself as the Mahdi, sent to reform Islam and overthrow the rule of 'the Turks'. In its place he would set up a theocracy and liberate the holy cities of Arabia in a recreation of the life of the Prophet Mohammed. From the pious to those who had lost out in the suppression of the slave trade, his message was a seductive one.

Khartoum moved quickly to quell the nascent rebellion and sent soldiers to arrest the Mahdi, but he escaped and fled to Kordofan. Here he continued to gather followers and began to build an army of the Ansar (followers), swelled by the nomadic Baggara to whom he promised freedom from taxation in return for their fighting ability. By the end of 1882 the whole of Kordofan had fallen to the rebellion, including El Obeid, Sudan's second largest town.

The loss of El Obeid rang alarm bells in Cairo and London. An Egyptian army led by the British officer William Hicks was sent to recapture the town and restore rule. The resulting Battle of Sheikan was a disaster for the colonial powers – the Ansar massacred the entire army of 10,000 men. Darfur and Bahr al-Ghazal fell soon after and the Beja tribes of eastern Sudan rose in support of the Mahdi under the leadership of the mercurial Osman Digna. Only Khartoum and Suakin held out against the rising tide.

The British Prime Minister Gladstone was in a bind. He had no appetite for an expensive military adventure, but in the wake of the disaster at Sheikan the public demanded that something be done. The cry went up: send for Gordon. It was the ideal face-saving solution. Carried away with the romantic idea that the power of one good British officer might be enough to face down an entire country in rebellion, Gordon was re-appointed governor general of Sudan and hurried to Khartoum, arriving in March 1884.

There was fatal confusion in his orders. London expected him to carry out a face-saving evacuation of the Egyptian garrisons. Gordon interpreted this to mean that he should leave behind some form of native administration to stand against the Mahdi. He initially proposed handing power over to the slaver Zubeir Pasha, reasoning that he was the only person capable of holding the country together. Anti-slavery campaigners who had lionised Gordon were aghast and the plan was shelved. Instead he resolved to hold Khartoum himself and refused to withdraw the garrisons, petitioning London to send a relief expedition.

The Mahdi's noose drew tighter. He arrived at the gates of the capital in September to lay siege, making his camp in Omdurman. The arms of the two Niles made Khartoum easy to defend but the Mahdi began to slowly starve the city into submission. Gordon's steamers – his only link to the outside world – were blockaded.

Again the cry went up from the British public: having expected him to do the impossible, they now wanted him to be rescued. The government dawdled but eventually dispatched a flying column to save their hero. Inexplicably it was sent along the Nile instead of making the short dash from Suakin where the garrisons, supplied by sea, had kept Osman Digna's men at bay. Instead the army fought not just the Ansar but also a huge logistical battle by boat and camel. Even then there was no perceived rush as everyone still expected Gordon to carry the day, scarcely imagining how perilous his situation was. As the Nile waters dropped, Khartoum's defences became increasingly exposed.

An advance party of British soldiers reached Khartoum on January 28 1885, only to be sent packing by Mahdist gunfire. They were too late – the city had fallen just two days earlier and Gordon had been stabbed to death on the steps of the Governor's palace. Britain wept, canonising Gordon as a Victorian warrior-saint. The relief column withdrew to Egypt and left Sudan to the Mahdi.

THE MAHDIYA
Sudan under the Khalifa

Mohammed Ahmed never got to enjoy the spoils of victory. Within five months of capturing Khartoum he was dead, probably from typhoid. Contemporary accounts describe him as retreating to his harem to grow prodigiously fat with his pick of any slave girl – accounts which probably say as much about Victorian ideas of an oriental despot as they do about what actually happened.

The Mahdi's successor was the Khalifa Abdullah, a Baggara from Darfur. The Khalifa had no less theocratic zeal than his master and set about reshaping the country. Omdurman grew as the new capital and the slave markets were reopened. Mahdism became the new orthodoxy and pilgrimage to the Mahdi's tomb was made incumbent on all Muslims. In other ways the Mahdiya was little different from what had preceded it. The taxation burden returned to crippling levels, swelling the Khalifa's private treasury. The Baggara tribes, the shock troops of the new ruler, were exempt from taxes and were moved to Khartoum where they lived as an army of occupation.

The Khalifa still maintained the Mahdi's expansionist dreams. In Equatoria, the last vestiges of Egyptian rule clung on under Emin Pasha, the German governor, before he was extricated by the famed explorer Henry Morton Stanley in 1889. The Ansar were sent to the corners of his land for further conquests but once there suffered grievous defeats. The Khalifa's best armies were beaten back in an attempted invasion of Egypt in 1887 and in the same year he barely won a massive fight against the Ethiopians, suffering the loss of thousands of his men.

At the same time Sudan was hit by a devastating three-year drought that led to widespread famine. The Khalifa succeeded in creating a state from a revolution, but at a terrible cost. His wings had been clipped and Sudan began to stagnate again.

The Anglo-Egyptian Conquest of 1898

For ten years Britain had turned its face away from Sudan, but in 1895 it suddenly ordered its reconquest. Calls to avenge Gordon had always been loud, but the renewed interest was more the result of European politics. The 'Scramble for Africa' was at its height and several powers had been eyeing up the waters of the Nile, claiming that Egypt had abandoned its claim there. The French were reported to be sending an expedition to claim the Nile headwaters for themselves, while the eccentric Leopold II of Belgium was hatching his own plans to add parts of Sudan to his Congo Free State. Britain's position in Egypt demanded control of the Nile from source to sea, so an army was dispatched under the command of General Kitchener to re-establish control.

Kitchener took Dongola in 1896 and made plans to lay a railway across the desert from Wadi Halfa to ferry troops closer to Khartoum. Slowly he inched toward the Khalifa. In early 1898 he smashed the Ansar at Atbara and held Khartoum in his grasp.

The British and Mahdist armies met outside Omdurman on September 2 1898. In one of the most mis-matched battles in the British army's history the Ansar were utterly laid to waste in a clash of the industrial and medieval worlds. The Khalifa fled, leaving 10,000 Sudanese dead on the field.

Kitchener didn't waste time enjoying victory. Barely pausing to give a eulogy to Gordon and order the demolition of the Mahdi's tomb, he headed south by steamer for another showdown. The French captain Jean-Baptiste Marchand had spent a hellish two years dragging his boats from the mouth of the Congo to claim Fashoda on the White Nile (near modern Malakal) for France, arriving two months before the Battle of Omdurman. Kitchener's arrival provoked the Fashoda Crisis, which nearly brought the two countries to war in Europe before the French renounced their claim. Further south, Leopold's men tried and failed to claim Emin Pasha's Lado Enclave for Belgium. Sudan returned to nominal Egyptian control, but there was no doubting who was really in charge.

THE ANGLO-EGYPTIAN CONDOMINIUM
British rule in Sudan

Egyptian money had largely paid for the expedition but Britain was reluctant to hand back control to the Khedive. Many blamed the harsh and corrupt rule of the Egyptians for provoking the Mahdist rebellion in the first place. As a result, the hybrid state of the Anglo-Egyptian Condominium grew up in its place, a British colony in all but name. A British governor-general would take all political decisions, with a token Egyptian military force remaining as a fig leaf for Cairo's nominal political role.

The early years of the Condominium were focused on pacification. The Khalifa was run to ground and killed in Kordofan in late 1899, but Mahdist revolts continued for another nine years. In Darfur, Ali Dinar had re-established the Fur Sultanate in the wake of Mahdist collapse and remained independent until 1916, when a military campaign brought the province under control, settling Sudan's western borders. Southern Sudan had experienced little but slave raiding from Khartoum and early British measures to establish control were also of a military nature, with local wars with the Nuer continuing well into the 1920s.

Britain set about remodelling Sudan along the lines of its other colonies. The primary imperial purpose was commerce – providing raw materials for the factories at home and markets for the products of empire. Sudan was to be no exception. Under the energetic Governor-General Reginald Wingate, a massive programme of building and agriculture was initiated. The railway network was expanded and vast cotton projects were implemented in the fertile Gezira region. A dam was built at Sennar to improve irrigation, with workers encouraged to settle in the area to make up the chronic labour shortage. Cotton and crops were sent to the coast for export and the docks of Port Sudan were founded for this purpose. An education system aimed to produce a westernised elite to run the civil service. Local government had a light touch, with Native Administration using tribal structures overseen by British district commissioners.

As modernisation proceeded apace in Khartoum, attitudes towards South Sudan were markedly different. There had never been any development here, just exploitation of people and resources. A Southern Policy aimed to administer the region as an entirely separate entity from northern Sudan. The Closed Districts Ordinances effectively sealed the South from Arab influence. Arab merchants were excluded and the spread of Islam discouraged – even Arab dress was outlawed. The aim was to develop the South at a slower pace and reconstruct tribal traditions disrupted by the slave trade. The education policy was entrusted to the Church, with the South parcelled out to different missionary groups.

Southern Policy was initially expected to see South Sudan assimilated into British East Africa. As a result there was frequent mistrust between the pro-Arabist administrators in Khartoum and those working in the South, who were often derided as 'Bog Barons' for their paddle-steamer headquarters ploughing through the Sudd.

The road to independence

Egypt formally gained its independence from Britain in 1922. Many Sudanese, products of the new education system and largely detribalised, took inspiration from this to give birth to the Sudanese nationalist movement.

One of the first to call for self-determination was the Dinka army officer Ali Abd al-Latif, who in 1924 formed the White Flag League, a non-tribal organisation that agitated for independence. Demonstrations led to Abd al-Latif's arrest. In November of the same year the governor-general Lee Stack was assassinated on a visit to Cairo. The killing prompted mass unrest and the mutiny of a battalion of the Sudanese Defence Force. The British response was uncompromising. The mutineers were brutally suppressed, putting the lid back on the nationalist movement for over a decade. The Egyptians, suspected of fomenting much of the trouble, were expelled from Sudan.

By the late 1930s Sudanese Islamic groups started to encourage nationalist sentiments. The Ansar, still followers of the Mahdi, formed the Umma Party led by the Mahdi's grandson Siddiq al-Mahdi, and called for complete independence. The opposing wing of the movement was the Khatmiyah, led by Ali al-Mirghani, scion of the influential Sufi brotherhood from Kassala. The Khatmiyah (later to form the Democratic Unionist Party) favoured federation with Egypt.

The two factions made up the Graduates General Congress, which began to lobby the government for political power. In 1943 they issued a memorandum calling for self-determination for Sudan and an end to the administrative separation of North and South Sudan. Britain demurred, but faced with nationalist movements throughout its colonies recognised that independence would soon become inevitable. As a concession it proposed electing an advisory council for North Sudan, but the Congress successfully pressed for it to have legislative powers.

The new Legislative Assembly forced a rethink on Southern Policy. At the 1947 Juba Conference the British proposed giving Southerners a place in the assembly, which led to the full abandonment of separate administration. In elections the following year the Umma Party swept the board and entered into formal negotiations with the British over self-determination.

Egypt was enraged at having been excluded from the process. They tore up all the existing treaties with Britain and unilaterally declared Egyptian rule over Sudan, although they had little means to back their claim up, the move having alienated many of their Sudanese supporters. The impasse was only broken with the Egyptian Revolution in 1952 that overthrew the monarchy. The new government in Cairo signed the Anglo-Egyptian Accord a year later that called for a three-year transitional period of government to be followed by self-determination.

Elections to the government brought in a DUP majority led by Ismail al-Azhari, who abandoned calls for unity with Egypt. The government immediately announced a policy of Sudanization to bring about a quick transfer of power, sacking many British officials and replacing them with Sudanese. This had the greatest effect in South Sudan, where all but a handful of positions were given to Northerners. Calls for outright independence became deafening. On January 1 1956 the British and Egyptian flags were lowered for the last time and the Republic of Sudan was born, with al-Azhari as its first president.

SUDAN SINCE INDEPENDENCE
The First Civil War

Independent Sudan had an inauspicious birth. Sudanization had already begun to produce disquiet in the South, where an army mutiny broke out in Torit even before the handover from the British. The shooting of striking southern workers sparked the outbreak, which spread as far as Malakal. In the face of government reprisals, the rebels fled into Uganda.

From 1956 the exiles continually slipped back across the Sudanese border to carry out guerrilla attacks on government targets. There was little organisation and they were badly equipped, relying mainly on captured arms. It wasn't until a military coup in 1958 that brought General Abboud to power in Khartoum that the security situation really started to decline. Abboud was fiercely pro-Arab. Islamic conversion was encouraged, Arabic replaced English as the language of education, and missionaries – who were running the majority of the South's schools – were harassed and eventually expelled altogether. As the South became more disaffected the level of violence increased. The exile community coalesced around the Sudan African Nationalist Union (SANU) in Kampala.

The formation of the Anyanya movement in 1962 tipped South Sudan into civil war. The Anyanya was the military wing of SANU, taking their name from a traditional poison concocted from snake parts and fermented beans.

The Anyanya was a loose-knit organisation and its many militias often seemed as interested in fighting each other as they did in fighting the Sudanese government.

SANU reflected these internal fault lines. The movement was dominated by the Equatorians, who were the best educated of the Southerners. The Equatorians wanted full Southern independence. The few Dinka in SANU, led by William Deng, supported a federalist solution for the entire country. Following the return of civilian government in Khartoum in 1964, SANU split and Deng went to the North to seek rapprochement. A proposed government conference on the South a year later was a whitewash. The Anyanya refused to participate and the government handed the Southern problem over to a committee dominated by Northerners. Fighting intensified and in 1968 Deng was assassinated by the Sudanese army.

The Anyanya had become a formidable fighting force. Southern divisions were overcome by the unifying figure of Joseph Lagu. Now called the South Sudan Liberation Movement (SSLM) they received arms from Israel and succeeded in driving the government from huge areas of southern territory. The SSLM set up their own civil administration in these areas and the situation reached an uneasy stalemate.

Coups and elections

Sudan had not settled easily into democracy after independence. The six years of military rule by General Abboud were punctuated by a declining security situation in the South and repression in the North. In October 1964 a series of protests by students and trade unions led to a general strike and ultimately the October Revolution that forced Abboud from power. A transitional government oversaw the return to democracy the following year.

The elections of 1965 were split between the Umma and the DUP, with a profusion of smaller parties, including the communists and the radical Muslim Brotherhood contesting the election. A power struggle within the Umma eventually led to Sadiq al-Mahdi, great-grandson of the Mahdi, forming a government. He held together an unstable coalition, but economic problems, an inability to produce a new constitution, and the escalating civil war resulted in weak administration. The military stepped in again and in May 1969 a second coup brought civilian rule to a close.

The rule of Jaafar Nimeiri

The leader of the Free Officers Movement that took power was Jaafar Nimeiri. A smooth political operator, he moved quickly to establish himself as leader of a left-leaning secular Sudan. In his first year of power he drew the teeth of the Umma Party by engineering a showdown with its followers, the Ansar. Demonstrations against him were met with force, culminating in an army assault on Aba Island, the spiritual home of Mahdism. Thousands were killed including the Ansar leader, Sadiq al-Mahdi's uncle.

Nimeiri's government initially relied on the support of the communists, but in July 1971 they attempted to take power in a coup of their own. Foreign support and popular protests helped Nimeiri, who prevailed and came out stronger than ever. He formally announced his presidency and amended the constitution to make his Sudan Socialist Union the only legal political party in the country.

His power base firmly established, Nimeiri moved to tackle the civil war in the South. He started a dialogue with the SSLM over a ceasefire and regional autonomy. Long negotiations led to the Addis Ababa Agreement of February 1972 that formally ended the 17-year conflict. South Sudan was granted regional self-government and a voice in Khartoum, a peace deal that brought Nimeiri much international prestige.

For the first time since independence Sudan was united in peace, and the economy started to boom. Development loans flooded in from the West and the Arab states as plan after plan was announced to turn Sudan into the breadbasket of Africa. The sugar and cotton industries were massively expanded. The ambitious Jonglei Canal scheme was begun to divert the waters of the White Nile for irrigation rather than letting them disappear in the swamps of the Sudd. Unfortunately for Nimeiri the projects were over- ambitious and badly managed. Many of the big infrastructure projects were white elephants, losing millions of dollars and forcing Sudan's economy into crisis.

In an attempt to avert a political crisis Nimeiri announced a policy of national reconciliation. Sadiq-al Mahdi, the DUP and Hassan al-Turabi's Muslim Brotherhood were brought back into the fold, all winning seats in new elections to the People's Assembly. At the same time, much of the government's leftist polemic was dropped, moving Nimeiri closer to the USA.

As the economy worsened, the influence of the Islamic parties grew. All put pressure on Nimeiri to renounce the Addis Ababa Agreement and reduce the powers of the Southerners in Juba. As attorney general, Hassan al-Turabi had widespread Northern support for a new Islamic constitution for the entire country. Under pressure, the Southern Assembly in Juba was suspended in 1981. Two years later, the autonomous Southern Region was broken into three parts. This was followed by the September Laws, which decreed that Islamic *sharia* law would apply in the South as well as in the North.

Mutinies in Southern battalions flared up into open revolt. The Anyanya guerrillas started operating openly again and were joined by a new rebel group, the Sudanese People's Liberation Movement/Army, led by the Dinka army defector John Garang. By the end of 1983 South Sudan had slid back into civil war.

Nimeiri lurched from crisis to crisis throughout 1984. The army seemed unable to deal with the Southern rebels, and in the North a state of emergency was declared in response to increasing strikes and protests. Support for the government ebbed away up until April 1985, when Nimeiri was swept from power in the same way that he had originally seized it – by military coup.

Another democratic interlude

The new Transitional Military Council in Khartoum inherited a shambles. The International Monetary Fund declared Sudan bankrupt; inflation went through the roof. The generals said they had taken power only as a last resort to save the country and promised a handover to civilian government within a year. To everyone's amazement they were true to their word.

Elections in April 1986 saw Sadiq al-Mahdi return as prime minister. He relied on a fractious coalition in cabinet including Osman al-Mirghani of the DUP and Hassan al-Turabi, who had reorganised his Muslim Brotherhood into the National Islamic Front. Sadiq proved to be no better a ruler than he had been the first time around. Pro-Arab, he had no answers to the escalating conflict in the South. The SPLM/A were well organised and were capturing great chunks of territory. His only solution was to arm the Baggara Arab tribes along the North-South border to fight his war by proxy. The *murahilin* militia raided deep intoDinka territory, particularly in Bahr al-Ghazal, causing the population to flee. In a throwback to the 19th century, the Arabs repeatedly carried women and children into slavery. Combined with a severe drought, the disruption to the civilian population resulted in a famine in 1988 in which it is thought a quarter of a million people died.

In the North, the economy struggled through disaster after disaster. The currency was devalued and the population rioted when price controls on food and fuel were lifted. Sadiq's coalition repeatedly collapsed, only to be reformed with the same cast.

Attempting to break the political impasse, al-Mirghani secretly negotiated with the SPLM/A, agreeing to a ceasefire and the suspension of *sharia* in the South. The army pressured Sadiq to follow suit, which he did in 1989. The NIF left the coalition in disgust at his alleged abandonment of Islamic principles.

The deal with the SPLM/A would repeal the September Laws and build a new national consensus to finally bring peace to the country, but not everyone was happy. A small group of army officers plotted against Sadiq and on June 30 1989, as he prepared to sign the protocols into law, he was tumbled out of office in yet another military smash-and-grab for power.

National Islamic Front government

The coup was led by Omar al-Bashir, who set up the Revolutionary Command Council for National Salvation. They immediately suspended the constitution and dissolved parliament, banned trade unions and muzzled the press and judiciary. Hassan al-Turabi's fingerprints were all over the new regime and although he was never given a formal role in government it soon became apparent that the National Islamic Front was really running the show.

Bashir and Turabi were uncompromisingly Islamist. Despite the growing successes of the SPLM/A, they saw only a military solution to the civil war, calling for a *jihad* or holy struggle against the rebels. Sudan also allied itself with radical foreign Islamic causes, isolating itself from the political mainstream.

The NIF had their watershed year in 1991 as events in the South began to turn in Khartoum's favour. The Ethiopian dictator Haile Mariam Mengistu, who had been the SPLM/A's main sponsor, was overthrown, leading to the loss of the rebels' training camps and supply lines. At the same time, the Nuer SPLA commander Riek Machar launched a rebellion against John Garang that succeeded in splitting the SPLM/A down the middle. For the next few years the Southerners would spent as much time fighting each other as the Sudanese army, as the region became increasingly split along ethnic lines. The government took advantage of the disarray to launch a series of offensives that recaptured much lost territory. Following the old Turkiyah maxim of divide and rule (literally 'setting a slave to catch a slave') they even managed to buy off Riek Machar, who switched between calls for Southern independence and fighting on behalf of the North to extend his personal power base.

The government, meanwhile, was doing little to win friends overseas. Turabi gave vocal support to Saddam Hussein during the Gulf War, giving Sudan instant pariah status and causing an economic blow through loss of remittances from Sudanese workers expelled from the Gulf. Also expelled from Saudi Arabia was the al-Qaeda firebrand Osama Bin Laden, who was offered sanctuary by Turabi and went on to set up training camps in Sudan. Khartoum also played host to the terrorist Carlos the Jackal and the Palestinian group Hamas. In 1993 the USA placed Sudan on the list of state sponsors of terrorism. This had only a temporary chastening effect – that year's dry season offensive in the South was cancelled, as US intervention in Somalia prompted Sudanese fears that it would be followed by open American military support for the SPLM/A.

Sudan's radical politics also played themselves out on a regional level. Islamic groups waging a guerrilla campaign in Eritrea were given support, and aid given to the Lord's Resistance Army in northern Uganda led to Kampala breaking off relations with Khartoum in 1995. The same year the Sudanese government was implicated in an assassination attempt on the Egyptian president Hosni Mubarak in Addis Ababa. International pressure led to the expulsion of Bin Laden to Afghanistan in 1996, but events came to a head in August 1998 when President Clinton ordered cruise missile attacks on the al-Shifa pharmaceutical company in Khartoum, in retaliation for the bombings of US embassies in Nairobi and Dar es Salaam. Clinton claimed that the factory was manufacturing chemical weapons and was linked to both al-Qaeda and Iraq, but when the factory turned out to have been making valuable veterinary drugs, the US government quietly compensated the owner a few years later.

Despite this, the Sudanese government ended the 1990s on a high. Revenues from the oil fields in Upper Nile finally came online in 1999 and the majority of the proceeds were spent on the army who were increasingly convinced of victory over the SPLM/A. In a struggle for control with Turabi, Bashir gained the upper hand and consolidated his personal power base.

Sudan today: prospects and problems

Now firmly in control and with oil exports finally bringing economic stability, Bashir began to seek international rehabilitation. In February 2001 Turabi was placed under house arrest: in a sign of how far against the government he had moved, the ideologue had begun to make ties with the opposition parties, leading to the signing of an agreement with the SPLM/A in support of bringing down Bashir.

The events of September 11 2001 gave Sudan the chance to come in from the cold. Khartoum renounced terrorism and gave the USA access to its files on al-Qaeda and Iraq. For the first time the government became open to serious negotiations to end the civil war and accepted a US peace envoy, Senator John Danforth, to aid the process. By January 2002 a ceasefire had been brokered with the SPLM/A in the Nuba Mountains, allowing peace talks to take place in earnest.

While fighting continued elsewhere, the two warring parties sat down in Kenya and hammered out the Machakos Protocols in July – a statement of intent to end the war. Khartoum agreed to a six-year interim period after the signing, followed by a referendum on self-determination for the South. *Sharia* law would not apply in the South. Garang again pledged support for a strong federal state instead of independence. By the end of the year a ceasefire was declared across the entire South.

Talks dragged on throughout 2003, throwing up disputes of power sharing and the status of the disputed regions of the Nuba Mountains, Abyei and the Southern Blue Nile that straddled the North–South border. Other opposition groups, most notably the umbrella body the National Democratic Alliance overseen by Sadiq al-Mahdi, complained at being excluded from the talks, but progress continued to be made. In September 2003 hostilities were formally declared over. Khartoum agreed to equally share oil revenues with the South. Stretching into 2004, the status of the disputed areas was settled by granting varying degrees of autonomy, and the shape of the interim government was clarified – Bashir would remain president, with the vice-presidency going to Garang. By the summer of 2004 all the pieces were in place for a final, comprehensive peace agreement.

But excitement over the settling of the war was overshadowed by events in the west of the country. Regions long ignored by repeated governments clamoured for part of the peace dividend. Old grievances in Darfur began to spill over into insurrection with the formation of new rebel groups in 2003, the Sudan Liberation Army and the Justice & Equality Movement, who gave voice to the disenfranchised Fur, Masalit and Zaghawa tribes in the face of Arab expansion. Early military successes were rapidly turned around when the government began to arm Arab militias, the *janjawid*, in much the same way as it had once done in the South. Able to move troops from the Southern ceasefire zone, it backed the *janjawid* with aerial bombing of villages.

The international community initially made little comment, anxious not to rock the boat during the peace negotiations over the South. By the start of 2004, however, the situation had become critical, with over a million displaced to the Chad border region and the government accused of complicity in ethnic cleansing. Attempted ceasefires were repeatedly broken and no measures taken to rein in the *janjawid*. The United Nations declared Darfur the world's worst humanitarian disaster.

Previous page Mosque near Erkowit, Red Sea Province, eastern Sudan (MP)

Above left Rashaida girl near Suakin, eastern Sudan (MP)

Above right Kababish girl from Sudan's northern desert (MP)

Below left Girl carrying water in El Geneina, western Darfur (MP)

Below right Dinka grandmother and child, New Cush, Equatoria region, southern Sudan (MP)

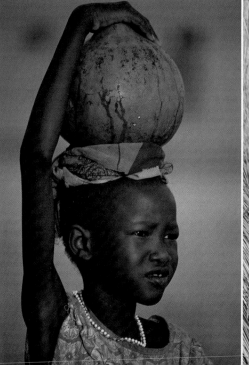

African Union observers were sent to Darfur at the end of spring 2004, followed by troops from Nigeria and Rwanda to monitor the situation. International pressure finally seemed to have a mixed effect on the Sudanese government – humanitarian access to refugee camps improved, but *janjawid* attacks largely continued. With a UN Security Council resolution pressing for action and threatening sanctions, and the USA defining events in Darfur as genocide, the Sudanese government continued to play for time – even managing a political clampdown in Khartoum, claiming an alleged coup attempt by Turabi's Popular Congress Party.

In January 2005, the finalised peace deal between the government and the SPLM/A was signed in Nairobi to universal acclaim, although the dragging on of the Darfur crisis cast a shadow over events. With the interim period of government due to start in the following July, it was hoped that the settling of Africa's longest-running civil war would give new impetus to the stalled negotiations to stop the conflict in the west. Optimism in the South, continued crisis in Darfur; Sudan's immediate future is hard to divine.

Planning and Preparation

WHEN TO VISIT

Sudan is a seasonal destination. The north is hot and dry throughout the year, but between April and October temperatures are ferociously hot, typically reaching over 40°C. Sandstorms are also commonest during this time. Khartoum is a little cooler but more humid, receiving rain in July and August. November to March are the best months to travel, although northern winter nights can be cold.

If you're interested in scuba diving, the conditions in the Red Sea are ideal for diving all year round, but operators tend to close for the months of July and August, when the heat in Port Sudan makes living unbearably hot – temperatures pushing 50°C are not unknown.

In the south and west, the best times to travel will be after the complete end to fighting and implementation of a comprehensive peace deal, something that was looking far likelier for the South than for troubled Darfur at the time of going to press. Heading south, the climate becomes increasingly tropical, with summer rains making swathes of the country impassable overland between May and August.

TOURIST INFORMATION (ABROAD)

Sudan does not maintain any tourist offices outside the country. While embassies usually only give scant tourist information, several maintain useful websites giving information on everything from visa regulations to modern Sudanese art. The Sudanese embassy in the UK is a good place to start (www.sudanembassy.co.uk). Given the variable nature of Sudanese politics, it's worth consulting the travel advisories issued by the British and US governments (www.fco.gov.uk and http://travel.state.gov/travel_warnings respectively).

PAPERWORK
Visas

All visitors to Sudan require a visa. Arab nationals can pick these up on arrival; all other nationalities need to apply in advance. Tourist visas are normally valid for a one-month stay, to be used within a month of issue. However, the wheels of Sudanese bureaucracy turn slowly, so timing your visa application carefully is important. Visa fees can vary considerably – at the time of going to press the price of a one-month visa was £56 in London and $150 in Washington DC.

Visa applications made in Europe or North America require a letter of invitation from a company or individual in Sudan. This must be approved by the Ministry of Interior in Khartoum and then sent with your forms to the embassy where you are applying for your visa. If you are travelling on an organised tour, your travel company will arrange this. A local Sudanese tour operator such as Globtours (see *Tour operators*, page 53) can also arrange this invitation for a fee.

If you cannot get a letter of invitation you can still apply for a visa, but you are entering uncharted waters, as your application will be sent to Khartoum for approval. Embassy staff in London freely admit that applying this way can take up to 12 weeks, with no guarantee of acceptance! Persistence in this paper chase may help but is no guarantee of success, and given that visas are valid for a month from the date of issue, applying too early adds another element of risk to the process. If you apply this way, the embassy only asks for your passport and visa fee once Khartoum have approved your application.

Sudanese embassies in Africa seem to make up their own rules. The embassies in Cairo and Addis Ababa are particularly useful for travellers as they are allowed to issue visas without reference to Khartoum, speeding up the application process considerably. It is common to request a letter of introduction from your home embassy, which bumps up the price considerably for British passport holders. The embassy in Chad is consistently reported as a hard place to get a visa without an invitation letter. Typical visa fees in Africa are around $55.

If you are travelling as part of an organised tour, some operators may arrange for you to collect your visa on arrival in Sudan. This is particularly common if you are visiting Sudan on a diving trip. You'll need to provide a photocopy of your passport, after which they will send you a copy of your visa authorisation from the Ministry of Interior (which you will need to board the plane to Sudan). The operator will meet you on arrival and whisk you through immigration.

If your passport contains evidence that you've visited Israel – including entry or exit stamps from Egyptian or Jordanian border posts with Israel – your visa application will automatically be rejected.

Visa extensions

If you need to extend your stay in Sudan, visa extensions can be obtained at the Aliens Building of the Ministry of Interior in Khartoum. You need to take a photo and pay a fee of 6,000SD/US$24. It's a relatively painless experience with extensions of up to a month granted. When completing the form you are asked to provide a guarantor for your stay – most mid-range hotels will provide this service, as will local tour operators. If you don't have a guarantor you can still get an extension, but the normal processing time of two days can drag on and you'll need to be persistent in visiting the office to make sure your application doesn't slip to the bottom of the pile.

Visa extension applications are only accepted when you have a few days left on your visa, with a similar grace period allowed after expiry – I had no problems extending my stay when applying two days after my current visa had expired.

Other paperwork

A valid yellow fever certificate is required if you're arriving from an endemic area, such as a neighbouring African country, although immigration officials seem lax about checking this. You will definitely need a yellow fever certificate if you plan on leaving Sudan by ferry to Egypt – Egyptian officials check your documentation before you board the boat at Wadi Halfa. I once did this trip with just one week left on my ten-year yellow fever certificate and it took a long argument before I was allowed on the boat!

All visitors to Sudan must register with the Ministry of Interior within three days of arrival (see page 57).

SUDANESE EMBASSIES AND CONSULATES

Austria Reisnerstrasse 29/5, Vienna 1030; tel 1 710 2343/44; email: botschaft.d.rep.sudan@chello.at

Belgium 12 Av Franklin D Roosevelt, 1060 Brussels; tel: 2 647 9494; fax: 6483499

Canada 354 Stewart St, Ottawa K1N 6K8; tel: 613 235 4000/4999; fax: 613 235 6880; email: sudanembassy_canada@rogers.com

Chad Rue de la Gendarmerie, Ndjamena; tel: 525010

Egypt Embassy: 4 Sharia al-Ibrahimy, Garden City, Cairo; tel: 2 794 5043; fax: 2 794 2693. Consulate: Building 20, Atlas, Aswan; tel: 097307321; fax: 342563

Eritrea Hazemo St, Asmara; tel: 1 124176; fax: 1 129287

Ethiopia Ras Lulseged St (off Mexico Sq), Addis Ababa; tel 01 516 477; fax 01 518141; email: sudan.embassy@telecom.net.et

France 56 Avenue Montaigne, 75008 Paris; tel 01 42 25 55 71/73; fax: 01 45 63 66 73; email: ambassade-du-soudan@wanadoo.fr

Germany Kurfürstendamm 151, 10709 Berlin; tel 030 890 6980; fax: 030 890 6982; email: post@sudan-embassy.de

Italy Via Spallanzani 24, Rome 00161; tel: 06 4404377; e-mail: info@ambasciatadelsudanaroma.org

Japan Chiyoda House, 2-17-8 Nagata-cho, Chiyoda-ku, Tokyo 100-0014; tel: 3 3506 7801; fax : 3 3506 7804

Libya 68 Mohamed Ali Mosadak Street, Tripoli; tel: 21 4778052; fax: 21 4774781; email: sudtripoli@hotmail.com

Kenya Minet ICDC building, Mamlaka Rd, Nairobi; tel: 2 720853; fax: 2 710612

Netherlands 81 Laan Copes Van Cattenburch, 2585 EW, The Hague; tel: 70 360 5300; fax: 70 361 7975

Nigeria 28 Kofo Abayomi St, Victoria Island, Lagos; tel: 1 615889; fax: 1 615945.

Norway Holtegata 28, Oslo 0355; tel: 2269 9260; fax 2269 8344; email: sudan.oslo@c2i.net (also accredited to Denmark)

Saudi Arabia Embassy: Sharia 30, Riyadh 11693; tel: 1 488 7979; fax: 1 488 7729. Consulate; Jeddah; tel: 2 647 6003

South Africa 1203 Pretorius St, Hatfield 0083, Pretoria; tel: 12 342 4538; fax: 12 342 4539; email: embassy@sudani.co.za

Sweden Drottninggatan 81A, Stockholm; tel: 8 208041; fax: 8 201621

Switzerland 49 Avenue Blanc, 1202 Geneva; tel: 22 731 2663/6; fax: 731 2656

Uganda Nakasero Road, Kampala; tel: 41 243518

UK 3 Cleveland Row, St. James's, London SW1A 1DD; tel: 020 7839 8080; fax: 020 7839 7560; email: admin@sudanembassy.co.uk
USA Embassy: 2210 Massachusetts Av NW, Washington DC 20008; tel: 202 338 8565; fax: 202 667 2404; email: info@sudanembassy.org. Permanent Mission: 655 Third Avenue Suite 500-10, New York 10017; tel: 212 573 6033; fax 212 573 6160

GETTING TO SUDAN
By air

Sudan's national carrier is **Sudan Airways** (London office tel: 020 7436 6423/ 020 7931 3373; email: lonmgr@sudanair.com; www.sudanair.com). They mainly operate inside Africa and between Africa and the Middle East, but they have two direct weekly flights between Khartoum and London, their only European connections. Potentially useful regional connections include flights to Cairo, Addis Ababa, Asmara, N'djamena and Lagos. Flights to Nairobi were suspended at the time of writing; there is no service to Kampala.

Within Africa, Ethiopian Airlines, Kenya Airways, Regional Airways and Egypt Air all serve Khartoum. Ethiopian Airlines have the best connections throughout the continent and the Addis Ababa-Khartoum service also continues to Cairo or N'djamena depending on the day of the week. Regional Airways (a partner of British Airways) link Khartoum to Asmara and Nairobi. As well as flights between Cairo and Khartoum, Egypt Air has a useful weekly flight to Port Sudan.

Sudan has excellent connections to the Middle East. The Gulf Arab airlines of Emirates, Gulf Air and Qatar Airways all have regular services to Khartoum and are good for onward connections. Saudi Airlines, Syrian Air, Royal Jordanian and Yemenia also run flights to their respective capitals.

Lufthansa are currently the only European carrier flying to Sudan. Although both British Airways and Air France maintain offices in Khartoum, at the time of going to press neither carrier were offering direct flights. If the peace deal holds, expect services from Heathrow and Paris to resume. KLM announced a Khartoum service as we went to press.

There are no direct flights between Sudan and North America or Australia.

London abounds with travel agents offering cheap flights to Africa – check the ads in the Sunday travel supplements, *Time Out* and *TNT* before booking. Two long established agents are **STA Travel** (tel: 0870 1676769; www.statravel.co.uk) and **Trailfinders** (tel: 020 7938 3939; www.trailfinders.com), who have branches across the UK. A good agent in London specialising in Africa is the **Africa Travel Centre** (tel: 020 7387 1211; www.africatravel.co.uk).

There is a departure tax of US$20 when leaving Sudan by air.

By land

A glance at the map suggests that Sudan, with its nine neighbours, should present a wide choice of entry points for those arriving overland. A closer look cuts down the options. Only the borders with Ethiopia and Egypt can be said to offer truly reliable access – good news for those on the classic 'Cairo to Cape Town' overland route. Access across other borders either depends on the political climate, or have been firmly shut for years.

Entering Sudan from Ethiopia is a straightforward affair, with transport links much improved in recent years. Further north, those heading to Sudan from Eritrea should beware ongoing tensions between the two governments means that this border is generally closed more often than it is open although there are good air connections between Khartoum and Asmara. The land border between Sudan and Egypt is closed due to a long-running dispute over ownership of the Haleib Triangle, making the ferry along Lake Nasser the only transport option.

It is unclear under present circumstances whether it is possible to enter Sudan from Libya. Officials in Khartoum indicate that the border post at Awaynat is open, but given the restrictions on travel in Libya and the remote desert location of the border, this is unlikely to become a major crossing point.

Approaching Sudan from the west, the most common entry point into Sudan is from Chad at El Geneina, although at the time of going to press this border was closed due to the ongoing conflict in Darfur. Under other circumstances the truly adventurous might be tempted by the remote crossing at Um Dafog from the Central African Republic, although CAR itself is hardly a model of stability. These borders are seasonal as rains in the spring and summer can make tracks impassable.

There are currently no official border crossings into Sudan from Kenya, Uganda or the Democratic Republic of Congo, as these countries border regions controlled by the SPLM/A. In recent years, unofficial access has been available through Kenya and the border town of Lokichoggio, the operating base for many international aid organisations. Should the peace process take hold, expect this border to open first, along with the crossings from Uganda at Kaya and Nimule, leading to the SPLM/A town of Yei and the southern capital of Juba respectively. None of the crossings into the west or south can currently be recommended because of safety concerns.

Nothing in Sudan is set in stone and events on the ground can change quickly, so keep your ear on the travellers' grapevine. In most cases air links exist should closed borders force a change of plan – particularly from N'djamena or Asmara to Khartoum.

For more information on getting around with your own vehicle, see *Travel in Sudan*, page 62.

By boat

The weekly ferry along Lake Nasser (or the Nubian Lake as the Sudanese prefer to call it) is a leisurely way to enter Sudan from Egypt. The ferry usually tows a barge should you need to ship a vehicle. An alternative is to cross the Red Sea from Saudi Arabia. Vehicle and passenger ferries run regularly between Jeddah and Suakin. The service occasionally continues up the Red Sea to Port Suez, but this is too unreliable for advance planning.

MONEY

The standard advice for travellers in most parts of the developing world is to take the majority of funds in travellers' cheques with a supply of cash that can be changed quickly and easily anywhere. Sudan is an exception, however, and for the time being it's a country where hard cash does most of the talking.

Travellers' cheques are both difficult and expensive to change in Sudan. Large banks in Khartoum such as the Sudanese-French Bank will cash travellers' cheques but at a price, charging up to US$30 on a US$100 cheque. Due to US sanctions, American Express travellers' cheques are not accepted at all, and a few travellers have reported difficulties changing anything other than cheques in euros or sterling. Also, as a result of sanctions, credit cards are useless in Sudan.

If you are travelling on an organised tour, carrying cash shouldn't be a problem, but backpackers may worry about having to carry the sum total of their trip funds in folding money. For the time being the only answer is to divide and hide your money well in your baggage, give thanks that Sudan is relatively crime-free and hope that the finalisation of the government-SPLM/A peace deal and a resolution of the Darfur crisis will lead to the dropping of sanctions.

US dollars are the most convenient currency to carry, although euros and sterling are accepted without problems in large towns.

Budgets

Sudan is not an expensive country to travel around. In Khartoum, a budget traveller could get by on less than US$10 a day and still stay in reasonable accommodation and eat well. Decent hotels start from US$20 or so with meals thrown in. Outside Khartoum, the cost (and choice) of accommodation drops considerably, but even taking travelling from A to B into consideration, a basic daily budget of US$15–20 should be fine.

Prices start rising when you start making special arrangements. The most obvious example of this is if you plan on diving in the Red Sea. If you plan on hiring a vehicle, perhaps to explore some remote archaeological sites, bear in mind that this will also add significantly to your budget. A 4WD with driver/guide typically starts at US$150 a day. Archaeological permits are another thing to be considered. At US$10 a time, you'll need to carefully plan which sites you want to visit to avoid costs spiralling unexpectedly. The price of bureaucracy is high in Sudan, so you'll need to budget for registration on arrival (around US$20) and any visa fees if you're travelling on from Sudan.

WHAT TO TAKE
Luggage

A rucksack is the best way to go in Sudan, or else a hardwearing soft bag. A bag that can be padlocked is good for deterring opportunistic theft and is a sensible precaution given the current need to carry large amounts of hard currency in Sudan. This should particularly be considered if you anticipate staying in *lokandas*, with their communal sleeping arrangements. If your rucksack allows you to fold away the shoulder straps in a separate compartment, so much the better, as this reduces the risk of damage at airports; leaving at the end of my last trip I forgot to do just this at Khartoum airport and my rucksack arrived home one strap short. Sudan's dust can be incredibly pervasive against even the best-sealed bags, so you may want to consider putting your belongings in bags inside your pack for further protection.

Clothes

Pack as lightly as possible. As a general rule, bring clothes for a hot climate. A couple of pairs of trousers (or long skirts), three shirts or T-shirts and a week's worth of underwear should be ample. A light fleece or jacket is also a good idea, particularly in winter when nights and early mornings can be cold. Natural fabrics such as cotton are best, although most outdoor shops are bulging with excellent lightweight fabrics that when washed will dry in minutes in Sudan's heat. A sun hat is invaluable, as is a scarf or bandana to protect against dust.

The issue of dress can be a delicate matter in Sudan. Muslim dress codes, for both men and women, are based on modesty. For this reason you shouldn't wear tops with bare shoulders. You sometimes see travellers wearing shorts in Sudan (mainly those who have spent a long time overlanding through Africa). It should be noted that anywhere in the Muslim parts of Sudan shorts are not acceptable. A Sudanese will generally be too polite to mention this, but in *their* eyes you will appear as if you're dressed in your underwear.

Sudan doesn't have enough accessible hiking to warrant heavy walking boats, so trainers or light walking shoes should suffice. Sports sandals are a good alternative. Flip flops (thongs) are useful when negotiating the floors of communal showers.

Camping

There is little need to bring any camping equipment to Sudan. Most hiking areas such as Jebel Marra are currently inaccessible, so the only reason to bring a tent along is if you have your own vehicle and will be camping in the bush.

That said, a sleeping bag is a good idea. Cheap hotels in Sudan are somewhat less than generous when it comes to providing bedding, so at the bare minimum a sleeping sheet would be useful. Even in the desert north, winter nights be distinctly chilly, so upgrading to a lightweight sleeping bag can make for a better night's sleep.

Miscellaneous

Toiletries are plentiful and relatively inexpensive in Sudan's larger towns. Toilet paper is a must unless you fancy the local 'hand and water' technique of cleaning. Don't expect to find toilet paper anywhere outside mid-range hotels. Women should bring enough tampons or sanitary towels to last the trip, although these can be found in Khartoum. The contents of a recommended medical kit are discussed in more detail in *Chapter 5*. A mosquito net is also useful, and don't forget to pack insect repellent and sunblock. A small towel is as much as you'll need for the odd shower.

Keeping clean on the road can sometimes seem like a battle against dust, and washing facilities are often lacking at roadside stops. Baby wipes are great to clean up with, or better still a small bottle of anti-bacterial disinfectant hand gel that can easily be slipped into a daypack.

A penknife and torch should definitely find their way into your pack. Power cuts are common in cities and in more remote parts electricity is rare so you might want to supplement the torch with candles, although these can easily be picked up locally.

Dental floss is the world's best sewing thread as well as having a more obvious application. You'll need a large needle for running repairs. Safety pins are equally useful.

Padlocks have been mentioned in connection with bags, but one is also useful to lock doors in cheap hotels where keys are sometimes lacking. Other useful sundries include a water bottle and purification treatment, a multi-fit travel plug, a washing line and (biodegradable) detergent.

Entertainment options are limited in Sudan, so bringing a good book or two is essential. English-language books are very hard to find outside Khartoum and there isn't even a great selection there. A short-wave radio can make a great travelling companion, although the truly 21st century traveller probably carries an iPod or similar music player these days. Whatever your technological inclinations, a pack of cards also provides a worthwhile distraction.

PLANNING AN ITINERARY

Itineraries in guidebooks are highly subjective affairs. Each traveller has their own personal interests, length of time available for their trip and preferred type of travel. If you are travelling independently you may also need to consider whether you're visiting Sudan as part of a trip that includes neighbouring countries, as entry and exit points will have a significant bearing on the shape of your trip.

NUBIAN EXHIBITS ABROAD
It's not necessary to wait until you get to Sudan to see some of its archaeological gems. Listed below are the museums with the best collections of Nubian artefacts outside Sudan:

The British Museum, London (*www.thebritishmuseum.ac.uk*)
One of the best Nubian collections outside Sudan and Egypt. There are many treasures on view, including a beautiful sphinx with the face of Taharqa from Kawa, a pair of granite lions from Soleb, and finds from continuing excavations in Sudan.

Museum of Fine Arts, Boston (*www.mfa.org*)
Easily the most important Nubian collection in the USA, representing all the periods of ancient Nubia. Highlights include the massed *shawabti* statues of Taharqa, Aspelta's 12-tonne sarcophagus and a wealth of funerary goods from Nuri and Meroe.

Royal Ontario Museum, Toronto (*www.rom.on.ca*)
A dedicated gallery represents the history of Nubia told through one ancient

When planning an itinerary, always remember that Sudan is not always a fast country when it comes to getting things done. It's a huge place, so getting from A to B can take up significant chunks of your time unless you choose to fly between destinations. Where transport infrastructure is poor, most notably in the desert north, long travel times can also be physically exhausting, so it's wise to allow for rest days between longer trips. Another thing that can eat up your time is paper-chasing in Khartoum. Factor in extra time if travel and archaeological permits need to be arranged. A final point to remember when planning your trip is whether you will be dependent on infrequent transport connections. The weekly Khartoum-Wadi Halfa train and the ferry to Aswan in Egypt are the most notable examples here, and a bit of forward planning can save unnecessary waiting or missed connections.

For all Sudan's vast size, the number of draw-cards that are accessible to visitors is still fairly restricted, largely due to conflict in the South and in Darfur. In a way, Sudan is the attraction in itself, as it's a country still relatively unknown to travellers but that's incredibly welcoming to visitors. The warmth and hospitality of the Sudanese is the abiding memory of Sudan for many people. For others, the emptiness and solitude of the deserts are a major draw. Those with particular tastes, however, will still find plenty to attract them.

Archaeological sites
Sudan's ancient sites, the remains of Kush and medieval Nubia, are strung out along the Nile north of Khartoum. Each requires a permit from Khartoum to visit and at US$10 a head it's worth considering whether you have merely a

town, on the Sudanese-Egyptian border. Alongside everyday items, there are accounts and artefacts from ancient Egyptian expeditions to Nubia.

Ägyptisches Museum, Berlin (*www.smb.spk-berlin.de/amp/e/s.html*)
Contains many fine artefacts brought back from Nubia in the early days of modern European exploration, including statuary and the gold treasure of Amanishakheto, found in Meroe by the adventurer-cum-vandal Ferlini in 1834.

National Museum, Warsaw (*www.ddg.art.pl/nm*)
Home to over 60 frescoes from the medieval cathedral at Faras, rescued by Polish archaeologists from the Aswan Dam flood. The other half of the collection is found in the National Museum in Khartoum.

Nubia Museum, Aswan (*www.touregypt.net/nubiamuseum.htm*)
Housed in a stunning new building and packed with objects representing both ancient and modern Nubia. The history has an undeniable pro-Egyptian slant, but it's worth a look for anyone passing through Aswan to or from Sudan.

casual interest in ancient Sudan or are really an archaeology buff, as costs can quickly mount up. The most popularly visited site is the Royal Cemetery of Meroe, better known simply as the Pyramids. As well as being probably the most stunning of Sudan's archaeological sites, it's also the most accessible; it's sat just off the highway between Khartoum and Atbara, and with an early start it can be visited as a day trip from the capital. Close by, near the town of Shendi, are the temples of Naqa and Musawwarat. There is no public transport, so you'll need to hire a vehicle to reach them. Naqa is particularly rewarding, with several intact temples. These sites are all covered in *Chapter 7*.

Futher north are the cluster of sites around Karima and Dongola – notably Jebel Barkal, Nuri and El Kurru (see *Chapter 8*). The Jebel Barkal site is open to all visitors but a permit is required to enter the locked temple, something which is probably only of interest to dedicated archaeologists. Nuri's crumbling pyramids and El Kurru's delightful tomb wall paintings are also definitely worth a visit.

The medieval Nubian sites of Old Dongola and Ghazali are harder to reach and require more planning to visit. The same goes for the West Bank temples of Soleb, Sesibi and Sedeinga (*Chapter 9*). These are particularly ruined, although their remoteness is likely to deter casual visitors. On the other hand, getting there is half the fun and many people will relish the challenge of ferry hopping and hitchhiking to reach them.

The problems of access mean that many sites are best reached by hired vehicle, although for independent travellers this can increase costs considerably. If you do have your own vehicle, or are travelling as part of an organised group, the isolation of the sites becomes one of their greatest assets. You will normally have each place to yourself, without a single tout or souvenir seller in sight.

A word of caution if you enter Sudan from Egypt. By doing so you are unfortunately penalised when it comes to archaeological sites, as there is nowhere to get a permit until you reach Atbara. The ruins of the West Bank temples (Soleb, Sesibi and Sedeinga) are so remote that it is usually possible to visit them without a permit, but you'll almost certainly be out of luck trying to access El Kurru and Nuri. Jebel Barkal should present no such problems, but if you have your heart set on particular sites, you'll probably need to back-track once you reach Khartoum. The National Museum in Khartoum should be visited by everyone with an interest in ancient Sudan (see page 115).

Scuba diving

Sudan probably has the best diving sites in the Red Sea (see pages 189–93). Sanganeb and Sha'ab Rumi are world-beaters in terms of their large schools of sharks, their coral and their reef fish. The latter is also the site of Jacques Cousteau's famous Conshelf II experiment in underwater living, which can still be explored by divers. Most divers visit the Sudanese Red Sea as part of a self-contained package, but the opening of an on-shore dive centre with full equipment hire in Port Sudan has created new opportunities for devotees of the underwater world. Summer heat shuts down diving centres throughout July and August.

Trekking

Sudan has plenty of potential as an interesting trekking destination. The weirdly shaped granite mountains around Kassala (*Chapter 10*) in the east are ideal for day walks and scrambling. The Red Sea Hills run along most of the coast and could be great for trekkers who want to head out on their own. The best starting place is the old hill resort of Erkowit in the heart of Beja country (see *Chapter 11*).

The gradual opening of the Nuba Mountains should set any trekker's mouth watering, although the security and permit situation is still unclear and needs to be checked out on arrival in Khartoum. The green rocky hills of the Nuba Mountains rise out of the Kordofan plains and their people suffered greatly during the civil war – infrastructure is minimal, so it's best to be as self-sufficient as possible here. The ideal time to visit is during the autumn harvest, as this will give you the best chance to experience the many festivals (see *Chapter 12*) that take place in the region.

In the event of a peaceful resolution to the Darfur crisis and reconstruction in the area, the Jebel Marra plateau beckons the truly adventurous. This fertile hill country was once Sudan's best trekking destination and may yet be again.

Culture

Sudan is one of the most ethnically diverse countries in Africa. One of the pleasures of any trip is seeing the many tribes that make up the country. Even standing at a juice bar in Khartoum's Souq el-Arabi you can see a microcosm of Sudan pass in front of you in a few minutes.

The best place for people-spotting in the capital is at the Omdurman Souq, Sudan's largest market. The Camel Market on the western edge of the city is a meeting place for the Arab tribes of Darfur and Kordofan. In Khartoum North it's possible to see Nuba wrestling on Friday afternoons, although this unfortunately clashes with the 'whirling dervishes', a Sufi order who dance and pray at sunset in Omdurman – definitely one of Sudan's must-see events.

Kassala has one of the best markets in Sudan. It's sprawled across the town and is full of the shock-headed Beja and the Rashaida, with their veiled and bejewelled women. The men of both tribes frequently wear their swords to market.

Along the Nile in northern Sudan you can experience the hospitality of the Shaqiyah Arabs and the Nubians, whose land stretches into Egypt. Kordofan, a mix of Arab in the plains and Nuba in the mountains to the south of the province, is one of the most ethnically rich parts of the country. Troubled Darfur is similarly diverse, but here ethnic differences are playing themselves out through violence, and the region is currently closed to travel.

Off the beaten track

In many respects you'd be hard pressed to describe anywhere in Sudan as on the beaten track as the country has still largely to be discovered by travellers. Even the most popular route along the Nile north of Khartoum could hardly be labelled as particularly busy, but just stopping in a town or village for a couple of days to experience the gentle pace of life can be incredibly rewarding. The opportunities for exploration are almost endless.

The long-isolated Nuba Mountains are potentially one of the most attractive places to visit, subject to the evolving security and permit situation discussed above. East Sudan is little visited, but the area around Kassala is particularly interesting. The agricultural heart of Sudan, between Gedaref and Wad Medani and in the Gezira area between the Niles, is low on 'attractions' but is arguably just as fascinating once you get exploring – you can learn at least as much about the country by talking to a farm worker in a tea house in the Gezira as you can by visiting any amount of archaeological sites. Any reasonably sized town will have at least one place to stay and if there is a bus heading there, that should be reason enough to go for many travellers.

The most tantalising prospect for the adventurous is the on-going peace process between the government and SPLM/A that could potentially open up swathes of South Sudan for the first time in over 20 years. Even if this happens, however, real safety concerns will persist, making it essential to check the current security situation before even thinking of attempting a trip. Thoughts on possible travel options in South Sudan – from boats up the Nile to Juba to who controls where – are discussed in *Chapter 14*.

TOUR OPERATORS

The majority of tour companies offering trips to Sudan are based in the UK:

Exodus Grange Mills, Weir Rd, London SW12 0NE, UK; tel: 0870 240 5550; fax: 020 8673 0779; email: info@exodus.co.uk; www.exodus.co.uk. Two-week camel trekking trips in the northern deserts, led by desert-exploration and Sudan expert Michael Asher.

Explore Worldwide 1 Frederick St, Aldershot, Hants GU11 1LQ, UK; tel: 01252 760000; fax: 01252 760001; email: info@exploreworldwide.com; www.exploreworldwide.com. Ten-day camping and cultural tour of the main archaeological sites of North Sudan and combined 22-day Egypt–Sudan tour.

I Viaggi di Maurizio Levi Via Londonio 4, 20154 Milan, Italy; tel: +39 02 3493 4528; fax: +39 02 3493 4595; email: info@deserti-viaggilevi.it; www.italtoursudan.com. Group and tailor-made travel throughout North Sudan.

The Traveller 92–93 Great Russell St, London, WC1B 3PS, UK; tel: 020 7436 9343; fax: 020 7436 7475; email: info@thetraveller2004.com; www.thetraveller2004.com. Five-day 'city break' tours of Khartoum and the highlights of ancient Kush.

Overland tours

The following operators offer trips to Sudan as part of a larger 'trans-Africa' tour. While some run itineraries travelling Egypt-Sudan-Ethiopia (or vice versa), others pass through Sudan as part of an west-east traverse: before booking check contingency plans should events in Darfur mean the continued closure of this route.

Dragoman Camp Green, Debenham, Stowmarket, Suffolk IP14 6LA, UK; tel: 0870 499 4475; fax: 01728 861127; email: info@dragoman.co.uk; www.dragoman.co.uk

Guerba World Travel Wessex House, 40 Station Rd, Westbury, Wilts BA13 3JN, UK; tel: 01373 826611; fax: 01373 858351; email: info@guerba.co.uk; www.guerba.co.uk
Oasis Overland The Marsh, Henstridge, Somerset BA8 0TF, UK; tel: 01963 363400; fax: 01963 363200; email: info@oasisoverland.co.uk; www.oasisoverland.co.uk
Overland Club Salters House, Salters Lane, Sedgefield, Stockton-on-Tees TS21 3EE, UK; tel: 0845 658 0336; fax: 0845 658 0337; email: info@overlandclub.com; www.overlandclub.com

Scuba diving

There are many scuba diving companies that sell packages to Sudan, most of which buy into places on the various liveaboard boats that operate out of Port Sudan. A web search or diving magazines such as *Diver* will produce a more comprehensive list.

Aqua Action for Water Sports Via Borodin 19, 56122 Pisa, Italy; tel: 0333 64 33 254 (Mobile Italy), 0123 41282 (Mobile Sudan) email: info@sudandiving.it; www.sudandiving.it. Operates the *Don Questo* liveaboard.
Emperor Divers Hilton Hotel, Port Sudan; tel/fax: 0311 24815; email: reservations.sudan@emperordivers.com; www.emperordivers.com. Operates Sudan's only dive centre (5-star PADI rated and fully equipped including equipment hire). Operators for the dayboat *Empress Isa*, as well as tours on the *Elegante*.
Red Sea Divers 19 Westfield Rd, Cupar KT15 5AP, UK; tel/fax: 0870 4430311; email: info@redseadivers.com; www.redseadivers.com
Scuba Snacks Attic Office, 11 Jew St, Brighton BN1 1UT, UK; tel: 0870 7461266; email: info@scubasnacks.com; www.scubasnacks.com. Offers tours on the *Baron Noir* and *Freedom*.
Tony Backhurst Scuba The Scuba Centre, Smithbrook Kilns, Cranleigh, Surrey GU6 8JJ, UK; tel: 0800 0728221; fax: 01483 272163; email: travel@scuba.co.uk; www.scuba.co.uk. Trips on the *Freedom*.
Xplore 360 Zeedijk 776, 8300 Knokke, Belgium; tel: 050 61 17 85; fax: 050 62 75 05; email: info@Xplore360.com. Trips on the *Elegante*.

Sudanese operators

There aren't many travel companies in Sudan that can offer anything more to travellers beyond car hire and booking flight tickets. The two companies listed below can provide full services including guides, tents and vehicle hire for North Sudan (including the use of GPS). The full telephone code for Khartoum is +249 11 followed by the number.

Globtours Sharia Sayed Abdul Rahman, tel: 011 798111 (mobile: 0912 253 484); email: globtours_sudan@yahoo.com. Nubian-run company with long experience of dealing with overlanders, including shipping vehicles across Lake Nasser. Have recently started running tours to the Nuba Mountains.
Italian Tourism Company Sharia 27, Amarat; tel: 011487961; fax: 011 487962; email: italtour@sudanmail.net.sd. Partner company to I Viaggi di Maurizio Levi in Milan, specialising in visits to archaeological sites and running the Meroe Tented Camp and Nubian Guest House in Karima.

Travel in Sudan

TOURIST INFORMATION

Sudan isn't yet geared up for tourists, and as such there are few facilities offering information or services to visitors. The Ministry of Tourism on Sharia Abu Sinn in Khartoum can dig up a few old maps of Khartoum, but is vague when asked for specific advice. Atbara has a surprisingly good tourist office, and can arrange permits to visit certain archaeological sites. They can also provide pamphlets and postcards.

PUBLIC HOLIDAYS

The following are public holidays in Sudan. All government and most private businesses will be shut on these days:

Independence Day 1 January
Revolution Day   30 June
Christmas Day   25 December

In addition, many Islamic celebrations are public holidays. Dates vary each year, as the Islamic year is based on the lunar calendar, with the exact dates fixed by sightings of the moon. Easter Monday, another moveable feast, is also a public holiday.

Islamic New Year	February 10 2005, January 30 2006, January 19 2007
Prophet Mohammed's Birthday	April 21 2005, April 10 2006, March 30 2007)
Eid al-Fitr	November 3 2005, October 23 2006, October 12 2007 (three days)
Eid al-Adha	January 20 2005, January 10 2006, December 30 2007 (four days)

Eid al-Fitr celebrates the end of Ramadan, the month long dawn-to-dusk fast. Ramadan can be a tricky time for visitors – little seems to get done, offices shut early and restaurants and cafeterias are closed throughout the fast. That said, the breaking of the fast (*iftar*) every evening is a joyous occasion; restaurants burst at the seams and you'll often receive invitations to share food. It's a common joke that many people actually put on weight during Ramadan from over-eating in the evening and early mornings.

The festival of sacrifice, Eid al-Adha, is the most important holiday of the year, commemorating Abraham's sacrifice of his son Ismael. The Haj pilgrimage to Mecca also coincides with this feast. The entire country shuts down and transport is booked solid as people travel home to visit their families – Khartoum in particular undergoes significant depopulation. This can make things difficult for the traveller as many restaurants close for the entire holiday; in addition it is essential to plan your budget so that you don't run out of dinars while the banks are shut.

MONEY

The unit of currency is the Sudanese dinar (SD). Notes are printed in denominations of 2,000, 1,000, 500, 200, 100 and 50SD, with coins of 50, 20, 10 and 5SD.

The dinar was introduced in the mid-1990s, replacing the old Sudanese pound in an attempt to curb inflation. The population has taken slowly to the new currency, and most transactions are still quoted in pounds, a situation that can cause confusion for the unwary traveller. One dinar is equivalent to ten pounds, so a mango juice that costs 40SD may be quoted to you as costing 400 pounds.

To throw you off balance even more, it's common to drop even more zeroes from a price – particularly when it comes to taxi and minibus fares. If you're told that a ride will cost five, the chances are that the driver means 5000 pounds – or 500SD in real money. It can be hard to adjust at first to this seemingly random method of pricing, but once you're used to the prices of a few basic goods you'll get the hang of things. If in doubt, ask which currency you're being quoted in.

The Sudanese dinar is a surprisingly stable currency, and has kept its value against the US dollar and euro well in recent years. For quick mental arithmetic, one dollar is worth around 250SD, one euro 300SD and one pound 400SD – so a 1,000SD note is worth about US$4, € or £2.50. Given its stability, all prices are quoted in this book in dinars, unless payment is explicitly requested in dollars.

Changing money

There are no restrictions on importing hard currencies, and currency declaration forms are a thing of the past.

Sudan is a primarily a cash economy. Travellers' cheques are accepted at a very few banks in Khartoum, but charge huge commissions – up to 30% on a $100 cheque. Carrying cash isn't ideal from a security point of view, but for the time being it's the only realistic choice. Keep it hidden safely, but take comfort from the fact that Sudan is one of the safest countries in Africa.

US sanctions have meant that credit cards are useless in Sudan. If the peace process continues and sanctions are lifted it should be possible to get cash advances on plastic at major banks.

Banks are everywhere in Sudan, but only a few of them have exchange facilities. The Bank of Khartoum is the usually the best option, along with Baraka Bank and the Sudanese-French Bank. There are plenty of Islamic banks but they never seem to have exchange facilities.

A number of private exchange offices have opened in the last few years, and tend to keep longer hours than banks – very useful if you're short of money on a Thursday afternoon with the weekend approaching. Kalsan Foreign Exchange has branches in Khartoum and Port Sudan and can also arrange money transfers.

Sudan has a negligible black market, so it's hardly worth taking a risk for a couple of extra dinars on the dollar.

RED TAPE AND PERMITS

As the largest country in Africa, Sudan is also sadly cursed with the continent's largest bureaucracy. A few days chasing permissions in the heat of Khartoum can be enough to drive anyone to distraction. The trick is to forget any Western conceptions of speed and efficiency and adopt a more laid-back Sudanese approach to the quest. Offices might be closed or the clerk at an extended breakfast, but if he is then you're likely to be invited to join him for a bowl of *ful* or glass of tea anyway – so what's the rush?

Registration

All foreign nationals must register with the Ministry of Interior within three days of arrival in Sudan. Tour companies and top-end hotels will normally take care of this automatically. Most people will register in Khartoum, but it is also possible to register on arrival at most Sudanese border crossings.

In Khartoum, registration takes place on the top floor of the tall pink Aliens Building on Sharia al-Taiyar Morad. You need to take your passport plus a photocopy of the identification page and Sudanese visa (with entrance stamp), and one photo. No-one ever seems to pay exactly the same registration fee; it fluctuates around the 4,500SD (US$18) mark. On filling in the form, you need to get it counter-stamped by the hotel where you're staying. Mid-range hotels often have a supply of registration forms already stamped for you to take to the office. At the cheaper end of the spectrum some hotels might not even have a stamp, so you might have to do as I once did, and take along the receptionist with the hotel ledger to prove your residence! Registration consists of another stamp in your passport, which is checked on departure.

If you're arriving overland, the registration procedure can vary slightly at each border, although proof of residence is more flexibly interpreted (crossing from Ethiopia at Gallabat, where there is nowhere to actually stay, you register straight after immigration). The registration fees are consistently higher than Khartoum by around 1,000SD (US$4), due to further charges levied by provincial governments. If you have registered at a land border, it is not necessary to do so again in Khartoum. Some towns in Sudan – mainly in the west, where the security situation remains fractious – may insist on you registering again on arrival. There is no further fee, but the excess of stamps can quickly fill a few more pages in your passport.

Travel permits

Travel outside Khartoum is regulated by a series of travel permits. No permits are required to travel north of Khartoum to Wadi Halfa, east to the Ethiopian border, west to Kordofan as far as El Obeid and south as far as Kosti. Most other places require special permission. Permits are frequently checked when travelling by road, and when checking into hotels. The permit system generally applies to travel by land – if you fly to Port Sudan you don't need a permit, but if you take a bus you do.

Until the end of 2003, free travel permits were issued by the Ministry of Tourism in Khartoum – they were free and quick to get, and covered most areas. This system has now been abolished. Most areas of interest to tourists, such as the north, were declared fully open and all restrictions removed. Everywhere else now falls under the remit of the Ministry of Interior, with all the paper-pushing that implies. Travel permits cost 6,000SD (around US$24). Apply in good time – processing takes a minimum of three days.

You apply for travel permits at the Aliens Building in Khartoum, in the same office as for registration. One photo is needed, plus three passport photocopies. The application form allows you to list as many destinations as you like for as long a period as your visa will allow, so it's worth adding in places you're not even sure if you'll visit, just in case. Attach the photo and get the form stamped. Photocopy the form three times (there is a photocopier in the office), and attach to each a copy of your passport, Sudanese visa and registration stamp.

You then need to take everything across town to the Ministry of Humanitarian Affairs. The (unmarked) office is on the second floor, through the entrance on Sharia Zubeir Pasha. Applications usually take two or three days to process. If your application is successful the forms will be returned to you covered in stamps from External Security and Military Intelligence. These need to be taken to a sub-office of the Ministry of Interior on the opposite side of the building (the gatehouse on the Sharia al-Gamhurriya entrance) to be checked.

You are finally ready to get your travel permit. Everything is crosschecked against your passport and your application is stamped again. Once the officials are satisfied a permit is filled in (in Arabic), for which you'll need to provide another photo. Only at this final stage do you pay the fee of 6000SD (US$24). Once you've got your travel permit take several photocopies, as officials are fond of keeping them at checkpoints or when you're registering in a new town.

At the time of going to press, it was reported that the whole permit process had been consolidated into the Ministry of Interior sub-office at the gatehouse, so it is worth checking if the process has been streamlined before applying.

Currently no travel permits are being issued for South Sudan or Darfur, even for those wishing to take internal flights. The situation with the Nuba Mountains remains vague as control of the area is split between the government and SPLM/A, but it seems that some permits for Dilling and Kadugli and the surrounding area are being issued. If the comprehensive peace deal is stuck to by the two parties, it is hoped the travel permit system will be relaxed even further, making swathes of the country open to visitors again, but don't expect the wheels of Sudanese bureaucracy to move too fast.

Photography permits

Technically, all foreign visitors must get a photography permit to allow them to use their cameras. In practice, this rule seems to be commonly ignored or forgotten completely.

The permits are free from the Ministry of Tourism in Khartoum. It's a simple case of filling in one form and providing a passport photo. You list the subjects you'll be taking pictures of (and where), so it's best to be as encompassing as possible – 'tourist attractions' or 'cultural sites' seems to do the trick. You also need to list all of the provinces you're likely to visit. Once you've filled in the form and had it stamped, the staff will send you away to get two photocopies for their records. As you keep the original it's anyone's guess what would happen if you didn't return with the copies, although I doubt that the system would grind to a halt.

The permit is explicit regarding things you are not allowed to photograph, such as military areas, bridges and power stations – all common sense in a developing country with a large security apparatus. Photos of 'slum areas, beggars and other defaming subjects' are also strictly forbidden.

Whether or not it's worth getting a permit is an open question. Although I have always got one, I've never actually been asked to produce it by the authorities. In Khartoum people can be more sensitive about cameras, possibly because of the number of government offices in the city, but outside Khartoum things are more relaxed. Simply checking whether you can take a picture of building or scene (something you would do if taking a picture of a person as a matter of course) should be adequate. On the other hand, the permit is free and only takes ten minutes to get, and may be worth acquiring if you plan on taking a lot of photographs or filming with a video camera.

Archaeological permits

The Kushite remains of north Sudan are one of the highlights of a trip to Sudan. It's perhaps inevitable, then, that access is regulated by a series of permits. These are issued by the Antiquities Service in Khartoum, and the Ministry of Tourism in Atbara (for Meroe, Naqa and Musawwarat only). This is all well and good if you start your trip in the capital, but it's a real pain if you enter Sudan by ferry from Egypt, where it's clearly not practical to travel down to Khartoum and then retrace your steps, just so you can see the tomb-paintings at El Kurru.

A permit is required for each site and at US$10 each (payable in hard currency) the costs can quickly mount, especially if you're an archaeology buff. Those with a casual interest may want to restrict themselves to a couple of choice sites (see *Highlights*, page 49). Each permit is given to the *ghaffir* (caretaker) on entrance to the site.

It might seem simpler just to operate an entrance fee system at the archaeological sites but the Sudanese authorities are firmly against such an idea, apparently not trusting the *ghaffirs* not to line their pockets with the money. The irony is that at most sites the *ghaffirs* are so honest that if you turn up with no permit thinking you can slip them a few dinars to gain entrance, they'll send you away disappointed, having delivered a sermon in Arabic about doing things by the book!

The Sudanese Antiquities Service in Khartoum (tel: 011 780935) is on Sharia Jama'a, behind the Sudan National Museum. Permits are available from the Antiquities Officers on the third floor - you simply tell them where you'd like to visit, hand over your money and collect the permission.

If you think you might be eligible for a free permit (if you're an archaeology student, for example) you can request them by writing a letter to the Director General of the National Corporation for Antiquities and Museums. If you arrive early in the morning, this should be processed on the same day.

GETTING AROUND
By plane

Sudan Airways has domestic flights covering the entire country. The timetable is a moveable feast at best, and flights are liable to be changed or cancelled at short notice. Busy flights (such as Khartoum to Port Sudan) tend to run well; less popular routes are inevitably subject to the most change – the most common reason for cancelling a flight is that not enough passengers have booked tickets in advance. The following flight information is presented as a guideline only:

Port Sudan (daily), Dongola, Wadi Halfa, El Obeid, El Fasher, El Geneina, Malakal, Wau (all twice weekly), Nyala and Juba (three times weekly). At the time of research, the Kassala service was suspended. Flights to South Sudan and Darfur require a travel permit which is currently unobtainable for normal travellers, although it is hoped that these will become accessible during the life of this guide.

Sample one-way fares from Khartoum include Port Sudan (17,320SD/$68), Wadi Halfa (22,190SD/$87) and Juba (35,240SD/$138). There is a domestic departure tax of 100SD. Reconfirming your flight in person the day before travel is strongly recommended.

Sudan Airways planes are leased from foreign countries. In July 2003 a Sudan Airways 737 flight between Port Sudan and Khartoum suffered catastrophic engine failure minutes after taking off. The resulting crash killed 116 people; only a two-year-old child survived. Poor maintenance was blamed for the disaster.

By road

Wherever you want to go in Sudan, there's likely to be some sort of transport heading there, even if it means sitting on the top of a truck. Getting there is half the fun.

On my first trip to Sudan I constantly asked what time the bus would arrive, and was frustrated with answers ranging from 'soon' to 'we will sleep there tonight.' No-one is in a rush, so it's best to adopt a Sudanese outlook on the trip (and indeed your whole stay in Sudan). Even luxury coaches can get flat tyres, and the best drivers can get stuck in sand. The journey may take a while but you will get there eventually, *inshallah*.

Sudan is a huge country, and you should allow plenty of time to get around. Travel times are relatively quick on the paved highways, but as most roads in Sudan are dirt tracks of varying quality, you can easily spend as much or more time in buses as you do enjoying the rest of the country. Not only that, but bad roads and cramped buses can be physically very wearing, so make sure you factor in as much time as you can between long trips.

One thing to bear in mind when travelling by road is dust. As few roads are paved in Sudan, dust is a perennial problem, so it's useful to have a scarf or bandana handy to keep the stuff out. I often seem to come back from Sudan with a nasty cough, and I have no doubt that long hours travelling on dusty tracks are a major culprit.

Bus

Sudan has a large variety of transport options falling under the loose category of 'bus'.

At the top end of the scale, luxury coaches link Khartoum to Port Sudan, Kassala, Atbara and El Obeid. They are fast and comfortable, run to a set timetable, and for your money you get plied with hot and cold drinks and snacks between meal breaks. This is the most expensive bus option (the 14-hour Khartoum–Port Sudan fare is around 7,900SD), but the reclining seats are positively heavenly if you've been bumping around in a pick-up for much of your trip. Companies running these coaches include Saf Saf, Aslan, El Shihaab Express and Pan Express.

Mid-range buses ply the same routes, but are much slower and have a more relaxed attitude to squeezing in passengers. You can certainly forget about having your own dedicated seat. These bus companies are usually only signed in Arabic and many appear to have a coach body attached to a truck chassis.

In north and western Sudan where tarmac is rare, the Sudanese have truly made the bus their own. These vehicles really are just trucks masquerading as buses, with seats welded in the back, and open sides to let in the elements. Built to last, with little consideration for speed or comfort, they are the cheapest – and often the only – option available. Passengers and their worldly goods are crammed inside, while enough baggage is lashed on top to double the vehicle's height.

Minibuses (*hafla*) link towns relatively close together and are fast and convenient. There's no need to pre-book – just turn up at the bus station; the minibus departs when full.

At the bus station you'll find bus company offices where you can pre-book tickets. Long-distance transport usually departs early in the morning (typically around 06.00), so it's wise to check departure times in advance. While you wait there are stands to get a bowl of *ful* or a kebab, and the ubiquitous tea ladies with their stalls.

Large towns often have several bus terminals, so you need to check where your bus leaves from by asking for the correct *moghof* or station. If you're heading to Kosti, for instance, the buses leave from '*moghof Kosti*'. The term 'bus station' is often synonymous with Souq es-Shabi, or People's Market. In many cases, the Souq es-Shabi acts as the only bus station, and can be several kilometres outside the town.

Travellers will quickly come to think of Souq es-Shabi as transport hubs, but they are primarily market places, and passengers use them for shopping on their way home as vendors hold their merchandise up to the bus windows. Waiting for one bus to fill, in the space of half an hour my fellow travellers bought children's clothes, tea glasses, perfume, clothes pegs, biscuits, falafel, socks, soap, a clock and a cheesegrater – all without leaving their seats!

Finally, don't be afraid to use the touts who will approach you at most bus stations. Compared to many neighbouring countries they are generally very helpful, and you won't suffer an extra commission on top of the price of your ticket.

Boksi

The workhorse of rural Sudan is the pickup truck, known locally as a *boksi* (plural *bokasi*). Almost always a Toyota Hilux, these are the most common form of transport where there is no sealed road, particularly in northern Sudan. Quicker than a bus over the same ground, they are also slightly more expensive. A two-hour trip typically costs around 500–600SD.

Bokasi are a fast and furious way to travel. The cab has two seats next to the driver and the covered back of the pick-up has bench seating along each side, with five passengers crammed on each row. Any free floor space is taken up with baggage, with an unlimited number of children thrown in for good measure. Latecomers sit on the roof. The benches are hard and you can feel every bump. If you can, avoid the space over the tailgate – whenever the vehicle hits a pothole you'll be liable to go flying. Short trips are fine, but a long journey can leave you cramped and bruised if the road is particularly bad.

Most *bokasi* companies have offices where it's possible to book a seat a day in advance – look for a painted picture of the vehicle, with the destinations listed in Arabic. Your name is written on a passenger manifest, with payment usually collected just before departure. The more comfortable seats next to the driver cost a quarter to a third more than those in the back and are always the first to be reserved.

Your own vehicle

For many years travellers have visited Sudan as part of a larger trip through Africa. In fact, on recent trips to Sudan I got the impression that independent travellers with vehicles actually outnumbered the backpackers. Having your own vehicle gives you the ultimate freedom to travel where you want, and camping under the stars can really let you enjoy Sudan at its most spectacular and wild.

Detailed planning for a major overland trip is outside the scope of this guide, but there are several excellent resources out there to help you with your preparations. Bradt's *Africa by Road* by Charlie Shackell and Illya Bracht has comprehensive information on vehicle preparation, route planning and dealing with bureaucracy, and a handy gazetteer for the entire continent. Two other

GPS POINTS FOR ARCHAEOLOGICAL SITES

Many of north Sudan's archaeological sites are difficult to access without a vehicle, or have few or no landmarks to guide you there. A list of selected sites with GPS points are provided below, along with locations of vehicle ferries for overlanders.

Naqa	N 16°16,476	E 33°16,446
Musawwarat	N 16°25,570	E 33°19,278
Sesibi	N 20°06,614	E 30°32,519
Soleb	N 20°26,249	E 30°19,918
El Kurru	N 18°24'668	E 31°46'514
Deffufa	N 19°34,742	E 30°25,101
Kawa	N 19°08'000	E 30°30'000
Old Dongola	N 18°13,466	E 30°44,714
Ghazali	N 18°26,532	E 31°55,914
Atbara Ferry	N 17°40,254	E 33°57,984
Merowe Ferry	N 18°29,134	E 31°48,874
Dongola Ferry	N 19°10,615	E 30°29,999
Delgo Ferry	N 20°07'280	E 30°33'575

With thanks to Maurizio Levi of *Italian Tourism Company* in Khartoum.

guides also stand out – the encyclopaedic *Vehicle-dependent Expedition Guide* by Tom Sheppard and *The Adventure Motorcycling Handbook* by Chris Scott.

Four-wheel-drive is essential for overlanding in Sudan. In the north and west you can frequently find yourself driving on sand and will need the extra power to keep yourself from getting stuck. The Land Rover is still the vehicle of choice for most overlanders, and there are enough in Sudan to make spares readily available. There are several Land Rover dealers in Khartoum who can source unusual spare parts; at the other end of the spectrum local mechanics are often geniuses of improvisation when it comes to repairs. Sudan's most popular 4WD is the Toyota Landcruiser, a vehicle all garages will be familiar with. Spare parts can be hard to find for motorbikes.

Whatever your vehicle, there are several important points to consider. Fuel and water are top of the list. Carry as much fuel as you can to increase your range. Away from the large towns, fuel can sometimes be hard to come buy, so always make sure your spare container is kept topped up. This is more problematic for motorcycles as sandy conditions reduce your range. Anything less than a 35l-capacity tank may result in problems in the northern deserts or the west. Petrol (*benzene*) in Sudan is sold by the gallon and typically costs about 500SD/gallon (110SD/litre), but the prices increase the farther the fuel has to be transported from either Khartoum or Port Sudan. Wadi Halfa probably has the most expensive petrol – up to 800SD/gallon. Diesel is three quarters of the price but harder to find in smaller places. Along with fuel, carry as much water as possible, both for yourself and to cool your engine in case of

ACROSS SUDAN BY MOTORBIKE
Ulli Rubasch

Not many countries have so resisted collecting information about them as stubbornly as Sudan did for us two-wheeled tourists. We entered the country from Egypt, lacking any solid information. Thankfully the weekly boat from Aswan to Wadi Halfa takes – amid the tomatoes and Taiwanese fish-cans – a limited number of vehicles on board.

Fortunately we had put brand new off-road tyres on our two bikes (a Honda Africa Twin 650cc and a Honda Dominator 500cc) because the first few hundred kilometres along the river Nile are challenging – for the riders as much as for the bikes. From Wadi Halfa to Dongola, the piste changes from hard and stony corrugation to very soft sand. Even when you end up looking like a brown dust-monster, it's useless to clean your clothes as I did in Dongola. The pleasure of feeling clean and tidy lasted exactly 15 minutes. When the brief stretch of tarred road in town ended I immediately hit clouds of fine brown dust, and ended up looking exactly the same as before my time-consuming washing-up!

Travelling through Sudan with a motorbike is a mixture of hell and paradise: hell when you fight against the soft sand along the Nile or try to stand up your fallen bike for the fifth time in an hour while the winter sun burns your neck and paradise when you fly over the beautiful landscape of the Bayuda Desert and feel pure freedom on two wheels. The Sudanese people are exceptional – helpful, friendly and sometimes really shy. Whenever we stopped in a small village, a crowd of a hundred people would gather within minutes. Nobody touched our bikes; it was us they were interested in. Sometimes there would seem to be a competition between them: who would manage to invite the funny-looking strangers into their house? The prize definitely goes to the Nubian man who came running ten kilometres to our camp in the desert: 'I have seen you, I have seen you', he gasped. 'Please, come to my house, I invite every motor biker who is passing my village!'

A few hints that might make biker's lives easier in Sudan: take spare parts with you, especially things that might break when you fall – motorbikes aren't common in Sudan so don't expect to get many spares along the way; take tyres that are good on both sand and stony ground; don't drive at night; calculate your petrol reserves well; and finally, take your time – it always takes you longer than you think.

overheating. When travelling off-road, extra food is another essential precaution.

Other essentials to carry are a comprehensive tool kit and manual for your vehicle, key spare parts and tyres, and a first-aid kit. If you plan on doing any driving in the desert, sand mats are strongly recommended. Many overlanders also use GPS units these days and selected waypoints, such as ferry crossings along the Nile, are presented on page 63.

Road surfaces vary greatly. Throughout the book I have attempted to give a guide to piste quality, but local conditions can vary greatly, with a gravel surface suddenly giving way to a kilometre of windblown sand before changing to deeply rutted tracks. Sand presents the greatest problems for driving, most notably if you choose to follow the railway tracks from Wadi Halfa to Berber. Never speed across open desert as the surface can suddenly give way to gullies or soft sand, bogging your vehicle down. If you need to,

CYCLING THROUGH SUDAN
Rob Cassibo

I must admit I was a little apprehensive about crossing Sudan by bicycle, but to complete the 'Cape to Cairo' leg of my global adventure, I had little choice. I took a deep breath and plunged in.

I crossed the border from Ethiopia at Gallabat and was immediately greeted with 150km of road so diabolical that most trucks preferred to make their own tracks through the neighbouring fields. However, in Gedaref a wonderfully smooth highway appeared and carried me all the way to Khartoum. Hundred kilometre days were easy enough to reel off on the flat – mind-numbingly flat – terrain.

Finding a secluded spot for pitching the tent was never a problem, and offers of a free cot at the informal truck stops along the highway were plentiful. However, truck noise and the unquenchable curiosity of the locals made this an option I partook of only once.

From Khartoum I followed the paved road to Atbara. Unfortunately a stiff north wind cut my daily progress in half. Shortly after Atbara, the road deteriorated quickly into a sandy track. Double-digit speeds were possible on a few of the firmer sections, but for the most part it was like cycling on a beach.

I hit one patch of sand near Berber so soft that the bike dug in and ground to a halt. The wheels were buried so deeply that when I climbed off it stayed up by itself. Wadi Halfa was still 600km away. In the last hour I had covered a mere 5km. At that pace it would take 120 hours of cycling. With only one small town and two desert stations along the way, I would have to carry food for two weeks and water for at least four days. Neither seemed possible.

The weekly train from Khartoum to Wadi Halfa was due in Berber later that day. I bit the bullet and jumped on board.

Although Sudan is not the ideal destination for a two-week cycling vacation, I had fun and my worries and apprehensions were completely unwarranted. The Sudanese are among the friendliest and most hospitable people on the planet.

reduce the tyre pressure to increase the vehicle's footprint (motorcycles may profit from using wider tyres in Sudan).

As always, other travellers are the best source of up-to-date information on road conditions – the Blue Nile Sailing Club in Khartoum has been the de facto meeting place for Sudanese overlanders for several years.

Car hire
There are plenty of car hire places in Khartoum, mostly with showrooms strung out along Africa Road near the airport. Car hire is expensive in Sudan, with prices typically quoted at around $150 a day. If you plan on driving off-road – quite likely given the nature of the country – the vehicle will be supplied with a driver, pushing costs up even more. If you do want to head out into the desert, it's far better to organise things through a local tour company (see *Khartoum*, page 113), who should also be able to provide you will maps and GPS navigation along with the driver.

Hitching
In a country where public transport between villages can be patchy, locals use hitching to get around all the time. Most commonly this means flagging down the big slow trucks that criss-cross Sudan – there isn't usually room in the cab, so you have to climb on top of the load and hang on tightly. Free lifts are rare, however, and drivers will expect you to pay for the ride.

Taxi
Most medium-sized towns have taxis. Drivers instantly mark up their fares for a *khawaja*, so be prepared to haggle. Even in somewhere like Gedaref, drivers will often refuse to take fares for less than 500SD to cross town! Motor-rickshaws are a better alternative for short distances. In small towns, donkey carts or *caro* replace taxis. Sitting on the back of these is a good way to raise a smile from any passing Sudanese.

By train
At independence, Sudan had the most extensive and best-run railway in Africa. Years of under-investment and (often wilful) neglect mean that the Sudan Railways Corporation now runs a strictly limited service. From Khartoum it's possible to take a train north to Wadi Halfa, with a branch line linking Atbara and Port Sudan. A service also runs west from Khartoum to Nyala every couple of weeks. The narrow-gauge branch line from Babanusa south to Wau is no longer operable.

Rail is a relaxing way to travel, but certainly not a fast one. The line from Khartoum to Wadi Halfa usually takes around 36 hours although it has been known to take over two days. Trains aren't always maintained well, sandstorms can stop progress, and tracks often need clearing. Mysterious stops in the middle of nowhere for several hours do occur. As with so much in Sudan, the trick is not to be in a hurry and to enjoy the journey for what it is. The Sudanese seem to manage an almost saintly patience when faced with the

TRAIN TIMES AND PRICES
Khartoum–Wadi Halfa
Monday (returning Wednesday) approx 36 hours
1st class 6,100SD   2nd class 5,150SD   3rd class 4,100SD

Atbara–Wadi Halfa
Monday (returning Wednesday) approx 27 hours
1st class 5,100SD   2nd class 2,700SD   3rd class 2,060SD

Atbara–Port Sudan
Tuesday (returning Thursday) approx 24 hours
1st class 4,500SD   2nd class 3,500SD   3rd class 2,500SD

Khartoum–Nyala
Thursday (twice monthly) approx 4 days
1st class 6,700SD   2nd class 6,500SD   3rd class 5,100SD

limitations of the transport network, an approach worth emulating. Just remember, you will get there in the end!

Trains have three classes. First and second class have separate compartments off a corridor. There's no difference in the quality of the seats, merely in the amount of room. First class takes six passengers per compartment; second class squeezes eight into the same space. Third class is open seating, with just a thin layer of foam providing any padding on the wooden benches. After a few hours this can be excruciating, so a sleeping bag or similar can come in handy for a little extra cushioning. All human life is here in third class, packed in like sardines with precious little room to manoeuvre.

There's occasionally also a *mumtaz*, or excellent, class. This comprises genuine sleeper carriages with space to stretch out, a true luxury on a long trip. The Khartoum-Wadi Halfa service is meant to have one *mumtaz* carriage, but it isn't always attached. If it is used, demand is high so you'll need to book your ticket early.

On an overnight trip, space is at a real premium. Passengers seem to appear out of nowhere as everyone tries to bed down for some sleep. Not an inch of space is wasted. The corridors turn into dormitories, so navigating your way from one end of the carriage to the other becomes a real obstacle course as you try not to step on any slumbering figures.

There is a restaurant car on each train that serves up *ful* and omelettes and the like, and tea sellers walk up and down the carriages carrying huge kettles for thirsty passengers. The restaurant car does tend to run out of food near the end of a long journey, but the trains have frequent station stops where there are plenty of food stalls, while hawkers hold up fruit and biscuits to the windows. Untreated water is available on the train, but it's best to take your own supplies.

You can often see people riding on the roof of the carriages, claiming their ride for free. It's a precarious position to take. You need some genuine acrobatic ability to get up on the roof, and even if the train is only trundling along at 40km/h that can seem plenty fast enough when you don't have any hand holds. There's also no protection from the elements – most likely a beating sun in the day and a desert chill at night.

By boat

The Nile has long been Sudan's major transport artery, although travellers are unlikely to make great use of it. Compared to Egypt, the Nile in Sudan can often seem an empty river. The only long-distance passenger ferry in northern Sudan is the weekly service across Lake Nasser between Wadi Halfa and Aswan. Until ten years ago there was a regular service between Dongola and Karima when the Nile waters were high enough. The remains of this fleet can be seen rotting on the riverbanks just outside Karima.

Anyone travelling in the north will make use of the local ferries to cross the Nile, however, as there is just one bridge north of Khartoum. These ferries range in size from large flat-bottomed barges capable of carrying a bus or two, down to small dinghies with outboards for foot passengers. Fares are typically around 25SD for foot passengers and up to 700SD if you have a vehicle, depending on the size. Some crossings have a ticket booth; otherwise you pay the fare when you get on. Ferry crossings are part of the fabric of the north and all human (and animal) life seems to congregate at them – boys driving goats, women carrying shopping, mules being shooed out of the way of a slowly reversing pick-up. The busiest landing stages have a cluster of teahouses and food joints, and are great places to spend a few hours people-watching.

South of Khartoum, the Nile is navigable as far as Juba near the Ugandan border. Barges and the occasional passenger ferry depart from the White Nile port of Kosti, stopping at Malakal. It takes up to a week to sail upstream to Juba and around four days in the reverse direction. Slowly making your way through the swamps of the Sudd this could be one of Africa's great boat trips, but at present foreigners are not permitted to travel in the region.

ACCOMMODATION

Rooms in Sudan cover the whole spectrum of accommodation, from rope beds in courtyards to luxury hotels. You won't have any trouble finding somewhere to sleep, but in smaller towns your choice may be very restricted. For this guide, I have divided accommodation into three categories: budget, mid-range and international. Bedding is a rarity in Sudan at budget and many mid-range hotels so a sleeping sheet is highly recommended.

Budget

The mainstay of accommodation at the cheapest end of the spectrum is the *lokanda*. Most typically, a *lokanda* is a series of rooms around an open courtyard. Rooms are basic, but the majority of guests pull their beds into the courtyard to sleep in the open – very cooling on hot summer nights. Washing facilities are similarly communal, and squat toilets the norm.

Many *lokanda* owners will assume that as a foreigner you'll want to pay for a private room, rather than sleep communally. Prices will be quoted accordingly, so make it clear which arrangement you'd prefer. Single travellers can often get penalised here, particularly if the owner insists you rent a whole room with several beds. This will also be the case for female travellers, and if there are no whole rooms available you are likely to be turned away. Throughout the text I have indicated whether prices quoted are per room or per person.

Whether or not you have your own room, the communal nature of *lokandas* make them a good place to meet people, and it's easy to lose track of time answering questions from your curious Sudanese neighbours. Also keep in mind security considerations.

Lokandas can vary enormously in quality. In the smallest towns they may only have simple washing and toilet facilities, with water coming from a communal drum. At the other end of the spectrum, many are kept spotlessly clean, and offer laundry and kitchen facilities.

In cities, the line between a *lokanda* and hotel (*funduq*) can become blurred, although the trend is still towards communal sleeping arrangements. Rooms with four beds are commonest, but you can still find the occasional double.

Lokanda prices vary from around 300–2,000SD, depending on sleeping arrangements.

Mid-range

Hotels in the mid-range bracket are aimed at local businessmen – there is no tourist class per se in Sudan. As a rule, rooms tend to be en suite and often come with a satellite TV. Air conditioning (or at least a ceiling fan) is normal, although power cuts aren't uncommon, even in Khartoum. Hotels usually have a restaurant attached but it's rare for breakfast to be included in the price.

Prices depend more on location than on quality of service. You can find some real gems in this bracket, but rooms at the higher price range can often appear poor value (particularly in Khartoum). Look for facilities such as self-contained water heaters before making your choice.

Mid-range hotels tend to be priced between US$15–50.

Upmarket

Khartoum appears to be enjoying a boom in five-star hotels at the moment, and with a couple of exceptions in Port Sudan and Karima, the capital is where you'll find all the upmarket accommodation. These hotels would be classified as top-range anywhere in the world; room prices are upwards of US$90.

Camping

Sleeping under canvas is most likely to suit those travelling with their own vehicles. Indeed, the ability to strike off and make camp on your own is one of the great attractions of overlanding in Africa. There is certainly no shortage of space in Sudan. If you are camping near a village it's best to ask permission before pitching your tent. Avoid camping in or near dry riverbeds, as flash floods can and do occur with approaching rains. There are a couple of campsites in Khartoum, but nothing organised elsewhere.

With the exception of the Nuba Mountains and Jebel Marra, Sudan has little to offer the dedicated hiker, so if you're carrying your luggage on your back rather than in a vehicle and not planning on hiking, I'd suggest leaving your tent at home.

EATING AND DRINKING

Sudanese food is uncomplicated. It is based around a few staples with spices used only sparingly. Some people complain of bland repetition, but it is possible to eat a good and varied diet on the road. Many of Sudan's staples are vegetarian, although travellers should be aware that some dishes such as stewed vegetables often use meat stock as flavouring, or are cooked with a few small pieces of meat lurking in the pot. Most restaurants are of the cafeteria variety, with the kitchen and food on display at the front. With no menu to consult you'll often find yourself poking around the pots to see what's on offer. Cutlery isn't used so you eat with your right hand, using bread as a scoop.

Most cafeterias open in the morning in time for breakfast – the most important meal of the day in Sudan – which is taken any time between 09.00 and 11.00.

Food

Sudan's favourite dish is *ful*, brown beans stewed for hours in a large metal cauldron (*gidra*). The *ful* is ladled out into bowls, often mashed slightly and served with a generous squirt of oil, a sprinkling of spice, and a round of bread (*kisra*). At it's simplest, *ful* can be pretty uninspiring, but it's usually enlivened by adding salad (*salata*), cheese (*jibneh*), hard-boiled egg (*bayda*) or falafel (*taamiya*). Served this way a bowl of *ful* makes a delicious and filling meal.

In some places, a poor man's *ful* is served using the bean water left over in the *gidra*, mopped up with bread and onions. This dish is called *bush*, as it derives from the shortages of the early 1990s when the first President Bush cut aid to Sudan in response to the Sudanese government's support for Saddam Hussein in the first Gulf War.

Fasuliya is another bean dish, served in a tomato-based sauce – the Sudanese equivalent of baked beans. Yellow lentils are served as a thick broth called *adis*, which is usually made in the mornings. Other vegetable dishes include stewed potatoes (*batata*), okra (*baamiya*), and peppers or aubergines (egg plant) stuffed with rice (*maashi*).

In the south and parts of the west, beans are replaced by sorghum, which is made into porridge (*asida*) and served with a simple vegetable or meat sauce.

The most common meat dish is kebabs, although the meat is often tough and stringy. Kebabs are usually cooked on skewers, but one variety you'll often see is *sheya*, where very fatty meat is cooked on flat stones sitting on a bed of charcoal. In large towns, Western-style fast food joints serve *shwarma* kebabs from a vertical spit; these are most commonly lamb, but are occasionally chicken. The same places offer burgers in a bun, always with a fried egg on top. *Kibda* is fried chopped liver, a popular breakfast dish. A meat dish from western Sudan is *agashay*, where meat is flattened and breaded before being cooked over coals – a type of Sudanese schnitzel.

Along the Nile, fish (*samak*) is popular. Large fish such as Nile perch are filleted before being fried and are accompanied with bread and a fiery chilli dipping sauce (*shotta*). Smaller fish are cooked whole and it's possible to spend as much time fishing for bones as meat. Many places cook their fish throughout the day, piling them up in a glass cabinet on the street for customers to choose from. For some reason, the taste for fish doesn't extend greatly to the Red Sea, and good seafood can be difficult to find there.

Taamiya (falafel) is a popular street snack, although people used to the salad and yoghurt flat bread wraps from the Middle East might be disappointed. The chickpea balls are served dry in a bread roll with no accompaniment, or with a slice of tomato at best. I much prefer to buy a bag from a stand and eat them on the hoof.

If you're looking for dessert, the Sudanese love of sugar will provide. Every town has a sweet bakery, where you can splurge on cakes and pastries. The most popular is *baklawa*, a super-sweet confection of pastry, honey and nuts. *Zalabia*, a deep-fried treat that's similar to a doughnut is made in the morning at teashops as a light snack to tide people over until mid-morning breakfast.

Drink

Along with *ful*, Sudan runs on tea (*shai*) and coffee (*ghawha*). Teahouses tend to be dark and gloomy places, with a couple of old men invariably sucking on a water pipe. Far more common are the tea ladies you find on almost any street corner. These women run impromptu tea stalls consisting of little more than a brazier and a lockable chest covered in jars of tea, coffee and spices. Stools – or old cooking oil cans – provide the seating. They are a great place to watch the world go by over a drink, while the stallholder keeps court over a never-ending routine of kettle juggling, coffee pounding and fire stoking.

Different drinks are favoured throughout the day. Black tea (*shai saada*) can be drunk at any time, but drinking it with milk added (*shai bi laban*) is reserved for the early morning and evening. Hot milk (*laban*) is also popular at these times, and is often flavoured with nutmeg. Tea is also made with mint (*shai bi nana*) and spices, most typically cloves (*shai bi habahan*). Whichever you choose, the tea is always served with a vast amount of sugar (*sukar*), although as a sop to western sensibilities you'll sometimes be asked if you want it without sugar (*bidun sukar*).

Coffee is made by simply boiling up grounds, and can be slightly gritty. A Sudanese variation sees the coffee flavoured with ginger or cinnamon and transferred to a long-stemmed pot and served in small china cups. The distinctive pots (*jebana*) give the drink its name. Finally the tea ladies may offer you *karkaday*, made from hibiscus flowers. It's just as refreshing served cold.

Sudan abounds in fruit, and juice bars are deservedly popular. Availability varies, but some of the best are mango (*manga*), lemon (*limoon*), grapefuit (*grebfrut*) and occasionally banana (*moz*). A personal favourite is a mix of guava (*guafa*) and watermelon (*batikh*). A glass of cold juice can feel like the healthiest drink around, but be aware of the blocks of ice providing the cooling, as they are usually made from untreated water.

The usual international brands of fizzy drinks are available everywhere in Sudan, along with a few homegrown varieties, like the fizzy apple-drink Stim, and Pasgianos, a sort of fizzy *kardakay*. Mineral water is also widely available, but in small remote towns it can be expensive. Brands include Soba, Safia and Crystal. In Khartoum the water is generally safe to drink, although the tang of chlorine may put you off.

On any street in Sudan you will often see a couple of large earthenware pots on stands. Kept in the shade and covered, each pot (*zir*) is slightly porous – as water slowly seeps out it evaporates, keeping the contents cool for passers by to refresh themselves. Whether or not you want to drink from the never-washed cup tied to the *zir* (and in some places the water can be distinctly murky) is up to you, but it's a neat communal approach to drinking water in a hot country.

Alcohol is illegal in Sudan, a prohibition ignored by some. The most commonly encountered under-the-counter drink is *araki*, a lethal spirit made from dates that's roughly akin to rocket fuel. In the west and south you may come across *merissa*, a beer brewed from sorghum. A non-alcoholic beer called Birrell is available in large towns, although it hardly seems worth the effort.

You'll often see Sudanese men producing a small pouch of indeterminate green material, rolling it into a ball and inserting it between the gum and lip. This is *sa'oud* or snuff; it's actually tobacco soaked in spiced water. The nicotine rush from *sa'oud* is very strong, but if you try it make sure you don't swallow any of the juice or you'll suffer the consequences. Do as everyone else does and expel a gob of fluorescent green spit every so often. A mellower experience can be had smoking the *shisha* (water pipe) over a drink in a teahouse.

SHOPPING
In African terms, shops in Sudan are well stocked and travellers will find a general store, pharmacy, or other shop stocking what they need in most towns. In the cities it is also quite possible to find a good selection of hi-tech goods – very useful if you need to buy a new cable for a digital camera for instance.

Away from urban centres, the variety of goods on offer inevitably decreases. The stretch between Dongola and Wadi Halfa in the north is a good example of this, as 'luxury' items like bottled water become harder to find. In these cases it's a good idea to time your trip around market days, when amongst other things you'll find piles of fresh produce, as well as the best transport connections.

Handicrafts
For the handicraft shopper, Sudan has much to offer. The mother of all markets is the sprawling Omdurman *souq*, across the Nile from Khartoum,

where almost everything is on sale, including huge wicker baskets for you to carry it all home in.

Carved wood and painted leather goods are prolific. Sudanese attire also makes for good souvenirs, from white *jallabiyas* for men to bright *tobes* for women. Jewellery is also popular. You can sometimes find the chunky silver jewellery worn by Rashaida women; delicate gold bracelets are more favoured by the Nubians. Kassala is the best place for knives; some Beja men may even approach you to sell you a sword.

There are a lot of morally dubious animal products on sale in Sudan. Dried crocodile heads and stuffed lizards and snakes crop up with alarming frequency. Even more worrying is the ready availability of ivory. Elephants are classed as an Appendix II species by the Convention on International Trade in Endangered Species (CITES), which allows only a very restricted trade in ivory from certain southern African countries. When pressed as to the source of his ivory, one shopkeeper insisted that it was 100% Sudanese and assured me (incorrectly) that I would have no problem with customs at home. With no clear picture of the state of Sudan's wildlife it's impossible to say where the ivory comes from, but if elephants do still survive in southern Sudan the population is likely to be under extreme pressure. If you must buy pretty white trinkets, stick to carved camel bone.

MEDIA AND COMMUNICATIONS
Newspapers
In August 2003, President Bashir formally announced an end to newspaper censorship, although this has not prevented the banning of several newspapers. The popular English language *Khartoum Monitor* has been repeatedly banned, along with the Arabic *Al-Ayam*. The only available newspaper in English is *Sudan Vision*, printed by the government-run Sudan News Agency (SUNA). While the news is a dry mix of official and syndicated stories, some of the columnists can be surprisingly lively. A monthly magazine *Sudanow* is also available in Khartoum.

International newspapers are almost impossible to find in Sudan, unless you can read the Arabic *Newsweek*. For up-to-the-minute news, the online newspapers *Sudan Tribune* (www.sudantribune.com) and *The Sudan Mirror* (www.sudanmirror.com, based in Uganda) are excellent places to start.

Television
Even locals find the heavy output of Sudan Television hard to love. Satellite television is much preferred, beaming in everything from Egyptian soap operas to Hollywood blockbusters. The smallest hotels often have a satellite dish, but don't expect to be able to tune into the BBC or CNN – even in mid-range places Al-Jazeera news is king. Al-Jazeera's Khartoum bureau was closed down in December 2003 for alleged anti-government bias.

Internet
Cyber cafés are popping up in most major Sudanese towns, and you can expect to pay between 200–300SD for one hour. It should be pointed out that while

many places specifically advertise internet services (usually in Arabic), in smaller towns this is commonly an aspiration rather than a statement of fact and you might be disappointed to find computers offering little more than word-processing facilities. Where there is a connection, it's quite common for internet places to have Net2Phone facilities: headphones and mikes running through the computer allow you to make international phone calls for as little as 100SD per minute, so long as you don't mind the lack of privacy.

Post

Poste restante has been a victim of the rise of email, but it's still possible to receive mail in Sudan if you feel nostalgic for pen and paper. Letters should be sent 'c/o poste restante (main post office)' in the town where you wish to receive it. It's useful to have the sender underline your surname so that the letter can be filed correctly, although in practice all mail tends to get kept in a bundle which the clerk simply hands over for you to go through. There is no charge to collect letters. Mail sent to Sudan takes around two weeks to arrive. Poste restante seems to be kept indefinitely – on my last trip I collected a letter I'd been sent during a visit two years before, and it wasn't even the oldest mail there!

Mail out of Sudan can be erratic. Two letters I sent to the UK simultaneously arrived after ten days and six weeks respectively. It gets there in the end, but don't always expect your postcards to beat you home. Outside many post offices you'll find professional scribes who can sell you paper and envelopes and the like. They often have old or collectable stamps for sale for a small mark-up. A postcard anywhere in the world should cost around 100SD.

If you have a more valuable letter or package you might wish to entrust it to DHL, who have an office in Khartoum.

Telephone

Like much of the developing world, Sudan has taken the mobile phone to its heart, and coverage of the Mobitel network is ever increasing. Travellers will find fixed lines more useful. The national operator Sudatel operates phone booths in major towns.

Cards for Sudatel phone booths should be sold at newspaper kiosks, but can be tricky to track down in many places. If in doubt, head for a post office, as there will invariably be a Sudatel bureau next door. An alternative is to use a private phone kiosk. In towns these will have a line of booths in an office, and in smaller places just a phone on a desk with an operator who places your call. Local calls are cheap at just a few dinars, but making an international call at a private kiosk can be expensive – up to 600SD a minute.

HASSLES

On a day-to-day basis, Sudan is a very relaxed country to travel in. For some westerners, with their rigid timetables and their 'mustn't stop moving' frame of mind, Sudan can sometimes appear a little too relaxed, which could almost constitute a hassle in itself, particularly if you're chasing paperwork. The Sudanese attitude to life is often summarised by their joke that the country is run by IBM; not the computer giant, but by the three rules of *inshallah*, *bokra* and *malesh*. You'll hear these three words spoken a lot in Sudan.

Inshallah literally translates as 'if God wills it' and is applied to virtually any situation or question where an outcome is unknown (or even if it is known). Ask what time the bus will reach its destination and you'll receive an answer of 'four hours, *inshallah*', irrespective of whether you're on a smooth highway and can time your arrival to the minute or bumping on a back road where the journey could take half or double the time. Everything is in the hands of God.

If you want to know when something might happen further in the future – when an office might open or a bus might depart to a very remote location – you might be told *bokra*, which is Arabic for tomorrow. In reality *bokra* is more akin to the Spanish idea of *manāna*, an unknown hour sometime in the future.

Finally, *malesh* means sorry. If the office is closed, the bus isn't running or the cafeteria has just run out of beans, you'll be told *malesh*. In a country where things don't always run smoothly, *malesh* is a very important concept, offering regret and saving face at the same time.

Nothing is hurried in Sudan. You can go blue in the face with the bureaucracy of the place and sometimes wonder how anything gets done at such an easy pace. If you can remember who runs Sudan, and take *inshallah*, *bokra* and *malesh* with a smile, you'll enjoy yourself so much more.

Being a *khawaja*

Khawaja is the Sudanese term for a westerner, frequently heard on the lips of Sudanese to attract your attention. World events have made some people wary of travelling in the Islamic world, fearing that they may become targets for the resentment of locals over the policies of their governments – particularly Britons and Americans. Fortunately being a *khawaja* in Sudan is still overwhelmingly a positive experience.

Muslim resentments are very real and need to be understood, but in my experience of travelling in the Greater Middle East, people there generally seem quite able to distinguish between a person from a country and the policies of that country's government. Sudan typifies this attitude.

Researching this book I travelled through Sudan during a particularly bloody stage of the Coalition occupation of Iraq. Sudanese newspapers were filled with accounts of death and violence, with similar scenes replayed everywhere on Al-Jazeera television. Although I had many conversations about the rights and wrongs of the invasion of Iraq and the Israel-Palestine situation, I was never once held to be personally responsible for the actions of Tony Blair despite my nationality. Since the September 11 attacks, Khartoum has been anxious to curry favour with the West and has reined in some of its more overt anti-western Islamism. Sudanese attitudes to the USA are often particularly confused, with worries over its Middle East policies mixed with the recognition that the US government has genuinely played a constructive role brokering the peace deal between the government and the SPLM/A, and in 2004 the Sudanese government was feeling particularly prickly over Western 'interference' in the Darfur crisis.

MAKING THE BEST OF YOUR TRAVEL PHOTOGRAPHS
Nick Garbutt & John R Jones
Subject, composition and lighting
As a general rule, if it doesn't look good through the viewfinder, it will never look good as a picture. Don't take photographs for the sake of taking them; be patient and wait until the image looks right.

People
There's nothing like a wonderful face to stimulate interest. Travelling to remote corners of the world provides the opportunity for exotic photographs of colourful minorities, intriguing lifestyles and special evocative shots which capture the very essence of a culture. A superb photograph should have an instant gut impact and be capable of saying more than a thousand words.

Photographing people is never easy and more often than not it requires a fair share of luck. Zooming in on that special moment which says it all requires sharp instinct, conditioned photographic eyes and the ability to handle light both aesthetically and technically.

- If you want to take a portrait shot, it is always best to ask first. Often the offer to send a copy of the photograph to the subject will break the ice – but do remember to send it!
- Focus on the eyes of your subject
- The best portraits are obtained in the early morning and late evening light.
- In harsh light, photograph without flash in the shadows.
- Respect people's wishes and customs. Remember that, on occasion, candid snooping can lead to serious trouble.
- Never photograph military subjects unless you have definite permission.

Landscapes
- Good landscape photography is all about good light and capturing mood. Generally the first and last two hours of daylight are best, or when peculiar climatic conditions add drama or emphasise distinctive features. Never place the horizon in the centre – in your mind's eye divide the frame into thirds and either exaggerate the land or the sky.

Equipment
Keep things simple. Cameras which are light, reliable and simple will reduce hassle. High humidity in many tropical places, in particular rainforests, can play havoc with electronics.

For keen photographers, a single-lens reflex (SLR) camera should be at the heart of your outfit. Remember you are buying into a whole photographic system, so look for a model with the option of a range of different lenses and other accessories. Compact cameras are generally excellent, but because of restricted focal ranges they have severe limitations for wildlife.

Always choose the best lens you can afford – the type of lens will be dictated by the subject and the type of photograph you wish to take. For people, it should ideally have a focal length of 90 or 105mm; for candid photographs, a 70–210 zoom lens is ideal. If you are not intimidated by getting in close, buy one with a macro facility, which will allow close focusing.

For wildlife, a lens of at least 300mm is necessary to produce a reasonable image size of mammals and birds. For birds in particular, even longer lenses like 400mm or 500mm are sometimes needed. Optics of this size should always be held on a tripod, or a beanbag if shooting from a vehicle. Macro lenses of 55mm and 105mm cover most subjects and these create images up to half life size. To enlarge further, extension tubes are required. In low light, lenses with very fast apertures help (but unfortunately are very expensive).

For most landscapes and scenic photographs, try using a medium telephoto lens (100–300mm) to pick out the interesting aspects of the vista and compress the perspective. In tight situations, for example inside forests, wide-angle lenses (ie: 35mm or less) are ideal. These lenses are also an excellent alternative for close ups, as they offer the facility of being able to show the subject within the context of its environment.

Film

If yours is traditional film camera, be sure to take the right film. Film speed (ISO number) indicates the sensitivity of the film to light. The lower the number, the less sensitive the film, but the better quality the final image. For general print film, and transparencies taken for showing at lectures, ISO 100 or 200 fit the bill perfectly; under weak light conditions use a faster film (ISO 200 or 400). If you want to get your work published, the superior quality of ISO 25 to 100 film is best. Try to keep your film cool – it should never be left in direct sunlight (film bought in developing countries is often outdated and badly stored).

Different types of film work best for different situations. For natural subjects, where greens are a feature, Fuji Reala (prints) and Fuji Velvia and Provia (transparencies) cannot be bettered. For people shots, try Kodachrome 64 for its warmth, mellowness and superb gentle gradation of contrast; reliable skin tones can also be recorded with Fuji Astia 100. If you want to jazz up your portraits, use Fuji Velvia or Provia, although if cost is your priority, stick to process-paid films.

Nick Garbutt is a professional photographer, writer, artist and expedition leader, specialising in natural history; he is a past winner in the 'BBC Wildlife' Photographer of the Year competition. John R Jones is a professional travel photographer specialising in minority people.

In general, the overwhelming hospitality offered to visitors far outweighs any negative aspects. That said, it is never wise to be complacent and travellers should always keep one eye on world events to see if developments elsewhere may adversely affect their security, or merely the attitudes of their hosts.

In out of the way places, being a *khawaja* is a good way to attract local attention. You might sometimes find children following you and you may experience a surfeit of stares, but hassles beyond this are the exception rather than the rule. If the attention ever feels overwhelming it's worth remembering all the good things about being a *khawaja* – the spontaneous offers of tea or the way you are often pushed to the front of a queue to buy a bus ticket. As a guest, the Sudanese may be as curious about you as you are of them, but the hospitality and warmth of the people are still likely to be the strongest memories you take home.

Women travellers

The vast majority of women travellers in Sudan report favourable experiences and Sudan can generally be regarded as a safe country for single female travellers. The threat of crime and serious physical harassment is certainly lower than in many neighbouring – or indeed Western – countries.

Muslim perceptions of western women are sometimes clouded by images from western films and satellite television (available across Sudan) that portray females as 'morally loose'. To many Sudanese the idea of a woman travelling on her own is perplexing at best, and some travellers have suggested inventing an absent husband for the duration of their trip, with a fake wedding ring to back up their story.

Actual harassment is rare. Anke Röhl writes of her experience backpacking across Sudan with another female friend, travelling by *boksi* and truck and staying in *lokandas*: '[We] had a lot of travel experiences in other Muslim countries before coming to Sudan. And, yes, we really had a very relaxed time in Sudan, the locals being very polite, interested and very hospitable to us, without all the hassles one experiences in countries like Egypt, Tunisia, Morocco and the like.' This is a common theme among many female travellers, particularly those who have arrived from Egypt, which carries a notably bad reputation for harassment.

In Sudan women travellers are frequently received as a guest, or possibly an 'honorary' man, and you'll often receive help with things like buying tickets. One area that does have potential pitfalls is at the cheapest end of the accommodation spectrum. *Lokandas* are based on communal sleeping, so the arrival of a female traveller (even with male partner in tow) can sometimes provide managers with a headache as they wonder where they are going to put you. Most tend to be as accommodating as possible and have smaller separate rooms that you will be offered.

From a male perspective I have to report that Sudanese women are open in a way that you don't often find in many Muslim countries. Whereas in more conservative countries like Egypt or Pakistan it's possible to spend an entire trip without talking to a local woman, in Sudan I have often been pleasantly surprised by a Sudanese woman thrusting out her hand to engage me in conversation. This isn't usual, but I take it as yet more proof of the relaxed Sudanese attitude to Islam and the importance placed on hospitality.

While Muslim Sudanese women cover themselves with the all-encompassing *tobe*, it can still be quite a surprise to see Southern women in Khartoum decked out to the nines in short sleeves and tight-fitting dresses.

ETIQUETTE AND RESPONSIBLE TOURISM

The concept of responsible tourism has taken off in recent years. As well as travelling for personal gratification, people increasingly realise they are travelling through other people's homes. In a country like Sudan, that has been racked by civil war and is only now starting to open to foreign visitors, it is incumbent on tourists to travel in as responsible a manner as possible.

The adage of responsible tourism says 'take nothing but photos, leave nothing but footprints'. Personally I think that's too passive an approach. While it is certainly necessary to highlight the potentially negative impact of tourism, it doesn't take into account the positive effects your visit can have. There are several simple steps you can take to ensure that your visit is as rewarding for your hosts as it is for you.

Always behave in a manner that respects local customs. The particular vagaries of travelling in a largely Muslim country are discussed below. Try to ensure that as much of the money you spend goes directly into the local economy, spreading the benefits of your wealth. For independent travellers this is straightforward enough, but people on package tours using foreign-owned services and hotels can still do their bit by spending in local markets.

Always ask before taking a photograph of someone. Sudanese officialdom can be twitchy about photography at the best of times, but it is common courtesy to ask someone before turning them into a subject for your camera. If they say 'no', respect their reply. Men taking photos of Muslim women is a perennially touchy subject, so be extra considerate on this front. And if you promise to send someone a copy of the photo, please make sure that you do. It's easy to forget when you return to the busy pace of life at home but your photo is certain to be treasured by its recipient.

Don't waste resources. Many parts of Sudan face regular water shortages and drought. Electricity can also be in short supply, so turn off lights and air conditioning when you leave your hotel.

Disposing of waste is always a tricky one in the developing world. You'll see plenty of people casually throwing litter out of the window of buses or on the street, and on the outskirts of some towns you could swear that the locals have specially sown fields of plastic bags there are so many flapping in the wind. That said, there's no need to add to this yourself, so throw away your rubbish with care. It's also worth bearing in mind that just drinking bottled water carries a high environmental cost in plastic waste, so you might consider also using water treatment while in Sudan.

Continually banging the drum about the need to behave responsibly while travelling can make one sound like a po-faced do-gooder, so I'd venture that the best way to get the most out of your trip and leave positive impressions behind is simply to get out there and enjoy Sudan and meet its people. On first impressions many Sudanese can seem a little reserved, but once you make contact their natural warmth is infectious. The Sudanese are aware that their country has been internationally isolated for a long time and are anxious to show you the good things about their home, and to learn about yours. Meeting people is the best way of building bridges, however small, so get stuck in!

Muslim etiquette

Travelling in a Muslim country (accepting that the parts of Sudan currently accessible to tourists are almost entirely Muslim) involves different considerations to visiting other parts of the world. More than just a religion, Islam is a social code that presents a specific way in which society should be run. As such, visitors have a particular responsibility to behave in a manner that's sensitive to local traditions, although the Sudanese are very tolerant and foreigners are usually forgiven for minor cultural gaffes.

The issue of dress has already been mentioned in *Chapter 3*, but it should always be remembered that nowhere is it easier to give casual offence than through what you are wearing. Modest dress is incumbent on Muslim men and women, so both sexes should cover shoulders and legs, although wearing a scarf for women is unnecessary. Dressing in a clean and presentable manner will always gain the respect of the Sudanese you meet.

Always remove your shoes when entering someone's house unless specifically advised otherwise. Mosques are generally closed to non-Muslims, but shoes should likewise always be removed on entry. The left hand is ritually unclean in Islam (as it is used in bathroom ablutions), so you should eat with your right hand. This is particularly important when sharing food from a communal dish such as a big bowl of *ful*. Never walk directly in front of someone who is praying or point the soles of your feet at someone.

Most importantly, keep your mind open and don't be afraid to ask questions. The Islam practised in Sudan is a world away from the western clichés of fundamentalism or the Taliban. The people you talk to are as likely to be as curious about your life as you are about theirs. Holding forth on the merits of Zionism or atheism are unlikely to win you any friends, but just about everything else is up for discussion. Questions about your marital status, salary and lifestyle are typical conversation pieces.

Begging

As in any developing country, you'll see beggars on the streets in Sudan. Bus stations tend to attract the most beggars, with supplicants holding their hands up to the windows as you wait for your minibus to fill. Giving to beggars is an entirely personal choice, but it might be worth taking a cue from the locals. The giving of charity (*zakat*) is one of the pillars of Islam and Sudanese frequently give money to beggars. If you have a few spare coins in your pocket why not follow suit?

Gift-giving

No two travellers ever seem to agree on the subject of giving gifts to locals. The indiscriminate giving of pens and sweets to children is a cliché, and an unwelcome one to my mind. At best it's a selfish pursuit to make the giver feel better about themselves, and at worst it comes with the patronising baggage of 'the White Man's Burden', doling out presents to the grateful natives. A surfeit of sweets can quickly change a group of friendly children into grabbing beggars, which can easily sour relations between hosts and visitors.

The relationship between a host and their guest is massively important in Sudan. Even the most casual encounter is framed in this context. Someone may go out of their way to help you find a *lokanda* only signed in Arabic or navigate you through a crowded bus station and will usually expect nothing in return, except perhaps the chance to practise their English. In such instances, the best you can give in return is often your polite conversation or the offer to share a tea or coffee. When giving presents – or even trying to pay for drinks – your offer will often be refused once or twice before being politely accepted.

An exception to this is if you are invited to eat or stay with a Sudanese family. In such circumstances gifts are appropriate. Fruit and pastries make good gifts. If you want to bring something from home, I have found that photos of where you live or your family are usually welcomed with much interest. Such gifts are very personal to those you give them too, and I have often had Sudanese show off pictures of their foreign friends to me with much pride.

GIVING SOMETHING BACK
Aid organisations operating in Sudan

In the face of human suffering, the urge is to help. Sudan has limped through many crises since independence, crises of war and famine alongside a plethora of development issues it shares with many other emerging nations.

There are numerous international charities and Non-Governmental Organisations (NGOs) currently operating in Sudan, many of which have worked in the country for long periods, gaining expertise in dealing with conflict and its aftermath. The recent Darfur crisis has provoked major international appeals for funds for relief work as well as political pressure for a political settlement. At the same time, the majority of those NGOs responding to the crisis also run larger programmes across North and South Sudan, dealing with development issues from primary healthcare, sanitation and HIV/AIDS awareness to education, conflict resolution and providing opportunities to the economically disenfranchised.

A list (inevitably selective) of aid organisations (UK addresses) with programmes in Sudan is provided below as a starting point for those wanting to help. ReliefWeb (www.reliefweb.int) is a useful resource to keep up with humanitarian developments in Sudan, and who's doing what and where.

British Red Cross 9 Grosvenor Crescent, London SW1X 7EJ UK; tel: 020 7235 5454; email: information@redcross.org.uk; www.redcross.org.uk. British branch of the International Committee of Red Cross and Red Crescent. Heavily involved in emergency relief work in Sudan, both in Darfur and as part of OLS.

CAFOD Romero Close, Stockwell Rd, London SW9 9TY UK; tel: 020 7733 7900; email: hqcafod@cafod.org.uk; www.cafod.org.uk. Development agency working on conflict resolution, civic education and rights programmes in Sudan in conjunction with the New Sudan Council of Churches (NSCC), and with South Sudan Women Concern, to increase opportunities for economically excluded women.

CARE International 10–13 Rushworth St, London, SE1 0RB UK; tel: 020 7934 9334; email: info@uk.care.org; www.careinternational.org.uk. Part of OLS, working on food security, health and sanitation projects in Bahr al-Ghazal, Kordofan, Upper Nile and Nuba Mountains, as well as emergency relief in Darfur.

Christian Aid Interchurch House, 35 Lower Marsh, London, SE1 7RL; tel: 020 7620 4444; email: info@christian-aid.org.uk; www.christian-aid.org.uk. Medical emergency work in Darfur and Malakal, along with HIV/Aids awareness programmes, and Southern reconciliation projects.

Concern Worldwide Units 13 and 14 Calico House, Clove Hitch Quay, London, SW11 3TN; tel: 020 7738 1033; email: londoninfo@concern.net; www.concern.net. Primary education, HIV/AIds awareness programmes, food security and capacity building projects in South Sudan, plus relief work in Darfur.

Disaster Emergency Committee 15 Warren Mews, London, W1T 6AZ; tel: 020 7837 0200; email: enquiries@dec.org.uk; www.dec.org.uk. British umbrella body of over a dozen NGOs co-ordinating responses to emergency situations, including the Darfur crisis.

Intermediate Technology Development Group The Schumacher Centre for Technology and Development, Bourton Hall, Bourton-on-Dunsmore, Rugby, CV23 9QZ; tel: 01926 634400; email: itdg@itdg.org.uk; www.itdg.org.uk. Development agency providing community-led (and women-focused) skills training in food processing, building, manufacturing and rural transport. Based primarily in Kassala, Gedaref and North Darfur.

MedAir Willow House, 17–23 Willow Place, London SW1P 1JH; tel: 020 7802 5533; email: united.kingdom@medair.org; www.medair.org. Primary healthcare and community rehabilitation projects in the Nuba Mountains, Upper Nile and internal refugees in Khartoum.

Médecins Sans Frontières (UK) 67–74 Saffron Hill, London EC1N 8QX; tel: 020 7404 6600; email: office-ldn@london.msf.org; www.msf.org. Long-term health projects from immunisation and sanitation to anti-malarial drives across South Sudan, relief work with internal refugees in Khartoum and emergency projects in Darfur.

Merlin 4th Floor, 54–64 Leonard St, London, EC2A 4LT; tel: 020 7065 0800; email: hq@merlin.org.uk; www.merlin.org.uk. Emergency healthcare specialists, with primary healthcare and community health projects in Equatoria.

Mine Advisory Group 47 Newton St, Manchester M1 1FT; tel: 0161 236 4311; email: maguk@mag.org.uk; www.mag.org.uk. De-mining and community liaison work in South Sudan, supporting local NGO Operation Save Innocent Lives.

Oxfam 274 Banbury Rd, Oxford, OX2 7DZ; tel: 01865 311311; email: oxfam@oxfam.org.uk; www.oxfam.org.uk. Campaigning development NGO, also working on water supply, food security and education projects across Sudan.

Save the Children 1 St John's Lane, London EC1M 4AR; tel: 020 7012 6400; email: enquiries@scfuk.org.uk; www.scfuk.org.uk. Child protection and development NGO, providing education for internally displaced children around Khartoum, and Bahr al-Ghazal and Upper Nile, healthcare and sanitation projects and support for demobilised child soldiers.

Sudan Volunteer Programme 34 Estelle Rd, London NW3 2JY; tel: 020 7485 8619; email: davidsvp@blueyonder.co.uk; www.geocities.com/svp-uk. Long-term English teaching for volunteers in North Sudan. Placements are for a minimum of two months, with TEFL qualification preferred (but not essential).

Tearfund 100 Church Rd, Teddington, Middlesex, TW11 8QE; tel: 020 8977 9144; email: enquiry@tearfund.org.uk; www.tearfund.org.uk. Relief work in Darfur and emergency feeding programmes in South Sudan.

UNICEF Africa House, 64–78 Kingsway, London, WC2B 6NB; tel: 020 7405 5592; email: helpdesk@unicef.org.uk; www.unicef.org.uk. Part of OLS, wide-ranging international body working in Sudan on child health and immunisation, education and with child soldiers, as well as emergency relief in Darfur.

World Vision World Vision House, Opal Drive, Fox Milne, Milton Keynes MK15 0ZR; tel: 01908 841 000; email: info@worldvision.org.uk; www.worldvision.org.uk. Emergency relief and development work, including shelter, sanitation and child-protection projects in the Shilluk Kingdom (Upper Nile) and Darfur.

As well as international charities working in Sudan, there is a host of local organisations. The Gurtong Peace Project (www.gurtong.org) has a directory of indigenous South Sudanese NGOs carrying out development work, many of them based in Kenya or Uganda.

Health and Safety

Travelling in the developing world presents different issues regarding health and safety compared to Western countries. By taking sensible precautions you can greatly reduce your risk of catching any serious diseases, and visitors to Sudan are unlikely to encounter any medical problems more acute than a bout of travellers' diarrhoea. Before travelling you should check that you have all necessary immunisations and up-to-date advice on anti-malarial drugs.

TRAVEL INSURANCE

It is important to take out a comprehensive medical travel insurance policy before travelling to Sudan, and preferably one that covers medical evacuation. Personal effects insurance is also a good idea. Be aware that parts of Sudan are subject to government travel advice that may invalidate some clauses in your policy should you need to claim – it is important to discuss this with your broker when purchasing the policy. Areas covered by such travel advice currently include the southern half of the country, Darfur, and (occasionally) Kassala and the Eritrea border region.

IMMUNISATIONS

It is recommended that you visit your doctor or travel clinic a minimum of six weeks before departure to discuss all your medical requirements, and to allow time for any course of immunisations that may be required. Last-minute injections can give only partial cover for some diseases. Regular travellers will find keeping an immunisation record card useful. You doctor or travel clinic will also be able to give the most up-to-date advice on malaria prophylaxis.

A yellow fever certificate is a legal requirement if entering Sudan from a country where the disease is endemic – ie: all of Sudan's neighbours apart from Egypt and Libya. If you plan on travelling overland in Africa after Sudan you will also need a yellow fever certificate. The certificate is valid for ten years from immunisation.

You are also strongly advised to have immunisations against typhoid, polio and tetanus, as well as the water-borne hepatitis A. The hepatitis A vaccine (such as Havrix Monodose) initially gives protection for one year, but can be boosted with a second injection to provide cover for ten years – a worthwhile investment for travellers.

If you intend to travel more than 24 hours away from medical facilities, consider rabies immunisation. This is most cheaply arranged through a travel clinic as one vial can be used for eight patients; your GP is unlikely to have that number of applicants unless you are travelling as a group. Three rabies vaccinations offer the best pre-exposure protection and should be taken over a four-week period.

Vaccination against the blood-borne hepatitis B can be considered for longer trips or for those working in situations where contact with blood is likely or when working closely with local children. Three injections are ideal, given over a period of four to eight weeks before travel.

If you are planning a long trip, a dental check-up before travelling is a good idea. If you wear glasses, take a spare pair and a copy of your prescription. Contact lens wearers should take a pair of glasses too, as Sudan's dust can irritate the eyes.

MEDICAL KIT

Consider carrying a small medical kit with you. This should contain malaria tablets, aspirin or paracetamol, sticking plasters, antiseptic (avoid creams), antihistamines to treat insect bites, water purification tablets, oral rehydration sachets and diarrhoea tablets. On top of this, be sure to pack insect repellent, plus a high factor sunscreen (20+).

Some travellers like to travel with a course of antibiotics (such as Ciprofloxacin) as a precaution. You should always be hesitant to take them without medical advice, however; antibiotics are widely available from Sudanese pharmacies.

TRAVEL CLINICS
UK

British Airways Travel Clinic and Immunisation Service 156 Regent St, London W1; tel: 020 7439 9584. This place also sells travellers' supplies and has a branch of Stanford's travel book and map shop. There are BA clinics across Britain and six in South Africa. To find your nearest one, phone 01276 685040.

Fleet Street Travel Clinic 29 Fleet St, London EC4Y 1AA; tel: 020 7353 5678. MASTA (Medical Advisory Service for Travellers Abroad) Keppel St, London WC1 7HT; tel: 09068 224100. This is a premium-line number, charged at 50p per minute.

NHS travel website (www.fitfortravel.scot.nhs.uk) provides country-by-country advice on immunisation and malaria, plus details of recent developments, and a list of relevant health organisations.

Nomad Travel Pharmacy and Vaccination Centre 3–4 Wellington Terrace, Turnpike Lane, London N8 0PX; tel: 020 8889 7014.

Thames Medical 157 Waterloo Rd, London SE1 8US; tel: 020 7902 9000. Competitively priced, one-stop travel health service. All profits go to its affiliated company InterHealth which provides healthcare for overseas workers on Christian projects.

Trailfinders Immunisation Clinic 194 Kensington High St, London W8 7RG; tel: 020 7938 3999. Non-profit-making private clinic with a one-stop shop for health advice, vaccines and travel goods, visas and passport services, and foreign exchange.

Previous page Woman of the Bishariyyin, a nomadic Beja tribe of northeastern Sudan, making coffee or *jebana* (MP)

Above Nomad girl from Sudan's northern desert repairing a goatskin water bag or *ghirba* (MP)

Right Crossing the Sudd, the vast swamps of Sudan's southern region (MP)

Below Beja woman lighting fire, eastern Sudan (MP)

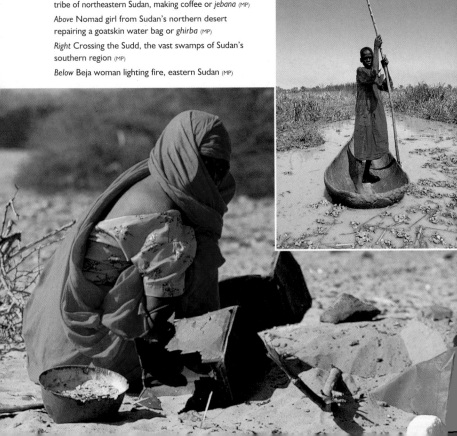

FIT TO FLY
Deep-vein thrombosis (DVT)

Evidence suggests that a small percentage of passengers on long-haul flights are at risk from developing DVT. It is estimated that around 30,000 Britons a year are affected by flight-induced blood clots. Those at highest risk on flights of four hours or more are:

- people suffering from varicose veins, heart disease or cancer
- people with a history of blood clots or who have undergone recent surgery
- people with leg injuries
- people over six feet and under five feet tall
- people over 40
- women who are pregnant or taking the pill

To reduce the risk of DVT

- exercise your legs while seated
- walk around the cabin during the flight
- drink plenty of water or soft drinks
- wear compression hosiery to prevent swelling

After landing, a DVT may develop. If you have severe swelling of the ankles, a swollen or painful calf or thigh, an increase in skin temperature or local skin discolouration, seek medical advice immediately.

Irish Republic

Tropical Medical Bureau Grafton Street Medical Centre, Grafton Buildings, 34 Grafton St, Dublin 2; tel: (353-1) 671 9200. This organisation has a useful website specific to tropical destinations: http://www.tmb.ie.

USA

Centers for Disease Control 1600 Clifton Rd, Atlanta, GA 30333; tel: 877 FYI TRIP; 800 311 3435; www.cdc.gov/travel. This organisation is the central source of travel information in the USA. Each summer they publish the invaluable Health Information for International Travel which is available from the Division of Quarantine at the above address.

Connaught Laboratories PO Box 187, Swiftwater, PA 18370; tel: 800 822 2463. They will send a free list of specialist tropical-medicine physicians in your state.

IAMAT (International Association for Medical Assistance to Travelers) 736 Center St, Lewiston, NY 14092. A non-profit organisation which provides lists of English-speaking doctors abroad.

Canada

IAMAT (International Association for Medical Assistance to Travellers) Suite 1, 1287 St Clair Av West, Toronto, Ontario M6E 1B8; tel: 416 652 0137.

TMVC (**Travel Doctors Group**) Sulphur Springs Rd, Ancaster, Ontario; tel: 905 648 1112; www.tmvc.com.au

Australia and New Zealand

TMVC Tel: 1300 65 88 44; website: www.tmvc.com.au. TMVC has 20 clinics in Australia, New Zealand and Thailand, including: *Auckland* Canterbury Arcade, 170 Queen St, Auckland City; tel: 373 3531; *Brisbane* Dr Deborah Mills, Qantas Domestic Building, 6th floor, 247 Adelaide St, Brisbane, QLD 4000; tel: 7 3221 9066; fax: 7 3321 7076; *Melbourne* Dr Sonny Lau, 393 Little Bourke St, 2nd floor, Melbourne, VIC 3000; tel: 3 9602 5788; fax: 3 9670 8394; *Sydney* Dr Mandy Hu, Dymocks Building, 7th floor, 428 George St, Sydney, NSW 2000; tel: 2 221 7133; fax: 2 221 8401

South Africa

There are six **British Airways travel clinics** in South Africa: *Johannesburg* tel: 011 807 3132; *Cape Town* tel: 021 419 3172; *Durban* tel: 031 303 2423; *Knysna* tel: 044 382 6366; *East London* tel: 043 743 7471; *Port Elizabeth* tel: 041 374 7471.
TMVC (**Travel Doctor Group**) 113 DF Malan Drive, Roosevelt Park, Johannesburg; tel: 011 888 7488. Consult www.tmvc.com.au for addresses of other clinics in South Africa.

Switzerland

IAMAT (**International Association for Medical Assistance to Travellers**) 57 Voirets, 1212 Grand Lancy, Geneva; www.sentex.net/~iamat.

DISEASES
Travellers' diarrhoea

The medical complaint that travellers are most likely to experience in Sudan is a bout of diarrhoea. Contaminated food is the most likely source of illness, but many factors can contribute to making the body susceptible to traveller's diarrhoea. Most obvious are a change in diet and different standards of hygiene from the western norm, but the rigours of Sudanese travel – long hours on the road, high temperatures and dehydration risks – can stress the body further.

Strict hygiene is the best way to avoid diarrhoea. Always wash your hands before eating – every restaurant provides soap and water for this purpose, as the Sudanese tradition is to eat with your hands from a communal bowl. Where washing facilities aren't available, I have found antibacterial hand gel invaluable. Food that is freshly cooked or thoroughly reheated should be safe. When it comes to food, the old adage 'boil it, cook it, peel it or forget it' is worth remembering.

It is best to stick to bottled or treated water. In Khartoum tap water has a distinct chlorine tang to it, so in theory should be safe to drink, but it may still be best to avoid it. The surest way to treat water is to boil it for at least one minute, but good portable filters can be bought in outdoor shops or water can be treated with iodine- or chlorine-based purification tablets. Bottled water is readily available in towns but less so in rural areas.

Most Sudanese restaurants provide each table with a single cup of water to be refilled from a bowl of water but this is best avoided. Ice (commonly used in making fruit juices) may be made with unsafe water.

Diarrhoea usually lasts between two and three days and clears up without any treatment. During this time it is important to maintain your fluid intake to prevent dehydration. Oral rehydration sachets are widely available in Sudanese pharmacies. An alternative is to add salt to a soft drink like Coke – it should be no saltier than tears. You should drink around three litres of fluids daily; sipping slowly throughout the day should keep you hydrated.

It is best to eat dry, bland foods and avoid fruit, vegetables and fatty foods. The bacteria that are responsible for most diarrhoea and related symptoms will normally die within 36 hours if they are deprived of food.

If possible anti-diarrhoea tablets (such as Imodium) should be avoided. While they control and reduce bowel movements they keep the bugs in your system and can prolong the symptoms. Better out than in is the adage of choice here. The tablets really come into their own if you need to travel or are staying in unsanitary conditions, however.

Should symptoms persist, you may require antibiotics. A fever, and blood and/or slime in your stools, can be indicators of more serious conditions, and you should seek medical assistance as soon as possible.

Malaria

Malaria kills about a million Africans every year, and is the leading cause of death in children under five. Of the travellers who return to Britain with malaria, 92% have caught it in Africa. You are 100 times more likely to catch malaria in Africa than you are in Asia. In most African countries, visitors are urged to take malaria tablets as a matter of course. Malaria is caused by the parasite *Plasmodium falciparum*, spread by the bite of the female *Anopheles* mosquito, which flies between dusk and dawn.

Malaria is present throughout Sudan, although the risk varies according to geography and season. Areas close to the Nile and its tributaries possess the highest persistent malaria risk, mainly south of (but not excluding) Khartoum. The Red Sea coast area is considered the lowest risk region in Sudan. At under 1,800m, the Nuba Mountains are not high enough to exclude malaria, which also affects the foothills of the Jebel Marra region.

Malaria outbreaks most commonly occur in low-lying areas after rains and flooding, where the abundance of water provides an ideal mosquito breeding ground. In August 2003, Kassala experienced a serious outbreak immediately following the devastating flooding of the River Gash. Further south, the cycle of floods and malaria outbreaks present a major problem for community health. The rains in north Sudan between June and August increase the malaria risk in the Khartoum area.

Preventing malaria is a two-pronged approach: taking anti-malarial prophylactics and avoiding getting bitten.

Mefloquine (Lariam) is the most effective prophylactic agent for Sudan but is not suitable for everyone, so should only be taken on a doctor's recommendation. If this drug is suggested, then start two and a half weeks before departure to check it suits you. Stop immediately if it seems to cause depression or anxiety, visual or hearing disturbances, severe headaches or changes in heart rhythm. Anyone who is pregnant, has been treated for depression or psychiatric problems, has diabetes controlled by oral therapy, who is epileptic (or who has suffered fits in the past), or who has a close blood relative who is epileptic, should not take mefloquine.

Doxycycline (100mg daily) is a good alternative if mefloquine is unsuitable and need only be started one day before arrival in a malarial region. It can only be obtained from a doctor. There is a possibility of allergic skin reactions developing in sunlight in approximately 5% of people. If this happens the drug should be stopped. Women taking an oral contraceptive should use additional protection for the first four weeks.

Chloroquine (Nivaquine or Avloclor) twice-weekly and proguanil (Paludrine) twice-daily are now considered to be the least effective. This combination should only be used if there is no suitable alternative.

Malarone (proguanil and atovaquone) is available on prescription. It has the advantage of fewer side-effects than mefloquine or doxycycline. It can be started the day before travel and continued for only seven days after leaving. However, it is expensive and because of this tends to be reserved for shorter trips although it can be prescribed for up to three months from the UK.

All prophylactic agents should be taken after or with the evening meal, washed down with plenty of fluids and, with the exception of Malarone, continued for four weeks after leaving the last malarial area. Be aware, however, that resistance patterns and thus the effectiveness of particular drugs are prone to change. Your GP may not be aware of new developments, so you are advised to consult a travel clinic for current advice, or phone 020 7636 7921 (in the UK) for recorded information.

Taking anti-malarial prophylaxis does not offer clear-cut protection against the disease, and you should take all reasonable steps to avoid being bitten by mosquitoes.

Insect repellents are vital. They should contain the chemical DEET, unless you are pregnant in which case a natural repellent such as Mosiguard may be recommended. Children should use a product with a lower percentage of DEET – take advice if you are in any doubt. Mosquitoes are attracted by heat so tend to bite where the skin is thinner, and blood vessels are closer to the surface; apply repellent to exposed skin, especially the wrists, elbows, knees, ankles and neck. Cover your arms and legs in the evening, and wear light-coloured clothing. A traditional and efficient insect repellent used across southern Sudan is a liberal dusting of cow dung ash. Hotels in Sudan do not usually contain mosquito nets, although it is not uncommon to see Sudanese in *lokandas* rigging up their own nets before turning in for the night. Take your own, preferably one that has been impregnated with permethrin. Mosquitoes are drawn to direct light, so leaving your hotel room light on with an open window (few are screened) is an open invitation to flying visitors. This can be problematic in many hotels, when the heat makes sleeping with doors and windows closed unbearable and ceiling fans cannot be relied upon.

Even if you take your malaria tablets meticulously and are careful to avoid being bitten, you might still contract malaria. Fever and chills are the most common symptoms. Headaches, a general sense of disorientation and flu-like aches and pains may also indicate that you have malaria. It is vital you seek medical advice immediately. Local doctors see malaria all the time; they will know it in all its guises (a blood test will confirm the presence of the *Plasmodium*, or otherwise) and know the best treatment for local resistance patterns. Untreated malaria can be fatal, but even prophylactic-resistant strains normally respond well to treatment, provided that you do not leave it too late.

If you are unable to reach a doctor, you may have to treat yourself. For this reason, it is advisable to carry a cure in your medical kit. Malarone is considered the safest and most effective treatment for malaria in Africa. Once again, this could change, so seek advice from a travel clinic before you leave for Sudan.

The life cycle of the *Plasmodium* parasite is four weeks, so it is essential that you continue to take malaria prophylaxis for this period after leaving Sudan (easy to forget if you are back in the routine of home life). If you suffer any malarial symptoms, even up to a year after your return, you should see a doctor, and advise them that you could have been exposed to malaria so that you can be tested and treatment started as soon as possible.

Bilharzia (schistosomiasis)

This is carried by a worm which spends part of its life inside freshwater snails, and infects people when they swim or paddle in still or slow-moving, well-oxygenated, well-vegetated fresh water. The worm's eggs become lodged in the body's organs, causing the worst effects of the disease. The first symptom of infection is an itchy patch where the worm entered your skin, then perhaps, a fortnight later, fever and other vague symptoms of being unwell. Much later, you may notice blood in the urine or motions if you have a heavy infestation. Although there is a very good cure for bilharzia, drug resistance is emerging. It is wise to avoid infection. A blood test performed six weeks or more after leaving an area of risk will establish whether you have been infected.

As a rule, a fast-flowing mountain stream is very low-risk, while a sluggish river or lake is high-risk. If you dry off promptly after spending ten minutes or less in the water, the parasite does not have time to penetrate your skin and so cannot infect you.

Bilharzia is prevalent in the Nile. Some travellers believe that the faster-flowing Blue Nile is bilharzia free, but this is not the case. Bilharzia is common in villages along the Nile, not only from people washing in the river, but also from the irrigation channels that provide an ideal breeding habitat for the snails.

AIDS and venereal disease

It is thought that around 600,000 people are infected with HIV/AIDS in Sudan – around 2.6% of the adult population. The condition is relatively new in

Sudan, where the civil war has restricted travel, migration and trade, thus containing the virus. It is feared that the end of the civil war and the opening up of the country will lead to a surge in infection. South Sudan already has higher infection rates (Yambio, on the border with the Democratic Republic of Congo, has infection rates of up to 21%), although Islamic taboos on discussing sexual matters have also hindered early education programmes in the north. Sudan's first voluntary counselling and testing centre was opened in Juba in February 2004.

The risks involved in having unprotected sex, particularly with a prostitute, barely need stating. Condoms and femidoms offer a high level of protection against HIV and other venereal diseases, and spermicides and spermicidal pessaries also reduce the risk of transmission.

Meningitis

This is a particularly nasty disease as it can kill within hours of the first symptoms appearing. The tell-tale symptom is a combination of a blinding headache and (usually) a fever. A vaccination protects against the common and serious bacterial form in Africa, but not against all of the many kinds of meningitis. Regional media normally report localised outbreaks. If you show symptoms, get to a doctor immediately.

Rabies

Rabies is carried by all mammals and is passed on to humans through a bite, a scratch, or a lick of an open wound. You must always assume any animal is rabid (unless personally known to you) and seek medical help as soon as possible. In the interim, scrub the wound with soap and bottled or boiled water, then pour on a strong iodine or alcohol solution. This helps stop the rabies virus entering the body and will guard against wound infections, including tetanus. If you intend to have contact with animals and/or are likely to be more than 24 hours away from medical help, then vaccination is advised. Ideally, three pre-exposure doses should be taken over four weeks. If you are bitten by any animal, treatment should be given as soon as possible, but it is never too late to seek help as the incubation period for rabies can be very long. Tell the doctors if you have had a pre-exposure vaccine. Remember, if you contract rabies the mortality rate is 100% and death from rabies is probably one of the worst ways to go!

Tetanus

Tetanus is caught through dirty wounds, so ensure that any wounds are thoroughly cleaned. Immunisation gives good protection for ten years, provided you do not have an overwhelming number of tetanus bacteria on board. Keep immunised and be sensible about first aid.

OUTDOOR HEALTH
Sun and heat

The sun in Sudan can be very harsh. Even in winter, daytime temperatures in Khartoum regularly top 35°C with little or no cloud cover; in the desert temperatures can be up to 20° higher. Sunstroke and dehydration are serious risks. The long *jallabiyas* worn by northern Sudanese men are well adapted to the climate; the loose cloth is cooling and the white material reflects the heat.

Wearing sunscreen and gradually building up your exposure helps to avoid sunburn. Prolonged unprotected exposure can result in heatstroke, which is potentially fatal. A hat with a brim will protect your head and keep you cooler. Stay out of the sun between noon and 15.00 – most Sudanese take a rest at this time for a good reason.

In such a hot climate you will sweat more, so dehydration is a serious risk. Don't rely on feeling thirsty to tell you to drink; if your fluid intake isn't high enough your urine will be dark yellow. The more colourless your urine the better. It's a good idea to carry water with you, although walking in towns you are never far from a drinks seller.

Wearing clothes made from natural fabrics such as 100% cotton help prevent fungal infections and other rashes. Athletes' foot is prevalent, so wear sandals/ thongs in communal showers. If you wear open footwear on a day-to-day basis, make sure you look after your feet, as skin can easily become dry and cracked.

Dust
After a week of travelling on unmade roads, you may consider Sudan to be the dustiest country in the world. *Bokasi* and many buses are open sided, exposing you to wind and dust. It's pervasive stuff, and you'll be amazed at just where it gets – even firmly sealed rucksacks aren't immune. And if it's getting inside your gear you can be sure that it's also settling in your lungs.

On short trips it's possible to ignore the fine particles in the air, but you can very quickly find that a tickly cough can develop into something more debilitating. During my my first trip to Sudan I learnt to cover up against dust the hard way, and had breathing difficulties and a wracking cough, which were only cured by a few days laid up in bed.

Wearing a scarf or bandana is strongly recommended if you plan on doing any amount of travel off tarmac roads – ie: the vast majority of travel in Sudan. Both Sudanese men and women use their scarves to protect themselves, and I recommend that you do the same.

Animals
It is unlikely that travellers are going to encounter many dangerous wild animals in Sudan. Feral dogs in towns are common, but are generally cowardly. The same cannot be said of the dogs used by nomads to protect their herds, and you should always approach nomad camps with care.

Hyenas are usually timid in their dealings with humans and sleeping in a tent should provide protection enough.

The chances of coming across a snake while walking are slim, and the chances of coming across a venomous snake are even less. Snakes are shy animals, and are likely to be more afraid of you than you are of them, so prefer to retreat when they sense a human approaching. One place where I was warned about snakes was walking in the jebels around Kassala. The rocky slopes seem like good snake habitat, and the nature of the ground might prevent a snake sensing your approach. Trousers, socks and solid boots provide good protection (while scrambling). If you do see a snake, don't approach it; let it slither off of its own accord.

MEDICAL FACILITIES

The Sudanese medical system produces excellent doctors – many doctors are in demand to work in the British National Health Service – with English widely spoken. Pharmacies in towns are well stocked in the main, and will be able to advise on the majority of travellers' complaints.

In Khartoum, the Teaching Hospital on Sharia al-Istbitaliya, across the street from the University of Khartoum Medical Faculty, is recommended. Many embassies also keep lists of recommended doctors.

SAFETY
Theft

By any measure, Sudan is a safe country when it comes to street crime and theft. Violent theft is almost unheard of. It would be naive to assume that it does not exist, however, and you should take simple precautions to help prevent yourself becoming a victim of crime. As the Prophet Mohammed said, 'Trust in God, but tie your camel.'

The most common form of theft is pickpocketing. The highest risk areas are busy spots like bus stations and markets, so keep a close watch on your belongings here. Keep your valuables (including your passport) in a money belt. Your daily spending money should be kept separate, so that you don't have to fiddle around with large amounts of money when all you are buying is a bowl of *ful*. Distribute your money throughout your luggage, keeping a separate small stash particularly well hidden for emergencies. Given the difficulty of using travellers' cheques in Sudan you are likely to be carrying large amounts of cash, so it's particularly important to take care here. Keep your insurance policy apart from the rest of your valuables.

If you are staying in a *lokanda*, communal sleeping arrangements can provide a tempting target for casual thieves. In these circumstances it is highly recommended that your baggage is lockable, and that you keep valuables out of sight. A padlock won't prevent a determined thief slashing your rucksack, but it will help deter opportunistic light fingers.

Banditry

Sudan's remote western provinces have always sat outside the rule of Khartoum to some degree. Many tribes have practised banditry – from highway robbery to camel rustling – as a way of life. The horse- and camel-mounted *janjawid* are the most recent manifestation of a traditional regional problem, albeit taking the practice to extreme levels and with tacit government support. The area between Nyala and the Chad border at El Geneina has always been lawless, and even before the recent fighting in Darfur was particularly notorious for banditry. In the event of a solution to the conflict in

Darfur, low-level banditry is still likely to persist. Travellers in their own vehicles present a particularly tempting target. Seek local advice before travelling by road.

If you are a victim to banditry, try to remain calm. Cooperate with your captors, and hand over your valuables. Your personal safety is more important than your possessions.

KEY TO STANDARD SYMBOLS

Bradt

—·—·—	International boundary
------	District boundary
------	National park boundary
✈	Airport (international)
✈	Airport (other)
✈	Airstrip
🚁	Helicopter service
▬▬	Railway
··········	Footpath
--🚗--	Car ferry
--⛴--	Passenger ferry
⛽	Petrol station or garage
P	Car park
🚌	Bus station etc
🚚	Boksi (pickup)
🛺	Rickshaw
⌂	Hotel, inn etc
Λ	Campsite
♦	Hut
♀	Wine bar
✗	Restaurant, café etc
⊠	Post office
✆	Telephone
@	Internet café
⊞	Hospital, clinic etc
🏺	Museum
🐘	Zoo
i	Tourist information
$	Bank
♟	Statue or monument
∴	Archaeological or historic site
🏛	Historic building
🏰	Castle/fortress
†	Church or cathedral
♣	Buddhist temple
⌂	Buddhist monastery
⚜	Hindu temple
ϛ	Mosque
🏃	Football Stadium
🏃	Stadium
▲	Summit
△	Boundary beacon
◉	Outpost
⤫	Border post
⌂	Rock shelter
▨	Souq
≍	Mountain pass
○	Waterhole
☀	Scenic viewpoint
⊦	TV/Radio antenna
♧	Specific woodland feature
🗼	Lighthouse
≔	Marsh
⚲	Mangrove
✈	Bird nesting site
⌇	Waterfall/Cataract
✳	Source of river
➘	Beach
✓	Scuba diving
➴	Fishing sites

Other map symbols are sometimes shown in separate key boxes with individual explanations for their meanings.

Part Two

The Guide

Khartoum

Sitting at the place where the waters of the Blue and White Niles meet before continuing their slow progress to Egypt, Khartoum has a fantastic setting. It's a melting pot of the many ethnic groups that make up Sudan, and to sit at a tea stall watching the world pass by is to watch a progression of tribes and nationalities, from Arab, Dinka and Shilluk to Nubian, Beja and Fur.

Khartoum is often called the tri-capital, as it is actually three cities in one. The oldest part – Khartoum proper – sits between the confluence of the Blue and White Niles. On the west bank is Omdurman, the old Mahdist capital, and on the north bank the semi-industrial city of Khartoum North (also sometimes called Bahri).

As the capital of a dry country, Khartoum is a quiet place and lacks some of the more obvious attractions of many cities. Don't expect great things of the nightlife. On the other hand, Khartoum has a relaxed charm that's hard to dislike, often feeling more like an overgrown village than a city. Friendly and safe, it's quintessentially Sudanese.

HISTORY

Human settlement in the Khartoum area stretches back into antiquity, but for most of its history it was little more than a fishing village, overlooked by Kushite and Funj rulers.

The strategic potential of the Nile confluence was first recognised by Mohammed Ali's Turco-Egyptian expedition to Sudan in the 1820s. The region's main market, at Shendi, was moved to Khartoum and a troop garrison converted to a permanent settlement. Within ten years the town was booming.

In the 1850s, Khartoum experienced its second boom, with the opening up of river passages to the south, allowing further exploitation of Sudan's resources. The most profitable trade was in ivory, dominated by Khartoum's European merchants, but as demand became insatiable this led to a parallel explosion of the slave trade, as forced labour went hand in hand with ivory collection. Khartoum rapidly became a slave centre to rival Zanzibar on the East African coast. European pressure on Egypt led to the closure of the city's public slave market in 1854, although slaves continued to be sold just outside the city limits and sent north to Egypt, or east to the Red Sea and Arabia. As

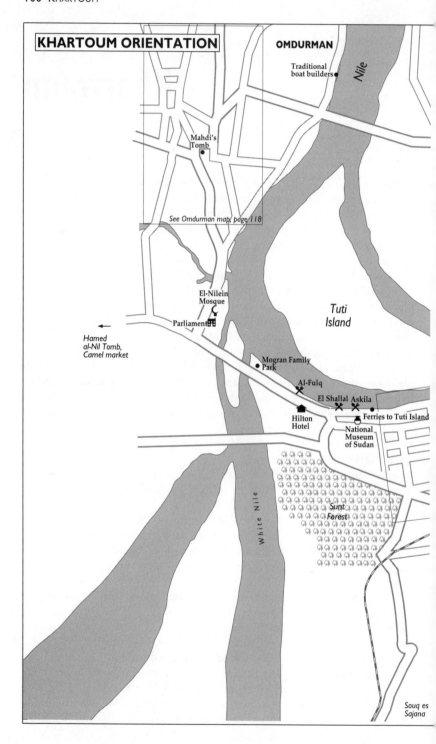

KHARTOUM ORIENTATION

OMDURMAN

Nile

Traditional
boat builders ●

● Mahdi's
Tomb

See Omdurman map, page 118

El-Nilein
Mosque

Parliament

*Hamed
al-Nil Tomb,
Camel market*

*Tuti
Island*

● Mogran Family
Park

Al-Fulq

El Shallal Askila

Ferries to Tuti Island

Hilton
Hotel

National
Museum
of Sudan

White Nile

*Sunt
Forest*

*Souq es
Sajana*

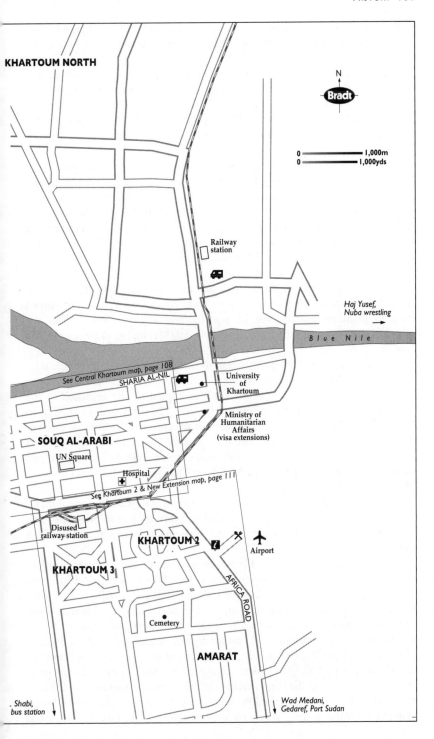

KHARTOUM NORTH

N

Bradt

0 |———| 1,000m
0 |———| 1,000yds

Railway
station

Haj Yusef,
Nuba wrestling →

Blue Nile

See Central Khartoum map, page 108
SHARIA AL-NIL

University
of
Khartoum

Ministry of
Humanitarian
Affairs
(visa extensions)

SOUQ AL-ARABI

UN Square

Hospital

See Khartoum 2 & New Extension map, page 111

Disused
railway station

KHARTOUM 2

Airport

KHARTOUM 3

AFRICA ROAD

Cemetery

AMARAT

. Shabi,
bus station ↓

Wad Medani,
Gedaref, Port Sudan ↓

well as the slave trade, Khartoum served as a base for European expeditions, most notably Samuel and Florence Baker's voyage up the White Nile to try and find its source in the 1860s.

At the start of the 1880s the Mahdist rebellion was prospering in the west of Sudan, and the Turco-Egyptian regime in Khartoum felt threatened. Only four years after resigning as Governor General of Sudan, Charles Gordon was sent to organise an evacuation of the Egyptian garrisons. On arrival in March 1884 Gordon was given a rapturous reception by a population feeling under threat.

Gordon felt that he could not simply withdraw the Egyptian forces and abandon Khartoum to its fate. Attempts to set up an acceptable administration failed, as did negotiations with the Mahdi. The decision was made to stay put and defend the city against the Mahdist advance. Khartoum's location between the arms of the Blue and White Niles made it easy to defend, and a trench and wall were thrown up between the two rivers. The Mahdist forces cut Khartoum's telegraph wires and harried steamer traffic, isolating the city from Egypt.

The siege of Khartoum began in earnest in September 1884. The city was shelled and by December food supplies were running low. Gordon worked hard to maintain morale, but he was fighting a losing battle. With the population reduced to eating rats, he expelled 5,000 citizens to the care of the Mahdi.

A British army column had been sent to extricate Gordon, but it made slow progress. The Mahdi sat tight, waiting for the Nile waters to fall and expose the city's defences. On January 26 1885, prompted by the approach of the British, the decision was taken to storm the city. The city was devastated in an orgy of looting. Gordon died on the steps of the Governor's Palace, speared to death; the Mahdi regretted the killing, saying that he had wanted to convert Gordon to Islam. The steamers of the relief column arrived in Khartoum just two days later, to be shelled by the Mahdists. They were too late, but Gordon's place in the canon of Victorian heroes was guaranteed.

The Mahdi preferred Omdurman to Khartoum and made his capital there, only to die soon after its capture. Omdurman thrived, but its prosperity was short-lived. An avenging British army retook both cities in 1898, and returned the capital to Khartoum.

Under Anglo-Egyptian rule, Khartoum was rebuilt and its street plan laid out in a series of interlocking grids in the shape of the Union Jack. Khartoum North was established as a dockyard and garrison, and a railhead to Egypt. Omdurman was largely neglected and left to the Sudanese, although some industrious British officials did set aside some land for a golf course.

Khartoum has been witness to the many coups that have shaped Sudan's post-independence history. Its large European (mainly Greek) population has mostly disappeared, the last exodus prompted by Nimeiri's establishment of *sharia* law in 1983 and the coup that brought the Islamists to power in 1989. In response to the bombing of the US embassies in East Africa, President Clinton ordered a Cruise missile attack on a pharmaceutical factory in Khartoum

North in August 1998, although there has subsequently been no evidence that it was involved in manufacturing chemical weapons as alleged.

The population has increased massively as a result of the civil war. Displaced people's camps filled with Southerners, which the government refuses to allow any permanent status, have sprung up around the edges of the city. The government controls access by international agencies and periodically demolishing the camps entirely. The status of Khartoum has been a sticking point in negotiations between the government and the SPLM/A, with the Southerners insisting that they should be exempt from *sharia* law in the capital.

GETTING THERE AND AWAY
By air
Khartoum International Airport is 4km from the centre of the city, off Africa Road. Arriving by air, there are slow queues for immigration, and then a further wait while all passengers have to open their bags for customs. There is a small kiosk for changing money just before you leave customs, but no exchange facilities after. Taxi drivers are aware of this and will usually demand ludicrous fees in dollars for the ten-minute ride into town, often refusing fares under US$10. If you want to use public transport, you'll need to leave the terminal area completely and walk to Africa Road, from where you can flag down a minibus for around 25SD. There is no public transport at night.

If you are leaving Khartoum by air it's sensible to arrive at least two hours before your departure time. For night and early morning flights when there is no public transport to the airport, arrange a taxi the day before as they can be very hard to find in the small hours. Before checking in, you need to complete a disembarkation card and pay the departure tax of US$20. Sudanese dinars aren't accepted, but there is a branch of the Farmer's Commercial Bank next to the check-in desks that will change money. Make sure you get a receipt for the departure tax as it's needed at check-in. Following this there is a customs check before you can proceed to your gate. If you still have excess dinars, you can blow them at the duty free, which stocks a dazzling array of perfumes, toothpaste and stuffed crocodiles.

By bus
Khartoum has three main bus stations. The largest is the vast Souq es-Shabi on the southern edge of Khartoum, a 20-minute minibus ride from the city centre. From here you can take transport to east and west Sudan. A market as much as a transport terminal, it's a huge site and it can be hard to find your way around. On the northern edge are the offices of the bus companies, from the mid-range options to the luxury coach operators. Coaches start leaving at around 05.00–06.00, particularly for more distant locations such as Port Sudan. The huge mosque with three minarets (run by the Samaniyah sufi order) on the northern edge of the *souq* is a good landmark to get your bearings. On the south side of the *souq* you'll find the minibuses, running throughout the day and departing when full. The stands are mixed up with

auto-shops and teahouses, but there are plenty of touts shouting out the destinations to guide you.

Near to the Souq es-Shabi is Sajana Bus Station, which has buses running north to Dongola and Karima.

Transport north to Shendi and Atbara departs from a small bus station in Bahri, just north of the Blue Nile Bridge. From the centre of Khartoum, take a minibus to 'Moghof Shendi' and get out by the Shell petrol station; the terminal is just behind it.

Omdurman has its own Souq es-Shabi, with transport links to west and north Sudan (ie: towns along the western bank of the Nile as far as Dongola, and Karima). If you are arriving in Khartoum from these towns, the bus will often stop at the Omdurman Souq es-Shabi before terminating at Sajana Bus Station.

By rail

The railway station is located in Khartoum North. Minibuses pass by on the main road heading into Khartoum. They're easily flagged down, and a ride to Souq al-Arabi costs around 25SD. You can buy tickets in advance – a good idea if you want to travel first class – for the weekly train to Atbara and Wadi Halfa (Mondays), as well as for the four-day trip to Nyala departing twice a month on Thursdays. The railway station also sells advance tickets for the weekly Wadi Halfa-Aswan ferry.

GETTING AROUND

Khartoum taxis are beaten up yellow affairs, and are uniformly expensive. On even short trips drivers ask for 500SD, a fare which increases dramatically should you want to cross the Nile. The only way I ever found to significantly reduce the asking price was to take a Sudanese friend along for the ride.

For travelling longer distances it's as easy to jump on minibus – a ride anywhere in the city will never top 50SD. The minibuses, liveried to some degree in yellow and blue, ply the main routes in the tri-city and stop when flagged down. Departure points from Souq al-Arabi in central Khartoum for major routes are indicated on the map. Most minibuses also terminate here, making navigation straightforward. Otherwise, stick out your arm and shout out your destination – you won't have to wait for long. It's worth noting that minibuses are slow to start in the morning, and can be hard to find before 07.00.

Motor rickshaws are popular in Omdurman, but are expensive for anything other than short trips.

ORIENTATION

Khartoum's grid system makes navigation easy, and streets are well signed. The heart of Khartoum is found at Souq al-Arabi, a small area teeming with minibus stands, juice sellers, *ful* joints and hole-in-the-wall shops. North of this is Sharia al-Nil, stretching the length of the Blue Nile bank, with large shady trees for pleasant walks. Khartoum has enough old buildings to maintain a certain faded colonial air; in some parts churches can seem to outnumber mosques.

Most embassies are located in the prosperous districts of Khartoum 2, New Extension and Amarat south of the city centre. Beyond these is the sprawling Souq es-Shabi, Khartoum's main bus station and open-air market.

West of Khartoum across the White Nile Bridge is Omdurman. Where Khartoum is slow-paced and relaxed, the Arab city of Omdurman is all bustle and business. At just over 120 years old, Omdurman lacks the winding streets and ancient bazaars of Cairo or Istanbul, but it makes up for this in a whirlwind of activity centred on its huge *souq*, Sudan's largest. Nearby, the Tomb of the Mahdi and the Khalifa's House offer pointers to Omdurman's history; on the edge of the city at the Sheikh Hamed al-Nil Tomb, Sufi dervishes dance and pray every Friday before sunset.

Across the Blue Nile from Khartoum is Khartoum North (Bahri). A sprawling, semi-industrial city, it has a rapidly expanding population. Travellers are most likely to visit Khartoum North for transport connections – buses north along the Nile and the train to Wadi Halfa. In the district of Haj Yousef it is often possible to see traditional Nuba wrestling on the edge of the *souq* on Friday afternoons.

WHERE TO STAY
Upmarket
Hovering on the edge of the upmarket bracket, the **Acropole Hotel** (Sharia Zubeir Pasha; tel: 772518; fax: 7700898; email: acropolekhartoum@yahoo.com) is a Khartoum institution. Run by the Greek Pagoulatos family, it's Khartoum's oldest hotel, and is popular with businessmen, journalists and archaeologists, as well as the occasional tourist. Rooms are simple and have a slightly old feel to them (a few lack bathrooms), but the service is excellent. Hotel staff can help with anything from vehicle hire to visas and permits. Room prices include internet access and full board in the attached restaurant (single/double US$95/145).

Well-located in central Khartoum is the **Meridien Hotel** (Sharia Sayed Abdul Rahman; tel: 775970; fax: 779087). As well as a pool, grand piano restaurant and coffee bar, the hotel is also home to the office for the British Airways franchise, Regional Air. Rooms are unfussy for the price, with the hotel's location being its strongest suit. Singles/doubles from US$150/173 plus 15% tax.

The **Grand Holiday Villa** (Sharia al-Nil; tel: 774039; fax: 773961; email: hovikha@sudanet.net) has a great location overlooking the Nile. The chandeliers and Old Masters oil paintings in the lobby feel a little incongruous in Sudan, but the rooms are of the quality expected from this international chain hotel. There are two restaurants and the Nile Terrace, with a live band in the evenings. The two pools are segregated for men and women, and there's a health club and tennis court. Singles start from US$120 and doubles from US$210 plus 15% tax. (Incidentally, don't bother trying to check in to the **Sudan Hotel** next door, as its leased by the Chinese National Petroleum Company, and is only open to it's employees.)

The **Hilton** (Off Sharia al-Nil; tel: 774100; fax: 775793; email: Hilonline1@sudanmail.net) is Khartoum's top hotel. Sited near al-Mogran, rooms on either side of the hotel have views of either the Blue or White Nile.

There are two restaurants (including the excellent Ivory Club), a bar (non-alcoholic), a pastry shop and a travel agent, along with a pool, gym and tennis court to keep guests happy. Due to the US embargo, the hotel cannot currently be booked online through the international Hilton website. Rooms start at US$190/210 for a single/double, plus 15% tax.

Khartoum is undergoing a five-star hotel boom. A **Pearl Continental Hotel** is being built on a plot next to the Hilton. The huge sail-like building past the Grand Holiday Villa built by the Libyans will be another.

Mid-range

The **Badr Tourist Hotel** (Sharia Sayed Abdul Rahman; tel: 782433) has basic but clean rooms. Rooms cost 3,640/4,940SD for a single/double with shared bathroom; there are a few ensuites. Choose your room carefully – while rooms at the front with balcony are good value, those without a bathroom (or a window) in the middle of the hotel can feel a bit claustrophobic.

There's not much to choose between the Badr Tourist Hotel and the **Hotel Safari Palace** a couple of doors down. (Sharia Sayed Abdul Rahman; tel: 782064). Rooms are slightly cheaper at 3,120/5,200SD for a single/double, but the place is in real need of a spring clean. All rooms are en suite.

Central Hotel (Sharia Sayed Abdul Rahman; tel: 772949; single/double 6,050/8,050SD) has cleaning ladies stationed on each floor to keep this hotel in good working order, and add a friendly bustle to the air. Rooms at the front have balconies. A great little place.

Another good choice is the **Shahrazad Hotel** (Sharia al-Jami; tel: 783577), which has comfortable modern rooms at 7,843/10,626SD for a single/double, with hot water and satellite television. Deservedly popular.

The **Taka Hotel** (Sharia Malik; tel: 776912) is popular with Italian tour groups. The hotel has a well-worn air and definitely needs a lick of paint, but at 7,500SD for either a single or double including breakfast, it's great value if you're travelling in a pair. Rooms are en suite with water heaters so guests are able to soak in a real bath rather than just to take the usual shower.

The **Gobba Hotel** (Sharia Istbitalya; tel: 784423) has aspirations to business class, with its comfy lobby and liveried staff. The plush rooms (10,660/12,740SD single/double) have television and hot water.

Finding the entrance to the **Sahara Hotel** (Sharia al-Jamhuriya; tel: 796541) can be confusing, as the hotel advertises itself on each corner of its block then does it's best to hide the front door down an arcade. Rooms are en suite (with bath) and have satellite television. Prices include breakfast; the attached restaurant is good for lunch and dinner. While the hotel is clean and modern, rooms still feel a bit expensive at 13,000/20,800SD for a single/double.

Somewhat out on a limb on the edge of Khartoum 2 is **Hotel Africa** (Africa Road; tel: 460744). Rooms start at 8,840/9,880SD for a single or double with bathroom and water heater; there are a few cheaper rooms with shared facilities. The hotel is well located for the airport and embassies, and minibuses ply the main road into the city. Attached is a great restaurant serving Chinese and Korean food.

Budget

Most of the budget options in Khartoum are clustered in and around Souq al-Arabi, placing you right in the heart of the action. The hotels below straddle the *lokanda-funduq* divide in terms of private/communal rooms and all have shared bathroom facilities. Don't expect hot water in this price range.

Set back from the road down a passageway and signed only in Arabic, the **Khalil Hotel** (off Sharia Hashim Bey) is a very welcoming *lokanda*. Rooms are large and airy, and the bathrooms are simple but clean. Next door is the equally friendly **Highcool Hotel**. Both hotels charge 2,000SD for a room of four beds and prefer you to take a whole room.

El Waleed Hotel (Sharia Istbitaliya) has no qualms about renting beds rather than rooms to *khawajas*, which it does at 500SD a bed. The rooms on the roof are the pick of the bunch, and you can pull your bed out to sleep in the cool if you prefer. It's clean and well run, and the toilets and showers are spotless.

Similar *lokanda*-fare is found around the corner at the **Riyadh New Hotel** (off Sharia Hashim Bey). Beds are 1,100SD, but you frequently get the whole room to yourself.

In the thick of the action in Souq al-Arabi is the **Haramein Hotel**. Slightly cramped rooms with three beds cost 1,800SD. During the day, the hotel is noisy from the bustle of the markets, but it's well placed above a row of cafeterias and juice bars for refreshment.

One of the few cheapies to offer genuine single and double rooms is the **Salli Hotel** (Sharia Sayed Abdul Rahman) at 1,900/2,800 single/double. The walls are painted with bright abstract murals, which makes the rooms themselves seem greyer and dustier than they might otherwise, and the bathrooms are even more rundown.

Camping

Situated on the river, the **Blue Nile Sailing Club** (Sharia al-Nil; tel: 0123 46790, mobile only) has long been a favourite campsite for overlanders in Khartoum. At the centre of the club is the Gunboat Melik, a relic from Kitchener's campaign against the Mahdi. It's now in impromptu dry-dock and used as the club office. The green lawns by the river are a great place to pitch a tent as they're kept cool by the Nile breeze throughout the day. Insect repellent can be handy in the evenings. Staff and club members are useful sources of information, particularly if you need to hunt down spares for a vehicle. Only the shower block lets the place down as it's in need of refurbishment. It's the best place in Khartoum to meet other travellers; if you're not staying here, it's still worth wandering over to have a cold drink and watch the sun set over the Nile. US$2 per person, US$2 bike, US$5 car.

WHERE TO EAT AND DRINK

Khartoum isn't overwhelmed with fantastic restaurants, but there is still a good variety to choose from. Although eating out is common enough, most places fall into the cafeteria or fast-food bracket. Here a meal won't set you

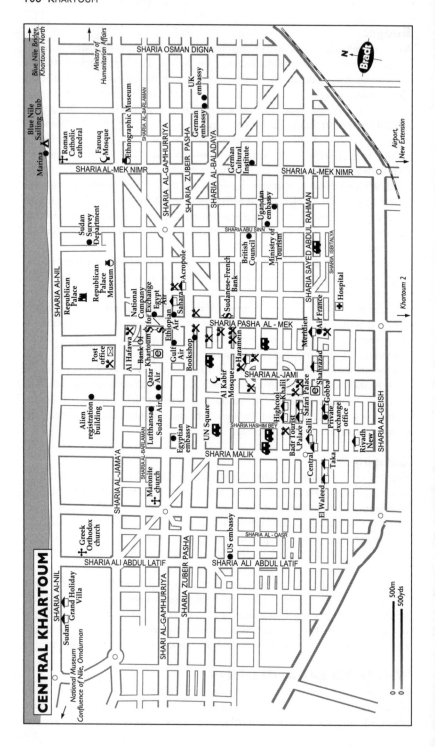

CENTRAL KHARTOUM

National Museum
Confluence of Nile, Omdurman

Blue Nile Bridge,
Khartoum North

Marina

Blue Nile
Sailing Club

Airport,
New Extension

N

Bradt

Ministry of
Humanitarian Affairs

SHARIA OSMAN DIGNA

UK
embassy

German
embassy

Ethnographic Museum

Roman
Catholic
cathedral

Farouq
Mosque

SHARIA AL-BARLAMAN

SHARIA AL-MEK NIMR

German
Cultural
Institute

SHARIA AL-MEK NIMR

SHARIA AL-GAMHURRIYA

SHARIA ZUBEIR PASHA

SHARIA AL-BALADAYA

Sudan
Survey
Department

SHARIA AL-NIL

Ugandan
embassy

SHARIA ABU SINN

British
Council

Ministry of
Tourism

SHARIA SAYED ABDUL RAHMAN

SHARIA ISBITALYA

Hospital

Khartoum 2

Republican
Palace

Republican
Palace
Museum

Acropole

National
Company
for Exchange
Egypt
Air

Sudanese-French
Bank

Sahara

Air France

Post
office

Al Hafawa

Bank Of
Khartoum

Qatar
Air

Sudan Air

Ethiopian
Air

Gulf
Air

Bookshop

Haramein

SHARIA PASHA AL - MEK

Merdien

Shahrizad

SHARIA AL-JAMI

Gobba

Alien
registration
building

Lufthansa

Al Kabir
Mosque

Highcool

Khalil

Safari Palace

Private
exchange
office

SHARIA AL-BARLAMAN

Egyptian
embassy

UN Square

SHARIA HASHIM BEY

Badr Tourist
Palace

Salli

Riyadh
New

SHARIA AL-GEISH

SHARIA MALIK

Central

Taka

SHARIA AL-JAMA'A

Maronite
church

El Waleed

US embassy

SHARIA AL - QASR

Greek
Orthodox
church

SHARIA ALI ABDUL LATIF

SHARIA ALI ABDUL LATIF

SHARIA AL-NIL

Sudan

Grand Holiday
Villa

SHARIA ZUBER PASHA

SHARI AL-GAMHURRIYA

500m

500yds

0

0

back much more than a couple of hundred dinars at most, including a soft drink or tea, with street snacks even cheaper. For something a little more fancy you'll generally have to head for a hotel or one of the few actual restaurants in the more upmarket districts of Khartoum 2 and New Extension south of the city centre.

Hotel restaurants

The pick of the bunch has to be the **Hilton Hotel** off Sharia al-Nil, which spoils you for choice with two restaurants. Dinner at the **Ivory Club** starts from about 5,000SD and is well worth the splurge. There's also a juice bar and pastry shop to tempt your sweet tooth.

The restaurant at the **Grand Holiday Villa** is open all day. Lunchtimes offer up delicious club sandwiches for 4,000SD, and a range of international dishes in the evening is available.

It's possible to eat at the **Acropole Hotel**, but you'll need to book in advance, as guests pay full board and they'll need to check there's space. A three-course meal costs 2,500SD, with a heavy slant towards Greek and Italian cuisine.

In the centre of Khartoum, the **Meridien Hotel** is good value and throws in someone tinkling on a grand piano for some ambience. The Nile Perch and soup is a steal at 1,600SD.

Restaurants

Sharia al-Nil has several open-air restaurants as you walk up to the Nile Confluence. Menus tend to feature grilled fish or meat with soup and a salad. The restaurants start to get going from around 18.00 and stay open late. **Askila**, with grassy lawns and liveried waiters opposite the National Museum, is the largest. A little farther along is **El Shallal**, which offers more of the same. For something a little different there's **Al-Fulq**, which actually floats out into the Blue Nile as you eat. Cruises last two hours and leave from next to the Tuti Island ferries, so check dining/sailing times carefully!

Al Hafawa (signed in Arabic) serves up good pizza at the top of Sharia al-Qasr on a green lawn, but the service doesn't lend itself to the term 'fast food'. Nevertheless a large 'Khartoum pizza' is good value at 800/1,400SD for a medium or large meal. If you order in advance they can do takeaway.

There are couple of good eastern restaurants on Africa Road near the airport. Technically a hotel restaurant is **Hotel Africa**, which serves up great Korean and Chinese food all day, and which is well worth a visit. A main course costs between 1000-2000SD. Slightly closer to the centre is **Panda Chinese**, another good place for noodles and chop suey.

In Khartoum 2, **Little India** has tasty curries (about the only ones on offer in Sudan).

Cafeterias and fast food

Khartoum is awash with cafeterias serving up the standard selection of Sudanese fare – *ful*, *fasuliya*, *kebabs*, *adis* and a variety of stews. The busiest and best are clustered around United Nations Square. They're always unnamed and unmarked so go wherever looks popular. *Ful* and *adis* tend to be served around Sudanese breakfast time. Several good places are marked on the map; one of the best has to be the one next to the Shell petrol station on Sharia Sayed Abdul Rahman – not only are the grilled quarter chickens great, but it seems to be the only place branching out into pasta – a bowl of macaroni slathered with tomato sauce costs 150SD.

Western-style fast food places dish out lamb and chicken *shwarmas* and a variety of different burgers in buns, topped with the obligatory fried egg. Kookie Burger is a particular favourite, but there are plenty to choose from.

Bear in mind that cafeterias and fast food places close up for several hours on Friday lunchtime.

THEFT AND SAFETY

Khartoum must rank as one of the safest cities in Africa. That said, there is always the risk of pickpockets, so pay attention to your belongings, particularly in the busiest areas around Souq al-Arabi, the Souq es-Shabi and the Omdurman *souq*.

LISTINGS
Airline offices

In addition to the airline offices below, Khartoum has plenty of travel agents, mostly clustered on or around the northern end of Sharia al-Qasr.

Air France Sharia al-Qasr; tel: 776606. Air France does not currently fly to Khartoum, but the office can sell code-share tickets with Kenya Airways.
British Airways Sharia Sayed Abdul Rahman (inside the Meridien Hotel); tel: 797277. Currently sells only tickets for Regional Airways, a BA franchise.
Egypt Air Sharia al-Qasr; tel: 780064.
Ethiopian Airways Sharia al-Gamhurriya; tel: 762088
Gulf Air Sharia al-Gamhurriya; tel: 774038
Lufthansa Sharia al-Taiyar Morad tel: 771322
Qatar Airways Sharia al-Gamhurriya tel: 761307
Sudan Air Sharia al-Gamhurriya; tel: 472375

Embassies

The majority of embassies are based in south Khartoum, in the modern districts of Khartoum 2, New Extension and Amarat. Relevant visa information for neighbouring countries is listed below.

Canada Africa Road; tel: 563673
Chad Sharia 57, Amarat; tel: 471084. One-month visa costs US$60 with two photos, passport photocopy and letter of introduction from your embassy. If flying to Chad, visas issued in 24 hours; visas for land entry are referred to N'djamena for authorisation, which can take several weeks. Open for applications Sat–Thu, 11.00–15.30.
Egypt Sharia Jamhuriya; tel: 772190. A one-month single entry visa costs 6,000SD, issued in 24 hours. Applications on Sat–Wed, 11.00–13.00.

KHARTOUM 2 & NEW EXTENSION

Eritrea Street 39, Khartoum 2; tel: 483834. One-month visa costs US$40 with two photos and passport photocopy. Issued in 72 hours. Open for visas Sat–Thu 09.00–14.00.
Ethiopia Off Sharia Al Qasr South, New Extension; tel: 471156. One-month visa costs US$63 with two photos. Issued in 24 hours. Proof that you are flying into Ethiopia is no longer needed. Applications on Sat–Thu, 09.00–12.00.
France Sharia 13, New Extension; tel: 471082
Germany Sharia al-Baladya; tel: 777995
Italy Sharia 29, Khartoum 2; tel: 471615
Jordan Sharia 33, Amarat; tel: 471146. One-month visa costs 4,200SD with one photo, issued in 24 hours. Open Sat–Thu 09.00–12.00.
Kenya Sharia 3, Khartoum 2; tel: 483834. One-month visa costs US$50 with two photos and photocopy of passport. Applications on Mon and Wed 10.00–12.00, visas issued on same day.
Libya Block 18, Riyadh; tel: 222545. Visas only granted to those nationalities that do not have a Libyan People's Bureau in their home country (which excludes those from

the UK and most of Europe, so check carefully before travelling). A letter of introduction from a Libyan travel agency is required.

Netherlands Sharia 47, Khartoum 2; tel: 471200

Saudi Arabia Sharia 29, Amarat; tel: 464646. Seven-day transit visa costs US$20 with one photo and visa for onward travel. Married couples must provide their marriage certificate as proof of their status. Visas are not granted to unmarried couples; women under 40 will be refused visas unless accompanied by their husband, father or brother. Visa applications on Sat–Thu, 07.30–14.00.

Switzerland Sharia 15, New Extension; tel: 471010

Uganda Sharia Abu Qarga; tel: 797867. One-month visa costs US$30 with two photos. Visa applications on Sat–Thu, 09.00–14.00.

UK Off Sharia al-Balaadya; tel: 777105

USA Sharia Ali Abdel Latif; tel: 774701

Maps

The Ministry of Tourism and Culture on Sharia Abu Sinn gives away free small-scale maps of Sudan and Khartoum, but the city map in particular is very old and outdated. The Map Sales Section of the **Sudan Survey Department** sells maps covering the entire country, based on detailed surveys carried out by the British Army in the 1930s and updated in the 1960s. As such they are excellent for topographical detail but need to be used in conjunction with modern equivalents to accurately place roads and railways.

The maps divide Sudan into blocks mapped at 1:1 million. Each block is then subdivided into 16 sections, each mapped at 1:250,000. Overlanders and archaeologists may find the sheets covering Dongola to Shendi (NE36) and Dongola to Wadi Halfa (NF36) particularly useful, although the latter sheet pre-dates the construction of the Aswan Dam and the flooding of the Second Cataract. Sheets NC35 and ND35 cover north and south Kordofan and Darfur respectively. The topographical information would be useful for explorations of the Nuba Mountains or Jebel Marra, but frustratingly both regions are on the corners of four large-scale maps!

The Sudan Survey Department is a little hard to find – it's off Sharia Abu Sinn, opposite the National Centre for Diplomatic Studies. The Map Sales Section is signed in English.

To purchase the maps it is necessary to write a letter to the office explaining why you wish to purchase each sheet, although this seems like a hangover from the Sudanese love of bureaucracy rather than any serious attempt to hinder the purchaser. The maps cost 1,400SD each.

The **New Bookshop** carries a decent selection of maps of Khartoum and Sudan, as well as the Michelin and Bartholomew Africa road maps. The ITMB map of Sudan is not available in Khartoum.

Medical

Well-stocked pharmacies can be found on most major streets in Khartoum and staff frequently speak English. For more serious complaints, head for the Teaching Hospital near the corner of Sharia al-Qasr and Sharia Isbitalya.

Shopping

Khartoum's shops are well stocked, with the main shopping area around Souq al-Arabi. A square off Sharia al-Qasr is dedicated to handicrafts such as painted leather, carved wood and unethical animal products. The shops are popular with Chinese workers and prices are consequently high. More fun is to head to Omdurman Souq, where you'll find many of same things on offer, along with a more interesting shopping experience.

Books

Good bookshops are thin on the ground in Khartoum. For a choice that extends beyond English language textbooks, your best option is the Greek-run **New Bookshop** on the corner of Sharia Zubeir Pasha and Sharia al-Qasr, which holds a reasonable selection of titles on Sudan, some useful maps and an eclectic mix of books from spy novels to Oscar Wilde plays.

Tour operators and booking agencies

Two reliable tour companies that can provide guides and hire vehicles are:

Globtours Sharia Sayed Abdul Rahman, tel: 798111 (mobile: 0912 253 484); email: globtours_sudan@yahoo.com
Italian Tourism Company Sharia 27, Amarat; tel: 487961; fax: 487962; email: italtour@sudanmail.net.sd

Tourist information

The Ministry of Tourism has an office on Sharia Abu Sinn. They're friendly enough but can't offer much practical help or advice, beyond issuing photo permits and 20-year old maps of Khartoum.

MEDIA AND COMMUNICATIONS
Internet

The internet has caught on in Khartoum and net cafes are popping up all over the place. The fastest and most consistently reliable connections are in the lobby of the **Meridien Hotel**, which charges 500SD/hour (almost worth it for the air conditioning alone). Elsewhere, expect to pay around half that. There are several unnamed net cafes further along Sharia Sayed Abdul Rahman and there's a handy place in the Kuwait building opposite the Blue Nile Sailing club.

Newspapers

Many newstands carry the English-language newspaper *Sudan Vision*. The monthly *Sudanow* magazine is harder to track down – try the stands near the Acropole Hotel.

Post

The main post office is on Sharia al-Jama'a. Stalls outside sell postcards, envelopes and stamps, including some good collectable issues. Poste restante can be collected here; there is no collection fee.

WHAT TO SEE AND DO IN KHARTOUM
Confluence of the Nile

Known locally as al-Mogran, the Confluence of the Nile is one of Africa's geographical highlights. From here you can look east along the fast and narrow Blue Nile stretching to Ethiopia; turning south you are faced with the White Nile, wide and lazy, exhausted by its passage from Lake Victoria through the swamps of the Sudd. The two Niles are distinct colours (or at least shades of muddy grey) due to the silts they carry, and you can see the streams flow next to each other before mixing to complete the mighty river.

During summer months when the Blue Nile is at its highest level, the flow of water is so strong that is causes the White Nile to back up, flooding parts of southern Khartoum in bad years. The difference in colour between the two rivers is particularly noticeable at this time.

In 1772 the Scottish explorer James Bruce passed through claiming to have found the source of the Nile in Ethiopia. He had traced the Blue Nile from its source at Lake Tana, and was disheartened to reach the confluence to find an equally mighty river joining the waterway. It would take nearly a hundred years more for the source of the White Nile to be located by John Hanning Speke.

In many countries, a site like the Nile confluence would be heralded with signposts and viewpoints. The Sudanese are happy to let things like this pass, as unhurried to draw attention to it as the lazy waters of the river itself. In fact, the less attention drawn the better as far as the security forces are concerned. Anyone pulling out a camera on the White Nile Bridge overlooking the Confluence is likely to have his or her film confiscated. The bridge is regarded as 'strategic', so photography (even with a permit) is expressly forbidden. Strangely, the postcard sellers outside the main post office will happily sell you a snap of the bridge, although this irony seems to have gone unnoticed by the authorities.

For photography, try the Mogran Family Park next to the bridge. Entry costs 75SD; for the best view of the Confluence, take a ride on the ferris wheel. You should be able to snap away happily from up there. Alternatively, hop on a ferry to Tuti Island and walk to its northern tip, where the blending of the Nile waters is at its strongest.

Nile Cruises

A boat trip on the Nile is a relaxing way to see Khartoum. From the water the city seems little more than an over-sized village – head even a short way along any arm of the river and you'll quickly find yourself cruising past arable land rather than urban sprawl. Boats can be hired from the **Blue Nile Sailing Club** and the **Marina** next door (signed only in Arabic, with a large Coca Cola logo). There are a variety of motor launches and pontoons on offer; prices typically start at around 10,000SD per hour. An hour upstream on the Blue Nile, the sandy beaches at Jazeera are a good place for picnic. For those who prefer life under sail, the season at the Blue Nile Sailing Club runs from the end of November to April, starting with a dinghy race around Tuti Island.

There is sailing most Wednesday afternoons, and volunteer crews are welcome.

Tuti Island

Situated at the Confluence of the Nile, Tuti Island is a snapshot of traditional village life in the heart of the capital. Tuti is a large farming village with few motor vehicles, and you can spent a pleasant afternoon wandering the island escaping from the press of people in Khartoum. Please be considerate when walking around farmer's fields. The steep banks on the south of the island are a good illustration of the seasonal variation in the level of the Nile, while the beaches on the north make a nice picnic spot.

Ferries to Tuti depart from opposite the Friendship Palace, and cost 25SD each way.

National Museum of Sudan

The National Museum holds many treasures of Sudan's ancient and medieval past. They're well presented and labelled, and give a good narrative of Sudanese history.

The museum is on two floors. The ground floor starts with Sudan's prehistory and covers the rise of Kerma and Kush in great detail. Kerma is particularly well represented through its famous pottery. The Kushite displays show the wide variety of cultural exchange in play throughout the kingdom. Egyptian culture is the strongest influence, shown particularly in the royal statues found at Jebel Barkal dating from around 690BC and the sarcophagus of Anlamani from his tomb at Nuri about 100 years older. A clear Hellenistic influence can be seen in the statue of the so-called 'Venus of Meroe' and a blue glass chalice from Sedeinga, with depictions of gods and bearing a Greek inscription 'You shall live'. A side room on the ground floor has space for temporary displays, often illustrating current archaeological digs.

The upstairs gallery holds the museum's most unexpected displays – frescoes from Christian Nubia. Despite lasting for 700 years, Sudan's early Christian kingdoms are little known in the outside world and repeated Sudanese governments have shown little interest in promoting this aspect of their history. I was as ignorant as most on my first visit, and was astounded to find beautiful frescos depicting Christ and the Virgin Mary, along with a host of archangels, saints and apostles. The style of the frescos is distinctly Byzantine, reflecting Nubia's links with the Roman Empire in the east. Most of the frescoes were painted between the 8th and 14th centuries, and were taken from the cathedral at Faras, now submerged under Lake Nasser.

In the grounds of the museum are three Egyptian temples also rescued from the rising waters of Lake Nasser in the 1960s. The temples, from Buhen, Semna and Kumma, all date from the 18th Dynasty (1550–1295BC), a time when Egypt was consolidating its southern borders with Nubia. Also outside are two rams with a figure of Taharqa between their front legs from the Temple of Amun at Kawa, and the massive granite statues of temple guardians from Tabo from the Kushite period.

FARAS

The Christian Nubian centre of Faras sat on an island roughly halfway between the Second and Third Cataracts, on the site of early Egyptian and Kushite settlements. With the coming of Christianity it was the seat of the kings of Nobatia, and had close ties to the church in Byzantium.

Some time in the 7th century AD, Nobatia was absorbed by the energetic Makurian kingdom and ruled from Old Dongola to the south. Faras continued to thrive, with a bishop, several churches, a monastery and two palaces. As a sign of Faras's continued influence, one of these palaces may have belonged to the Eparch, who governed Nubia's relations with its Muslim neighbours in Egypt.

However, Faras did not survive past the end of the Christian kingdoms, despite its key location to control trade along the Nile. More than any political factors, it was the desert that led to the town's eventual demise. Sand blown in from the Sahara perpetually threatened the site, filling the strait between the island and the bank. By the 13th century the cathedral was entirely filled, forcing services to be held outside. An entirely new church was later built on top of the covered cathedral.

The sands that engulfed Faras also saved it for history, helping to preserve the richly painted frescoes of the Nubian Church. Faras was excavated extensively in the early 1960s by a Polish archaeological expedition. While the site itself now lies under the waters of Lake Nasser, the frescoes – and more – were saved for the future. Polish archaeologists continue to work at the site of Old Dongola.

The museum was closed for much of 2004 after the theft of several displays. Minibuses from Souq el-Arabi to Omdurman go past the museum. Opening hours are 08.30–18.30, closed on Monday and Friday between 12.00 and 15.00. Entrance costs 50SD.

Ethnographic Museum

At the time of going to press, the Ethnographic Museum on Sharia al-Jama'a was closed for renovation. It has a large collection of material covering Sudan's ethnic diversity, and should be well worth a visit when it re-opens. One of the old highlights was a giant wooden ceremonial drum from the Azande, carved in the shape of an ox.

Unfortunately no one could give me an idea of when this would be, and there wasn't much evidence of work going on during the several visits I made.

Republican Palace Museum

Khartoum's old Anglican Church has been converted into a museum celebrating the history of the Sudanese republic. The problem here is knowing exactly which history to celebrate in a country whose post-independence period has been dominated by coups. The museum steers a middle path, with displays of medals, photos and presidential gifts. My personal favourite is the commemorative plate presented to President Bashir by the West Omdurman Abbatoir. At the back of the museum in the knave is a nod to the Condominium period – busts of Kitchener, memorials to missionaries and a chapel dedicated to Gordon. Outside is a display of vintage (and bulletproof) presidential Rolls Royces.

The museum is worth a visit for the building alone, a fine red sandstone church with some pretty stained glass, built in 1904. Entrance is 50SD; it's open Friday–Sunday and Wednesday, 09.00–13.00 and 16.00–20.00.

Commonwealth War Cemetery
The Commonwealth War Cemetery was established shortly after the Second World War. Khartoum was used as the base for the invasion of Abyssinia in 1940, to expel the Italians. Soldiers of the Sudan Defence Force supported emperor Haile Selassie. It was a remote theatre of war, but no less bloody than those elsewhere in North Africa. Rows of gravestones remember the war dead.

SIGHTSEEING IN OMDURMAN
Omdurman Souq
The *souq* in Omdurman is the largest in the country. The main part of the *souq* consists of endless alleys and side streets lined with shops and stalls. The buildings aren't particularly old but the sounds, smells and throngs of people capture the essence of the bazaar. Omdurman is said to be the heart of Sudan and you can well believe it. Rickshaws and donkey carts compete for space amid the bustle, street hawkers shout out their wares, and the smells and sounds of the city fill the air. With what feels like the highest density of people per square metre in the country, it's impossible to rush. Shopping in the *souq* is an invigorating, exhausting experience.

Minibuses drop you on the edge of the *souq*, or you can walk up from the Mahdi's Tomb. The *souq* is centred on two open squares. The southerly square has Omdurman's post office and several banks with exchange facilities. The second square, 500m farther north, has a large stand for local yellow minibuses. From here it's a case of diving into the side streets to explore. The streets closest to the squares sell clothes and household goods, but you can find everything here from food stalls to ironmongers. Stalls selling handicrafts and souvenirs from across Sudan are on the western side of the *souq*. There are plenty of food and juice bars if you want to get away from the crowds and revive flagging spirits.

The Mahdi's Tomb
Less than five months after the fall of Khartoum in 1885, the Mahdi died after a short illness. A tomb with a glittering silver dome was raised in his honour, and pilgrimage to the site was made incumbent on all Sudanese, replacing the Haj to Mecca as one of the pillars of Islam.

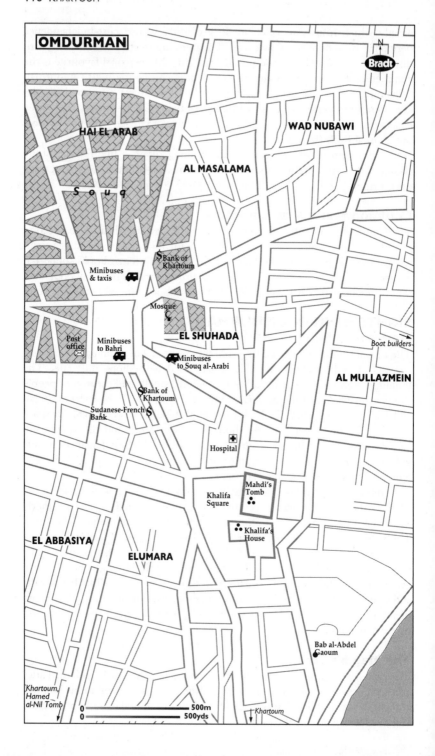

OMDURMAN

N

Bradt

HAI EL ARAB

AL MASALAMA

WAD NUBAWI

S o u q

Bank of Khartoum

Minibuses & taxis

Mosque

Post office

Minibuses to Bahri

EL SHUHADA

Boat builders

Minibuses to Souq al-Arabi

AL MULLAZMEIN

Bank of Khartoum

Sudanese-French Bank

Hospital

Mahdi's Tomb

Khalifa Square

AL ABBASIYA

Khalifa's House

ELUMARA

Bab al-Abdel Gaoum

Khartoum, Hamed al-Nil Tomb

0   500m
0   500yds

Khartoum

Soon after their reconquest of Sudan, the British blew up the tomb to prevent it from becoming a rallying point for disaffected Sudanese. The job was given to 'Monkey' Gordon, nephew of the dead general, who completed the job by throwing the Mahdi's ashes in the river. Kitchener wanted to use the Mahdi's skull as an inkstand, but decency prevailed and the head was buried at Wadi Halfa.

The present tomb – a straight copy of the original – was rebuilt in 1947, presumably once the British had got over their fears of its symbolic power. Non-Muslims are not permitted to enter the tomb itself.

Minibuses from central Khartoum to Souq Omdurman pass the Mahdi's Tomb.

The Khalifa's House

Across the street from the Mahdi's tomb is the house of his successor, Khalifa Abdullah. A low, two-storey building with a series of linked courtyards, the house has been turned into a museum of the Mahdiya period.

The first rooms are dedicated to the Battle of Omdurman that saw the end of Mahdist rule in Sudan. There is a collection of rifles and spears collected from the battlefield, as well as banners and the patched robes known as *jibbehs*, worn by the Ansar. The old muskets and crocodile hide shields on display give a good illustration of the total inadequacy of the Mahdist army in the face of British repeating rifles and Maxim guns.

Later, items contain coins struck by the Mahdiya and the rather flimsy bank notes issued by Gordon during the siege of Khartoum – little more than rubber stamped slips of paper. A letter from the Mahdi asking Gordon to surrender is proudly displayed, along with the Mahdi's copy of the Koran and a rhino-horn drinking cup belonging to the (more worldly) Khalifa.

The courtyards hold several interesting items – machine guns captured from Hicks Pasha at the Battle of Sheikan, the cupola saved from the ruins of the original Mahdi's Tomb, and the first car in Sudan, belonging to the Governor General. Looking more like a cart than any other contemporary motor vehicle, it's solid wheels look well suited to Sudanese roads, and travellers on a long and bumpy bus trip may reflect that not much has changed in nearly a hundred years

Known locally as Beit al-Khalifa, entrance costs 100SD; the museum is closed on Mondays.

If you continue walking east away from the Khalifa's House and Mahdi's tomb for 750m, you'll reach the Bab al-Abdel Gaoum, one of Omdurman's old city gates, now rather ignominiously tucked behind railings as traffic whizzes past.

MOHAMMED AHMED, THE MAHDI

Many Muslim Sudanese see the Mahdi as the first African anti-colonialist, a father of the nation who united the country under Islam and kicked out the Egyptians and British – no small achievement for the son of a boat builder.

Mohammed Ahmed was born in 1844 near Dongola. His father died at an early age (he would later claim descent from the Prophet Mohammed) and the boy was sent to Khartoum to receive a religious education. On completing his studies he went to Aba Island on the White Nile near Kosti and became a follower of the spiritual leader Sheikh Mohammed Sharif. The young Mohammed Ahmed was known for his piety and rigorous ascetism, traits that would bring him into conflict with his teacher. At a feast held to celebrate the circumcision of the Sheikh's sons, Mohammed Ahmed roundly condemned the music and dancing as sinful debauchery and was ejected from the Sheikh's company.

The devotee left Aba and wandered in Kordofan where he began to make a name for himself with his preaching, his sparse vision of Islam well received by the nomadic Baggara Arabs. He later returned to Aba where he took up with another leader, Sheikh al-Koreishi. On al-Koreishi's death, Mohammed Ahmed was joined by the son of a Baggara *faqi*, Abdullah ibn Mohammed, who would be his most faithful lieutenant and later succeed his master as ruler of Sudan. Abdullah declared his leader the Mahdi, a figure divinely called to renew the Islamic faith.

The Mahdi went further than his newly declared mission to expel Khartoum's colonial masters. He also gave himself the title 'Successor of the Apostle of God' and saw himself re-enacting the life of the Prophet Mohammed, claiming Mecca and Medina would be his ultimate goals.

No photographs of the Mahdi exist but Rudolf Slatin, the captured

Camel market

On the western edge of Omdurman is Sudan's largest camel market. It's open daily, although Friday is the busiest trading day. Darfur is the major camel-raising region in Sudan, and the majority of camels for sale here come from the west, bred by the many tribes of the Juhayna Arabs. Most camels are destined for the Egyptian market, which has a high demand for their meat. The Beja and Rashaida represent eastern Sudan; their Bisharin camels are highly prized in the Gulf States for racing. The market is also called Souq Abu Zayd.

Hamed al-Nil Tomb

Sheikh Hamed al-Nil was a 19th-century Sufi leader of the Qadiriyah order (*tariqa*), and his tomb is the weekly focus for Omdurman's most exciting sight – the dancing and chanting dervishes. Each Friday afternoon before sunset, adherents of the *tariqa* gather to dance and pray, attracting large crowds of

Austrian governor of Darfur, was one of the few Europeans to leave a first-hand account of meeting him, in his 1896 book *Fire and Sword in the Sudan*:

> I now had a good opportunity of making a careful study of Mohammed Ahmed; he was a tall, broad-shouldered man of light brown colour, and powerfully built; he had a large head and sparkling black eyes; he wore a black beard, and had the usual three slits on each cheek; his nose and mouth were well shaped, and he had the habit of always smiling, showing his white teeth and exposing the V-shaped aperture between the two front ones which is considered a sign of good luck in the Sudan, and is known as 'falja'. This was one of the principal causes which made the Mahdi so popular with the fair sex, by whom he was dubbed "Abu Falja" (the man with the separated teeth). He wore a short quilted jibba, beautifully washed, and perfumed with sandalwood, musk, and attar of roses; this perfume was celebrated amongst his disciples as Rihet el Mahdi (the odour of the Mahdi), and was supposed to equal, if not surpass, that of the dwellers in Paradise.

The success of the Mahdist rebellion was lightning fast, leading to the siege and capture of Khartoum and a crisis in Imperial Britain. General Gordon, another religious ascetic, had ironically found much to admire in the Mahdi. Pondering the relief expedition and a return home that never came, he wrote that he would 'sooner live like a Dervish with the Mahdi than go out to dinner every night in London'. For his part, the Mahdi professed regret at Gordon's killing, saying that he had wanted to convert him to Islam. The Mahdi never got so see his legacy in Sudan – within five months of capturing Khartoum he was dead, probably from typhoid.

observers and participants. A trip to see the dervishes should be a highlight of any visit to Khartoum.

The ceremony starts with a march across the cemetery to the tomb of the sheikh. It's an amazing sight as the dervishes carrying the green banner of the *tariqa*, their appearance a world away from the restrained white robes of most Sudanese. Instead, the *jallabiyas* are a crazy patchwork of green and red, often topped off with leopard skin, chunky beads and dreadlocks. As they march they chant, accompanied by drums and cymbals.

Outside the tomb, a large open space is cleared for the dervishes and the banner is raised for the ritual to begin. The pace of the chanting picks up, and the dervishes start to circle the clearing, bobbing and clapping.

The purpose of the frenzy is a ritual called *dhikr*. The *dhikr* relies on the recitation of God's names to help create a state of ecstatic abandon in which the adherent's heart can communicate directly with God. This personal communication with God is central to Sufi practices.

THE BATTLE OF OMDURMAN

Imperial Britain fought innumerable wars throughout the 19th century. Barring a few spectacular disasters, battles were often one-sided affairs, pitting a well-organised modern army against a poorly armed native force. The Battle of Omdurman was the apogee of such encounters.

On September 2 1898, General Kitchener led his men into the final confrontation with the armies of the Khalifa, in the shadow of the Kereri Hills outside Omdurman. His aim was not only to end the rule of Mahdism, but also to avenge Britain for the death of her hero, Gordon. The result of the fight was never in doubt.

Winston Churchill, then a lieutenant seconded to the 21st Lancers, is the keenest witness to the battle that we have, and captures the spirit of this clash of two worlds. The Mahdist army, with their glinting spears and proud banners, were of another age, reminding him of a scene from the Bayeux Tapestry. In contrast, the British officers drank champagne on the eve of battle, and luncheon that day had the air of a race day meeting rather than a military campaign.

Over 55,000 Sudanese faced the British and Egyptian troops, outnumbering them more than two to one. The numbers were less important than the products of British industry: repeating rifles, artillery and gunboats. The patched robes of the Ansar were meant to give protection from bullets, but the British volleys decimated them at a distance of several hundred yards.

For all his talk of the war as a splendid game, Churchill was at least an active participant, taking part in a cavalry charge – in fact, the last great charge of the British Army, which was soon to be faced with the horrors of the trenches and mechanised warfare.

At the end of the battle around 10,000 Sudanese lay dead. The Khalifa had fled the scene. The British and Egyptians lost just 48 men, with 434 wounded. Kitchener called this 'a good dusting'. On reading of the victory and bloodshed at Omdurman, the writer Hilaire Belloc penned the immortal lines that have characterised Victorian (and subsequent) imperial attitudes ever since: 'Whatever happens, we have got / The Maxim Gun, and they have not'.

The Sufis are often called 'whirling dervishes' but that's really a bit of a misnomer. Most are content to parade around the circle chanting and clapping. Occasionally a dervish will break off and start twirling by himself, spinning on one foot and lost in his own personal path to God. As they march, the dervishes repeatedly chant 'La illaha illallah', meaning 'There is no God but Allah', the first line of the Muslim profession of faith. Around the edge of the circle other adherents clap and join in the chanting, creating a highly charged and hypnotic atmosphere.

The chanting lasts up to 45 minutes. At the end of the ritual, the dervishes break off and enter the mosque to pray in the orthodox Islamic manner.

With Sufism so important to Sudanese Islam, *dhikr* rituals like this play a major role in religious life. There is a real festival air around the *dhikr*. Beside the tomb there are tea stalls and adherents selling Sufi pamphlets and tapes; before the ritual starts there is often drumming and chanting inside the tomb itself, and food provided for the needy.

OMDURMAN'S SQUATTER CAMPS

The Greater Khartoum area is host to around two million Internally Displaced People (IDPs), the majority of whom are clustered around Omdurman in a series of squatter camps. Most of the IDPs are from South Sudan, driven away from their homes by war, famine and in some cases land clearance for oil prospecting. Mixed in with these economic migrants from the South are people from the west, displaced by further drought and fighting.

The figures are startling. A 2003 survey by the aid organisation Care International reported over half of the camp's occupants were under 20. Female-headed households are common, with 65% of adults women. Approximately 11% of children were malnourished, with a further 15% 'at risk'.

The camps have received little or no help from the government, which has regarded the presence of so many Southerners as an irritant. The camps have been periodically bull-dozed, and the squatters moved to more distant sites with inadequate shelter and water supplies. At one stage in the 1990s, young boys were even rounded up and sent to Islamic schools.

International aid organisations have been able to provide limited infrastructure and access to water and health care, but the camps have remained desperately deprived. There are limited economic opportunities for the squatters, and Southerners are regularly discriminated against.

With the ongoing peace process, it is anticipated that the majority of those in the camps will return to their homes. The UN High Commission for Refugees has drawn up plans to aid travel and resettlement costs. Over one million returnees were expected in the South in the first six months following the signing of the peace protocols in May 2004, prompting worries that the war-shattered Southern infrastructure would not be able to cope. Despite this, both the government and SPLM/A have been keen to encourage the return as soon as possible. A new census will be carried out across Sudan for the first time since independence, and all sides want the returnees to be accounted for. More importantly for the SPLM/A they want all IDPs to return before the self-determination referendum after the interim period.

Photography is allowed, but it's best to be discreet. Don't dash in to the circle to fire off a couple of shots – the dervishes use ritual and atmosphere as the centre of their ceremony, and so shouldn't be interrupted in any way. This is an active religious community not a tourist attraction. If in doubt, ask for permission.

To reach the tomb, get on a minibus from Souq al-Arabi and ask for either Ghobba al-Hamed al-Nil or Ahlia (a nearby college); it should take around 20 minutes. The onion-domes of the tomb and mosque are clearly visible from the road. Get there in plenty of time; the ritual starts around an hour before sunset on Friday. The dervishes do not gather during Ramadan.

Boat builders
It's still possible to see wooden boats being built at Omdurman Boat Yard. The craft has traditionally been carried out by Nubians; indeed the Mahdi was the son of a boat builder from Dongola. There is little demand for the wooden-planked dinghies now, which are used by only a few fishermen. The yard is on the edge of the Abu Roaf district of Omdurman, just north of Shambat Bridge. The boat builders are usually happy for people to look around and take photos.

SIGHTSEEING IN KHARTOUM NORTH
Nuba wrestling
It's possible to see the traditional Nuba sport of wrestling on most Fridays in the district of Haj Yusef on the eastern edge of Khartoum North, although this annoyingly coincides with the 'whirling dervishes' in Omdurman. If you can, check in advance whether there will be wrestling that day as it is sometimes cancelled. The first time I tried – and failed – to watch them, the wrestlers were apparently called out on strike.

Wrestling is central to Nuba culture. A *sirwan* or wrestling ground is specially prepared and fighters are called out to meet their opponents. In the Nuba Mountains fights are usually performed to uphold the honour of the village. In Khartoum, the wrestling is organised municipally. Also in recognition of local custom, wrestlers in Khartoum are fully clothed; in their homeland they would be half-naked or adorned with animal skins. Bouts continue until everyone has wrestled. For more information on Nuba culture, see page 205.

The wrestling is a 20-minute bus trip from the centre of Khartoum. Minibuses leave from outside the Al-Shamal Islamic Bank on Sharia Sayed Abdul Rahman – ask for Souq Sita ('Market six') in the Wihda district of Haj Yusef. The minibus will drop you off on the edge of a large open-air *souq*. Walk east towards the area selling wood, cane and other building materials; the large open ground is where the wrestling takes place (and at other times, dangerous test drives for lads learning to drive). The mosques near by and rusty water tower are good landmarks to head for. The wrestling takes places about an hour before sunset.

Khartoum to Atbara

The geographers of classical antiquity knew the region between Khartoum and Atbara as the 'Island of Meroe', as it was the area bounded by the Blue Nile, the Nile and the Atbara rivers. Now called the Butana, it covers the centre of the Kingdom of Meroe, and contains its greatest sites. The pyramids of the Royal Cemetery of Meroe, isolated on the edge of the desert and a world away from the press of tourists at their more famous counterparts in Egypt, are a highlight of any trip to Sudan. Also worth visiting are the beautifully preserved Meroitic temples of Naqa and Musawwarat es Sufra.

The smooth tarmac road following the Nile north from Khartoum makes travel in this stretch of Sudan fast and comfortable. The Pyramids at Meroe can be visited as a day trip from Khartoum (as can Naqa and Musawwarat es Sufra) although you would want to time things to avoid sightseeing during the heat of the day. Alternatively you can base yourself in the old market town of Shendi and make arrangements from there.

SHENDI

Nowadays a nondescript market town, Shendi's appearance belies its history. Its location helped it to become the biggest market in Sudan during the Funj kingdom, and it only lost its pre-eminence with the establishment of Khartoum as Sudan's capital by the Turco-Egyptians in the 1820s. Now the town has the slight air of a backwater about it, with its current claim to fame being that it's the birthplace of President Bashir. Most of Shendi's inhabitants are Jaalayin Arabs and the town is mainly a market for cereals.

While there is little of interest to travellers in Shendi itself, the town's location makes it a good stopping point on the Khartoum-Atbara highway, and its proximity to the sites at Meroe, Naqa and Musawwarat es Sufra are enough to justify a stay here. Just before going to press I was told that it is now possible to get archaeological permits in Shendi to visit these sites – it would be interesting to know if any travellers succeed in doing this.

Getting there and away

Shendi sits about 3km east of the Khartoum–Atbara highway. Transport arriving in Shendi drops passengers at the train line next to the radio mast.

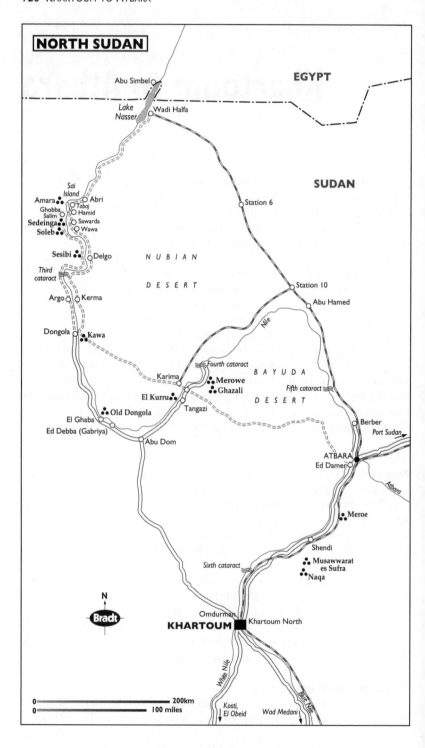

NORTH SUDAN

EGYPT

Abu Simbel

Lake Nasser Wadi Halfa

SUDAN

Sai Island
Amara Abri
Ghobba Tabaj
Salim Hamid
Sedeinga Sawarda
Soleb Wawa

Station 6

Sesibi Delgo

N U B I A N

Third cataract

D E S E R T

Argo Kerma

Station 10
Abu Hamed

Dongola Kawa

Nile

Fourth cataract
Karima *B A Y U D A*
Merowe
Ghazali *Fifth cataract*
El Kurru *D E S E R T*
Old Dongola Tangazi
El Ghaba
Ed Debba (Gabriya) Abu Dom

Berber
Port Sudan

ATBARA
Ed Damer

Atbara

Meroe

Shendi

Musawwarat
es Sufra
Sixth cataract Naqa

N

Bradt

Omdurman
KHARTOUM Khartoum North

White Nile

Blue Nile

0 ———————————— 200km
0 ———————————— 100 miles

Kosti,
El Obeid Wad Medani

THE SLAVE MARKETS OF SHENDI

Shendi was once a prosperous town. It drew its wealth from its location, as it straddled both the trade routes along the Nile and the caravan roads from West Africa to the Red Sea. From medieval times, Shendi was the market place of Sudan.

At its height in the 18th century Shendi had a permanent population of around 6,000. This was swollen greatly once a week when it hosted the largest market in the country. Merchants traded goods from as far afield as Venice and India for the leather, gold, wood and animals of the south. A further market specialised in camels and horses to make up the great caravans. But Shendi's real prosperity came from the trade in people. Around 5,000 slaves a year passed through the markets. Most were aged under 25, with a premium placed on girls and eunuchs. Some slave merchants would even allow their merchandise to be bought on a three-day sale or return policy, with the consequence that many girls were merely 'bought' for prostitution, only to be returned a few days later. Once sold, slaves would make the desert crossing to Suakin and from there they were shipped to Arabia and Egypt.

By the beginning of the 19th century Shendi was suffering as a result of the decline the Funj Kingdom, and the predatory attentions of the Shaqiyah Arab tribes on the caravans that were the town's lifeblood. With the advent of Turco-Egyptian rule, the centre of commerce moved to the new capital of Khartoum, and Shendi slid into decay. Despite the great wealth created there, there is no sign today of its past prosperity, or the terrible trade that made it possible.

Taxis and *caro* congregate here waiting for fares. Minibuses leave heading north and south leave from a different station, east of the train line.

Buses and minibuses out of Shendi leave at around 07.00. The run to Khartoum takes just under three hours. Despite what locals may tell you, there is no direct transport to Atbara. Instead, minibuses go to Ed Damer, where you must change. This isn't a problem – passengers from Shendi get out en masse and quickly fill a waiting onward minibus, so your wait will be measured in minutes rather than hours.

The train from Khartoum to Wadi Halfa passes through Shendi station on Monday afternoons. It returns some time on Thursdays, so it's much faster to travel by road.

It's possible to hire a *boksi* for the day to take you to Naqa and Musawwarat es Sufra – ask at the *boksi* lot next to the market. Haggle hard and be clear who is paying for the fuel. It's also wise to make sure that the driver knows the way, although you'll undoubtedly have to stop en route to ask for directions. Expect to pay around 16,000SD for the round trip, or more if you include the Pyramids at Meroe.

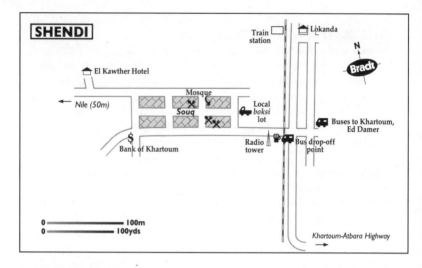

Where to stay and eat

There isn't a lot of choice when it comes to accommodation in Shendi. On the banks of the Nile, the upmarket **El Kawther Hotel** (tel: 0261 1997) seems out of place with its surroundings. The hotel has a pleasant garden, and the lobby is decorated with reliefs of Kushite rulers and gods from Naqa and Musawwarat es Sufra. Rooms with hot water and a balcony cost US$40 for one or two people.

The option at the other end of the spectrum is the *lokanda* next to Shendi train station. Conditions here are basic – water, for example, is collected from a large drum. Bring your own candles, as electricity seems to be at a premium here. Beds cost a rock-bottom 300SD per night, and you're unlikely to spend more than one night here.

Eating out in Shendi is centred on the market. As with many places, *ful* is served mainly in the morning for breakfast. Cafeterias offer the usual stews and kebabs, and a particularly tasty *fasuliya*. There are plenty of juice bars in which to quench your thirst, while *laban* (hot sweet milk) seems to be a favourite with locals and is dished out in tall glasses in the morning and evenings.

NAQA

The Meroitic temples of Naqa are situated about 30km east of the Nile and 35km southeast of Shendi. Together they form one of the best-preserved Kushite sites in Sudan.

The exact purpose of the site at Naqa is still unclear. As well as the Lion and Amun Temples there is a cemetery south of the site that has yet to be excavated. Surveys have shown little evidence of permanent settlement at Naqa. Far from the Nile as it is, the area is very dry and a nearby *wadi* could only have supported seasonal rain-fed agriculture at best.

On approaching the site, the first temple you will see is the **Temple of Amun**, on the western side near the foot of a rocky outcrop. The temple was built in the 1st century AD by King Natakamani, one of Kush's most prolific monument builders. It follows a traditional Egyptian floor plan of an outer court with a colonnade approaching a hypostyle hall containing an inner sanctuary chamber, and would originally have been around 100m long. The temple is approached through a short avenue of rams in a similar manner to the Temple of Amun at Jebel Barkal and Karnak (the latter is in Egypt).

German archaeologists are excavating in the temple, which has been partially reconstructed. The main entrances and walls show delicate relief carvings and many columns have been re-erected. The temple is aligned on an east-west axis and the eastern sides have been exposed to the abrasive effects of sand and wind, damaging the carvings on the soft sandstone. The rams have similarly suffered from the elements. Several statuettes of the king and his wife Amanitore have been recovered from the site.

West of the Temple of Amun is the Lion Temple and Kiosk. The **Lion Temple** is a beautifully preserved classic of Kushite architecture. Contemporary to the Temple of Amun, it is dedicated to the lion-headed Kushite god Apedemak. The temple is fronted by a massive pylon (gateway). To the left and right of the portal are massive carved reliefs of Natakamani and his queen Amanitore holding prisoners by the hair in triumphant pose. Lions sit at their feet devouring the vanquished. Who these prisoners are is unclear; it is possible they represent symbolic victories over Kush's foes, although records point to clashes with marauding desert tribes.

The edges of the pylon carry beautiful representations of Apedemak, represented by the body of a snake emerging from a lotus flower. On the sides of the temple the king is presented in the company of the gods Amun, Horus and Apedemak.

On the rear wall of the temple is the most famous depiction of Apedemak. He stands to receive offerings from Natakamani and Amanitore on either side. To allow him to do this he appears double armed and triple headed, facing both supplicants as well as the viewer.

The Lion Temple is a good key to trends in Kushite art. At first glance it may appear that the decoration is just a debased form of classic Egyptian forms. Certainly Egyptian tradition was important to the Kushites, heavily influencing their religion and culture. Indeed, when Kush invaded Egypt, establishing the 25th Dynasty in the 8th century BC, they regarded their veneration of the Egyptian pantheon as a legitimising factor in their rule. By the time the temples at Naqa were built, however, indigenous trends in art were becoming apparent as well as other external influences.

In figurative art we see round-headed, broad shouldered depictions of the body; the Kushites appear distinctly chunkier than their northern neighbours. This is particularly noticeable in the depiction of Queen Amanitore, who appears wide-hipped and very African looking. In the victory relief the queen also appears as the same size as her husband. This break from Egyptian iconography has led to some speculation that she may have ruled on equal terms with the king.

KUSHITE RELIGION

Kushite culture was heavily influenced by Egypt, a fact made inevitable by centuries of interaction – from Egyptian expeditions as far as the Fifth Cataract to the establishment of the Nubian 25th Dynasty in Thebes. The main gods of Egypt are represented in the Kushite pantheon.

Amun was the chief god of Kush, and temples dedicated to him have been found along the Nile from Kawa (near Dongola) to Naqa. Amun was thought to reside in Jebel Barkal. He was regarded as the Great Creator, and the Kushite kings were his champions on earth. Kushite representations show Amun with the head of a ram, crowned with a sun disk. The goddess Isis, the protector, was also important, with New Kingdom Egyptian texts even referring to her as the 'Mistress of Kush'. Isis was often depicted as the queen mother, from whom the king derived his legitimacy.

Isis was the sister and wife of the god of the Underworld, Osiris. The Kushites often preferred to portray her as a companion to an indigenous god Apedemak, who was particularly worshipped in the Island of Meroe. Apedemak is shown as a lion-headed god, often armed with a bow with captives at his feet. An inscription at Musawwarat es Sufra describes Apedemak as the 'splendid god at the head of Nubia, lion of the south and strong of arm'.

Two lesser gods, Sebiumeker and Arensnuphis, are though to have been guardians, sometimes in service of Amun.

The inability to decipher the Meroitic script has meant that many aspects of Kushite religious rituals are little understood. While many temples have been excavated, the impact of religion on daily life remains largely unknown. Only in funerary practises is the picture clearer, with the Kushites following Egyptian traditions of burying their dead with grave goods to help them in the next world, irrespective of their status.

The Kushites kept the flame of traditional Egyptian religion burning for several centuries after it was abandoned in its birthplace (with the adoption of Christianity). In the 6th century AD, missionaries finally brought the Word to Kush, and the old religion passed into history.

Another Kushite innovation is the depiction of Apedemak as a triple-headed god emerging from a lotus. This led some early archaeologists to speculate on cultural influences from India, presumably through trade routes from the ancient port of Adulis on the Red Sea (near Massawa in Eritrea), although this theory has now been discredited.

Inside the temple, a carving of the god Serapis is presented full face with a curly beard of Greek or Roman origin, and there's a second god with a sunburst crown possibly derived from Persian sources.

In front of the Lion Temple is a small **kiosk**. It is a showcase for the different influences on Kushite architecture, but the date of construction is disputed. Its entrance is Egyptian, topped by a flat lintel with a row of sacred cobras (*ureaus*), but the open sides are a riot of columns topped with florid Corinthian capitals and Roman-style arched windows.

The temple and kiosk are fenced off, and to gain access you'll need to ask the *ghaffir*. One reason for the fencing is the proximity of a deep well used by nomads, and the need to keep animals away from the site. If, as is likely, you visit during the winter, you can often see large herds of camels, goats, sheep and cows waiting to be watered. Donkeys are used to haul up the water in goatskin sacks.

You need your own vehicle to get to Naqa, which is best reached as a day trip from either Shendi or Khartoum, combined with Musawwarat es Sufra. The turning off the main Khartoum-Atbara highway is signed in English and is next to a Nile Petroleum station. Once off-road, the tracks are harder to follow and it's easy to get lost. Taking a guide or GPS is recommended (see page 63). A permit from the Antiquities Service in Khartoum or the Ministry of Tourism in Atbara must be given to the *ghaffir* on arrival, who will dutifully record your details in a logbook.

MUSAWWARAT ES SUFRA

The temple complex of Musawwarat es-Sufra is the largest set of Meroitic remains in Sudan. Covering 55,000m², its exact purpose remains unclear – a metaphor for our incomplete understanding of Meroitic culture. The site consists of a large complex called the **Great Enclosure**, a rambling structure of low walls and toppled columns, two reservoirs, and some distance away, a temple dedicated to the god Apedemak. The complex dates from the Napatan period of Kushite history and was expanded and rebuilt throughout the rule of Meroe.

At the centre of the Great Enclosure is Temple 100, surrounded by a finely carved colonnade and approached from the rear by a long ramped corridor. To the front (east) are two ruined tower-like structures. North of this is Temple 200, surrounded by a suite of rooms. Although both are colloquially called temples, it is possible that they may have served other purposes, possibly as throne rooms. A third, positively identified temple, Temple 300, sits on the eastern edge of the enclosure. Smaller buildings and corridors link these three structures, with the whole surrounded by a series of enclosing walls.

The Great Enclosure is liberally covered with carvings and ancient graffiti. Most typically these are of altars and images of Apedemak but more recent visitors have left their mark too, including the French adventurer Frederic Cailliaud in 1821.

The most favoured explanation for the existence of Musawwarat es Sufra is as a cult centre and pilgrimage site, possibly for Apedemak. The open parts of the Great Enclosure may have been used to house pilgrims, or animals used in religious ceremonies. The frequency of carvings of elephants throughout the complex suggests that elephants may have been used or possibly trained here, a view given credence by the number of low ramps inside the Great Enclosure that would have allowed access for the animals. Although there is no direct evidence that Kush captured elephants in this way, the Roman writer Arrian refers to the 'Ethiopians' (Kushites), using elephants in war and it is certainly possible that in historical times elephants ranged as far north as the Island of Meroe.

The size and scope of the Great Enclosure is a good illustration of the extent of Meroitic power, but those used to the more immediate grandeur of the ruins of the Classical world may find it difficult to project a vision of the living site on to the walls and columns of the enclosure. The complex is still an active archaeological site, and during the winter season you can find German archaeologists directing the work. The patient surveying work and digging of trenches is a world away from Indiana Jones, but for the amateur enthusiast no less thrilling. Be careful not to disturb any work.

Nearly 1km east of the Great Enclosure is a **Lion Temple** dedicated to Apedemak. The temple was built around 230BC by King Arnekhamani, one of the first kings to be buried at Meroe. The temple has a massive pylon entrance showing the king (in Meroitic styling) making offerings to the gods. At the base of the rear end of the temple are some beautiful carvings of a procession of elephants being led by bound prisoners.

The Lion Temple was reconstructed and beautifully restored by Humboldt University in Berlin in the 1960s, making it (along with Naqa) the finest standing Kushite temple. The inside of the building is a good illustration of the efforts of this rebuilding, starkly contrasting the smooth carvings of the long-buried block-work with the sand-eaten surfaces of the columns that have lain exposed.

A single permit for Musawwarat es Sufra covers entrance to both the Great Enclosure and Lion Temple, despite what cheeky *ghaffirs* may indicate. The *ghaffir* is needed to unlock the gate in the fence that surrounds the Lion Temple. Uniquely for archaeological remains in Sudan, information boards have been erected at both sites, giving excellent explanations of the ruins.

A private vehicle is essential to get to Musawwarat es Sufra. For more information see Naqa (page 131).

MEROE

The old Kushite capital of Meroe is a little over 30km north of Shendi. The area was occupied by the Kushites from around the fall of the 25th Dynasty in Egypt and had been a residence of the king, but sprung to prominence when the royal tombs were moved here from Nuri further down the Nile in around 270BC. The remains of the Royal City are more archaeologically significant than visually impressive, and casual visitors may happily choose to give them a miss. The star attraction is the Royal Cemetery – better known simply as al-Ahram, or the Pyramids.

Getting there and away

Meroe can be easily reached by private car from Khartoum in a couple of hours. It's best to time your visit for the early morning or late afternoon to avoid the heat of the day; the pyramids are particularly stunning at sunset. All buses running between Khartoum or Shendi and Atbara pass the pyramids. Ask to get off at Bajarawiya, a small village just south of the site. It's not easy to miss – every time I have travelled on this stretch of road other passengers have eagerly pointed the pyramids out to me. The site is half a kilometre from the road on the east side while the Royal City is 2km west of the road. For onward travel you'll have to stand on the road and flag down whatever's coming; there seems to be more traffic heading south than north, so be prepared to wait – make sure you have plenty of water and protection from the sun.

Where to stay

The Italian-run **Meroe Tented Camp** (tel: 011 487961, Khartoum; email: italtour@sudanmail.net) 3km north of the Royal Cemetery is a real taste of luxury in the desert. The camp has ten permanent tents, each with a veranda looking south to the pyramids and separate bathroom huts with showers. Meals can be provided on request in the dining building; in the evening a campfire is lit in front of a Beja-inspired 'nomad tent'. This is top-end accommodation with a top-end price: US$95/120 for a single or twin. The camp is frequently used by tour groups, so it's best to book in advance if possible.

If you have your own tent, you have the pick of the desert, although camping is not permitted within 100m of the pyramids or at the Royal City.

The Pyramids

Clearly visible from the Khartoum-Atbara highway, the pyramids of the Royal Cemetery of Meroe stand alone on a sandy ridge like a row of broken teeth. They are Sudan's most popular tourist attraction, although in a country where tourism is in its infancy, popular is a relative term. Visitors can often have the place to themselves and enjoy the rare sensation that they are discovering a long-hidden secret, without a tout offering a camel-ride or belly dance in sight. Instead, it's just you and the pyramids alone in the desert. The headline-grabbing treasures of Egypt have long overshadowed Sudan's ancient history, but at Meroe the charm of the unknown is the great attraction.

The site is divided into two main clusters – the Northern and Southern Cemeteries. In total there are around 100 pyramids, although in practice many of those are poorly preserved or exist only in outline traces. The South Cemetery is the oldest cluster, dating to around the 8th century BC, and the first kings who made the move from Nuri to Meroe were entombed here, before the switch was made to the Northern Cemetery. Kings and queens continued to be buried here until the fall of Kushite rule in the 4th century AD.

While clearly Egyptian in inspiration, the pyramids are quite unlike those at Giza. The most notable difference is in size and pitch. The largest pyramid at Meroe is just under 30m high, or would have been were it still intact, with an angle approaching 70°. The smaller size allowed the pyramids to be constructed much faster and with less manpower, using simple cranes. Tomb chambers were dug directly into the rock below and the pyramid then erected above – a marked difference to Egypt. The pyramids have a rubble core encased in local sandstone (or brick towards the end of the Kushite period). The pyramids were then covered with a render of lime mortar to give a smooth gleaming surface, and the bases were simply painted in red, yellow and blue stars. On the eastern face each pyramid has a funerary chapel where offerings could be made to the dead.

The Northern Cemetery is the best preserved, and contains over 30 pyramids in various states of repair. Most have been decapitated. Their sorry state is largely the work of a treasure hunter, Guiseppe Ferlini, who passed through in 1834. Ferlini was convinced that the pyramids contained great riches, and with the tacit support of the Turco-Egyptians, proceeded to pull them down. He struck gold on his first attempt. In Pyramid 6, that of Queen Amanishakheto, he found a hoard of gold jewellery in a chamber near the tomb's apex. This was highly unusual, as grave goods were normally placed with the body in the tomb chamber beneath the pyramid. Thus inspired, Ferlini laboured on with his destruction only to come up blank – his greatest haul after this was nothing grander some workmen's tools. The gold, showing distinct Hellenistic influences, eventually found its way to the Egyptian Museums in Berlin and Munich, while Sudan was left with a field of smashed pyramids.

Earlier damage was done to the pyramids by the tomb robbers of antiquity. As a result comparatively little is known about royal funerary practices. Bodies were probably entombed facing east to greet the rising sun. The funerary chapels contain a mix of passages from the Egyptian Book of the Dead and offering scenes, often with Isis in attendance.

At the centre of the Northern Cemetery is a small modern pyramid, its bright colour in stark contrast to the chocolate brown of its neighbours. This was restored in the 1980s as an exercise to recreate Kushite building techniques; its smooth rendered exterior gives some idea of how the pyramids would originally have appeared.

The older Southern Cemetery sits 500m south of the Northern cluster. There are over 60 smaller pyramids here, all belonging to the elite of Meroe. Many are totally ruined or lost altogether. A third, western, cemetery also contains noble tombs, including several well preserved or reconstructed pyramids.

A permit is needed to visit the pyramids. Travellers without them seem to have mixed success getting in, but the site is close enough to Khartoum or Atbara on a good road to make this less of a problem than some of the sites further down the Nile. The *ghaffir's* office is next to the Northern Cemetery. Note that a permit for the pyramids does not cover entry to the Royal City.

Above Rock shelter in Sudan's northern desert, one of the most desolate rocky plains in the southern Sahara (MP)

Below Granite domes of the Taka Mountains, Kassala (PC)

Right Dome of Hassan's Tomb,
Khatmiyah Mosque, Kassala (PC)

Below Apedemak and Kushite gods,
Lion Temple at Naqa (PC)

Below Kiosk at Naqa, showing
Egyptian and Roman influences (PC)

The Royal City

The ruins of the Royal City of Meroe are on the banks of the Nile. The site is now overgrown with low acacia trees and scrub, making it hard for visitors to envisage its original extent. The city was the capital of the Kushite Kingdom, and may have had a population of around 25,000 at its height. Evidence points to urban dwelling at Meroe from around the 8th century BC, but the city started to prosper as a seat of power from around 270BC, with the construction of its temple dedicated to Amun. Meroe grew from the trade along the Nile, and several Greek and Roman trade goods and coins have been recovered from the site. Also uncovered here was a bronze head of the Roman emperor Augustus, taken during the Kushite sacking of Aswan in 24BC. The city was abandoned in around AD350, with the decline of Kushite power.

At the centre of the city stood the royal palace and the Amun Temple, with a processional way. Residential areas lay on the periphery, surrounded by a boundary wall. Also amid the ruins are the Royal Baths, once thought to have been part of a gymnasium, but more likely to have been a sanctuary associated with the annual Nile inundation.

A separate permit is needed to visit the Royal City. The site is heavily ruined, often with little more than the outlines of buildings to be seen. For the amateur, it may be something of a disappointment, with the lack of clearly visible remains amid the scrub of thorn trees. Those with just a casual interest may will prefer to concentrate their attention on the pyramids.

ATBARA

The city of Atbara sits where the Nile receives its last tributary, the Atbara River. The Atbara rises in the Ethiopian highlands and has a very seasonal flow, swelling its banks from June to September but receding to pools and streams in the winter and spring. Atbara is the home of Sudan's railway and is known as 'the city of iron and fire'.

Atbara is very much a town of two halves. East of the railway tracks is what you would expect from any large Sudanese town – a sprawling mix of low buildings, concrete construction and lively markets full of business and people. West of the tracks is a completely different town. The railway quarter was populated by the British and is full of neat bungalows of café-au-lait brick and red roof tiles along quiet tree-lined avenues, giving it a distinctly provincial air. As railway workers in grey uniforms cycle to work you could almost imagine yourself in Surrey, or the cantonment of some Indian colonial town.

Atbara owes its popularity with the British to Kitchener's campaign against the Mahdiya. On Good Friday 1889, the kilted troops of the Highland regiments stormed the encampment of the 14,000 strong Mahdist army sent to meet them. With a little help from their Egyptian allies and a couple of Maxim guns, the Sudanese dead topped 2,000, and one of the Khalifa's best generals was captured and paraded in bondage. The defeat was the writing on the wall for the Khalifa's rule.

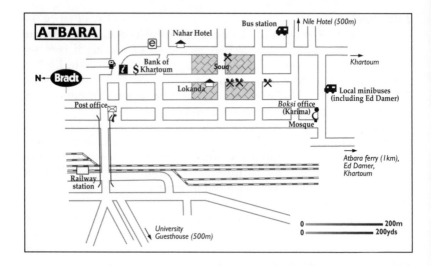

With the extension of the military railway from Wadi Halfa, Atbara was a natural junction for the branch line to Port Sudan. Atbara prospered as an industrial centre, and was the birthplace of the Sudanese labour movement. Throughout the 1940s and 1950s strikes and union activity were key in the growth of Sudanese nationalism. In the 1980s Nimeiri responded to strike activity by bringing forward plans to decentralise the railways and break the political power of Atbara – plans that sent the railways into a decline from which they have yet to recover.

Railway buffs will get the most joy out of Atbara, as the sound of engine whistles and shunting rolling stock is never far away. The best place to watch the trains come and go is from the large flyover near the stock yard, although there's nothing stopping you from wandering around the lines yourself, and Railway Corporation staff seem happy to show off the place to enthusiasts.

There's little else to see and do in Atbara and most people will visit it purely as a transport junction. Its relaxed air and well-stocked markets make it a good place to catch your breath and recharge, particularly if you have experienced the long haul by rail through the desert.

Atbara also has a useful and friendly tourist office (tel: 0211 24183), and can issue permits for the sites at Meroe, Naqa and Musawwarat es Sufra, which saves you a lengthy trip to Khartoum if you've come from the north.

Getting there and away

Given Atbara's pre-eminence as a railway town it only seems fair to take the train for onward travel. The train from Khartoum to Wadi Halfa arrives in Atbara on Monday evenings, returning some time on Thursday. Joining the train here does not necessarily guarantee you a seat, even in First Class. The branch line to Port Sudan has a service departing every Tuesday and also returning on Thursdays.

Atbara's bus station is close to the centre, and has a variety of buses and minibuses to Khartoum departing through the day, costing from 800SD. Buses also leave for Port Sudan on a partially-made road through the desert; check departure times in advance. A Saf Saf bus costs 3,500SD.

To head south to Shendi (or the Pyramids at Meroe), take a local minibus from a stand at the eastern side of the market to Ed Damer and change there, or take a bus to Khartoum and get off at the junction (although you'll have to pay full fare).

Just south of the Ed Damer minibus stand is a *boksi* office for the run to Karima. *Bokasi* don't run every day, so again it's wise to check in advance. Seats for the dash across the Bayuda Desert cost around 2,500SD, which takes anything from 10-14 hours. It's a very bumpy ride.

There is no bridge across the Nile at Atbara, so if you have your own vehicle and are making the crossing to Karima take the ferry on the southwestern edge of Atbara.

Where to stay and eat
North of the main bus station is the **Nile Hotel** (tel: 22111). Guests are immediately made to feel welcome by well-tended gardens, a theme carried on to the green and flowering courtyard at the rear. The Coptic owner lives in the hotel, giving it a warm personal atmosphere. Clean bright rooms have shared bathroom and a water heater. Singles/twins cost 3000/4050SD.

The **University Guest House** (tel: 22148) is farther out in the old British quarter, and indeed the place has an air of old establishment about it. There are large shady gardens in which you can imagine taking a gin and tonic before supper. All rooms are well sized and en suite, with the welcome addition of air-conditioning and a fridge – good value at 2,500/5,000SD for a single or twin, although a fair walk from the centre of town.

The **Nahar Hotel** is a good *lokanda*, laid out in the typical 'rooms around an open courtyard' style. There always seems to be someone sweeping up and keeping the place clean; there's also an attached laundry and kitchen. Beds are 400SD. The lack of small rooms may mean that female travellers could have trouble finding accommodation here.

A couple of less salubrious un-named *lokandas* lurk in the blank concrete blocks on the southern end of the market area.

The best eating spots are on the main street running through the southern edge of the market – cafeteria-style establishments offer the usual selection of kebabs and stews. With advance warning it's possible to eat in the Nile Hotel.

Ed Damer
Just 10km south of Atbara is the market town of Ed Damer. There's not much to distinguish it from many other towns of its size, but every Saturday it holds a large **camel market** that is certainly worth a look. The market is on the southern edge of town and, amazingly, it's signed in English. A minibus from Atbara costs 50SD. The market is at its busiest in the early morning. A small archaeological museum opened in Ed Damer in mid-2004.

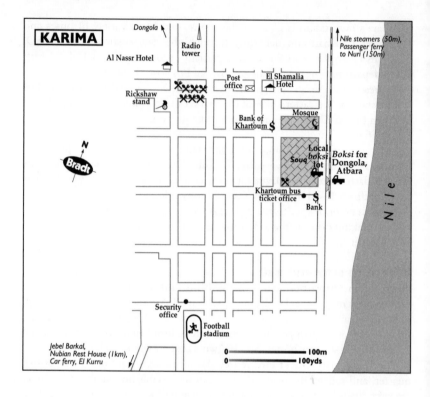

Karima and Dongola

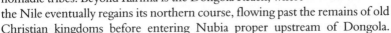

North of Atbara at Abu Hamed, the Nile suddenly loops south for several hundred kilometres. As it does so it passes through the ancient heart of the Kushite kingdom. Around the town of Karima is the old religious centre of Jebel Barkal and the first Kushite royal cemeteries of El Kurru and Nuri, collectively a World Heritage site. Either side of this loop of river is desert – the Nubian Desert to the north, the Bayuda Desert to the south – seemingly barren but home to several nomadic tribes. Beyond Karima is the Dongola Reach, where the Nile eventually regains its northern course, flowing past the remains of old Christian kingdoms before entering Nubia proper upstream of Dongola.

Transport connections are for the most part bumpy. There is very little tarmac, and unmade roads and desert tracks are the norm. To compensate for this, the remoteness of this region is one of the great attractions of this part of Sudan.

KARIMA

The market town of Karima is the largest town between Atbara and Dongola, but sandwiched between two deserts it seems like a long way from anywhere, with its low buildings and wide dusty lanes. Karima can sometimes give the impression of being the hottest place in Sudan, but stay a while and its lazy rhythms can grow on you.

Karima is the place to base yourself to explore the remains of the Napatan kingdom of Kush. On the edge of town is the incomparable Jebel Barkal, a landmark that dominates the area, with its ruined temples and perfectly preserved pyramids. Close by are the royal cemeteries of Nuri and El Kurru. Remains of a more recent nature are the boats of the middle Nile steamer fleet, hauled up on the riverbank to die.

Karima is one of the few towns in north Sudan that insist you register with the security police on arrival, despite the abolition of travel permits here. The security police are in an unmarked building on a large square next to the football ground; it has a gateway with green and white pillars. Inside, a man lounging on a bed will look up from watching Egyptian soap operas to enter your details in a ledger, and then hurry you away so he can get on with his viewing.

Getting there and away

Rickshaws are the most convenient way to get somewhere fast within Karima, or there are *caro* for the more leisurely-minded. A stand in the centre of town has minibuses serving outlying villages, including El Kurru. For reasons unknown, these are almost exclusively old Ford Transit vans.

Possibly due to its sprawling layout, long-distance transport out of Karima seems to favour the charming practice of picking you up rather than insisting you tramp to the bus stand with your bags at some crazy hour. This has happened to me for both bus and *boksi*, so I can only assume that it's standard procedure. For this reason if no other, it's best to book a seat the day before travel.

There are several offices around the town centre operating *bokasi*. The run to Atbara costs around 2,500SD and takes between 10 and 14 hours; it's a particularly uncomfortable journey, bumping through the Bayuda Desert. *Bokasi* to Dongola (2,000SD, four hours) is a smoother if sandier ride. For some reason the pickups that run this route are open-topped, so make sure you cover up against the sun. Even the most experienced drivers can find themselves stuck in sand on this trip and passengers are invariably asked to lend their shoulders to push the vehicle clear!

If you are attempting this route (or the Bayuda) with your own vehicle, sand mats are essential and lowering your tyre pressure is recommended to increase the footprint of your tyres. There are few genuine tracks – the route is technically marked by 2m high poles every kilometre, but in practice these can only be consistently followed closer to Dongola. If you're heading south you'll need to cross the Nile using the vehicle ferry at Barkal village over to Merowe, 6km southwest of Karima.

Buses run daily to Khartoum and they're good ones too, more akin to city life than the cattle-truck affairs you find further north. They cross the Nile to Merowe and follow tracks to the junction at Abu Dom, where the road becomes sealed and splits north to Dongola and south to the capital. The Khartoum bus (2,500SD, 10 hours) stops at Omdurman Souq es-Shabi and terminates at Sajana bus station.

There is no longer a passenger train service from Karima; goods trains occasionally run to the junction at Abu Hamed and on to Atbara.

Where to stay and eat

At the top end of the scale is the beautiful Italian-run **Nubian Rest House** (tel: 011 487961, Khartoum; email: italtour@sudanmail.net), possibly Sudan's only boutique hotel. A large compound opposite the north face of Jebel Barkal, it has ten rooms around a garden built in a traditional Nubian style. All are immaculately presented and the fluffy towels and hot water in the en suite rooms feel like genuine luxury. Breakfast is included with other meals on request; all are served in a high-domed dining room. Rooms are best booked in advance, costing US$95/120 for a single/double.

The best budget option is the **Al Nassr Hotel**. There's plenty of space (and room for parking) around the courtyard, plus a small shop at the front that sells bread and a few vegetables, and that dishes out *ful* and other staples throughout the day. Toilets are basic, but the showers look out to Jebel Barkal. A room of up to three beds costs 1,500SD.

The **El Shamalia Hotel** is very much a second choice in this bracket – it looks like a hurricane has hit it. It's a standard, if dirty, *lokanda*, with beds in the courtyard and a few side rooms. Its house rules hang over the front desk: 'Stay calm' and 'No strong drink to be taken'. If you can handle both of these, a bed will set you back 500SD.

Non-guests can dine out at the Nubian Rest House if advance notice is given. Three courses, a mix of Sudanese and Italian dishes, are a treat at 2,500SD. Otherwise, the usual *ful*, *taamiya* and kebab cafeterias are dotted around the food market in the centre of town. The Cafeteria El Durra is a good option. A side street between the centre and the Al Nassr hotel is lined with small restaurants and juice stands; you can find tasty *sheya* here.

Jebel Barkal

The holy mountain of Jebel Barkal (Jebel Barkal actually means 'holy mountain' in Arabic), a great sandstone butte that dominates this stretch of the Nile, is situated a couple of kilometres southwest of the centre of Karima. The ancient Egyptians and Kushites alike believed that the mountain was the home of the god Amun, the 'Throne of Two Lands' – Egypt and Nubia. The ruins of a temple dedicated to the god lie at the foot of the mountain. At dawn or dusk, Jebel Barkal still evokes a phenomenal aura and it's easy to understand why the ancients ascribed such religious significance to it.

Thutmose III, one of the first Egyptian kings to penetrate this far south, built the first **Temple of Amun** in the 15th century BC. Later pharaohs, including Rameses II, expanded it, turning it into an important cult centre, as well as a way station for goods from the south destined for the great Temple of Amun at Karnak. When Egyptian influence waned the temple fell into disrepair.

The rise of the Kushites changed the fortunes of the whole region. Jebel Barkal became the centre of the new kingdom and its kings resurrected the worship of Amun. In around 720BC Piye led his armies north into Egypt and captured Thebes. Ownership of the Temple of Amun gave legitimacy to his claim to be the true representative of Egyptian traditions; his successors set up the 25th Dynasty and ruled from Thebes and Memphis as pharaohs. Piye greatly expanded the temple at Jebel Barkal, as did his son, Taharqa. Over time the temple grew to over 150m in length, making it the largest Kushite building ever built.

The temple stretches out towards the Nile, near the bottom of a freestanding pinnacle of rock cracked from the sandstone cliffs. The significance of this pinnacle has puzzled archaeologists for decades. An early observer supposed that it was to have been a giant statue of a pharaoh, far surpassing anything in Egypt at 90m high. A more likely explanation is found in its profile, which (albeit roughly) resembles a *ureaus* – the protective cobra and symbol of the king. A relief in Rameses II's massive temple at Abu Simbel in Egypt shows Amun sitting inside a mountain, faced with a rearing cobra. This iconography is found in later Kushite art and almost certainly represents Jebel Barkal. In the 1990s, archaeologists discovered a niche at the summit of the pinnacle carved with hieroglyphics proclaiming Taharqa's military campaigns against his enemies. This was completely inaccessible (except to the gods) so would have been covered with a gold panel, allowing it to reflect in the light and provide a beacon for miles around. The light of Jebel Barkal would have been clearly visible from Taharqa's pyramid upstream at Nuri.

The temple is very ruined and much of the structure is covered with sand, but the ground plan is still clear, with a procession of two large colonnaded halls leading into the sanctuary at the base of the mountain, surrounded by several small rooms. At the southern entrance of the temple there are several wind-worn granite statues of rams; these were actually from Soleb further downstream and have been relocated here. There are many scattered blocks covered with reliefs and hieroglyphics.

At the immediate base of the pinnacle is the **Temple of Mut**, dedicated to the Egyptian sky goddess, the bride of Amun. Also built by Taharqa, the structure is again much ruined, but the two large columns with capitals carved in the image of the goddess Hathor are particularly striking. Engravings of the temple made in the 1820s show these columns interspersed with others carved in the form of the dwarf god Bes; these have now disappeared. The sanctuary of the temple is actually carved into Jebel Barkal itself, behind a modern metal door. Bes columns hold up the entrance and the walls are covered in hieroglyphics and relief carvings, many highly worn.

The presence of Bes, a protector of women in childbirth, and Mut, the divine mother, is intriguing. The symbolism is pretty overt: a womb-like cave temple sat at the foot of the highly phallic pinnacle of Amun's mountain. Royal wives possibly came here during pregnancy to give literal meaning to the divine origins of their lineage.

If you fancy a scramble, the best views of the temples are to be had from the top of Jebel Barkal – from here, the layout of the complex becomes immediately clear. You'll also be rewarded with stunning views of the Nile, bound by its thin strip of green fields and date palms holding back the desert. The best way up is from the north side of the mountain. It's not strenuous but there's no path as such, so some sturdy footwear is recommended. The climb to the plateau should take around 20 minutes. Coming down is much faster, as there's a sand drift covering the western side of the mountain that's great fun to skid down.

Also on the western side of Jebel Barkal is a small royal cemetery of around 20 **pyramids**. This was used briefly by Napatan kings who had abandoned Nuri at the turn of the 3rd century BC, before the centre of the kingdom was permanently moved south to Meroe. The reasons for this are unknown. The pyramids are the most intact in Sudan – steep-sided and faced with local sandstone. Sunset is a particularly good time to view them.

A permit is needed to get the *ghaffir* to unlock the Temple of Mut, but the site is otherwise open to be explored.

Nile steamers

Hauled up on the banks of the Nile at the northern edge of Karima is a small fleet of Nile riverboats. These used to take a day to sail between Karima and Dongola when the river was high enough, serving as passenger ferries, mobile markets and post offices. They have now been abandoned as slow and uneconomical; *bokasi* can do the desert run linking the two towns in around four hours. They're a sad sight stranded above the water, forgotten and slowly falling into disrepair, but they have a certain grandeur in the fading evening light, as you sit on the deck watching birds swoop for insects on the Nile. No-one seems to mind you clambering around them, but be on the lookout for rotten floorboards and the like.

NURI

One of the royal cemeteries of Kush lies a few kilometres upstream of Karima, on the opposite bank of the Nile. This means one thing: pyramids. Older than those at Meroe or Jebel Barkal, the pyramids at Nuri are weather-beaten and crumbling; you can almost see the desert reclaiming them before your very eyes. To my mind, this gives them a special charm and attraction of their own.

Nuri was adopted as the site of the royal cemeteries in the early 7th century BC. The great Napaptan king Taharqa was the first ruler to be buried here, breaking the tradition of interring kings downstream at El Kurru. The royal cemetery may have been moved here to place it within sight of the religious centre at Jebel Barkal. Taharqa was probably the most powerful ruler in Sudanese history. He came to power in the Napatan phase of Kushite history, and is best known as one of the 25th Dynasty pharaohs of Egypt – the so-called Nubian Dynasty. Taharqa's rule extended from the confluence of the Niles to the ports of Phoenicia in modern Lebanon and was part of a renaissance of Egyptian culture springing from Napata. Nubia's (and Taharqa's) rise on the international scene was short-lived, coinciding as it did with the expansion of another regional superpower, Assyria. The Assyrians poured out of their heartland and, under King Ashurbanipal, kicked the Kushites out of Egypt and back up the Nile.

As befits the grandness of the early period of his rule, Taharqa's pyramid is the largest at Nuri, in a cemetery that contains 19 royal tombs. The pyramid stands 29m square at the base above a large, rock-cut burial chamber. A funerary chapel on the east side of the pyramid has long disappeared. The tomb was excavated in 1917 by the pioneering archaeologist George Reisner, who uncovered a cache of around 1,000 *shawabti* figures, small statues of the king meant to accompany him into the afterlife and do his bidding there. It is not possible to enter the tomb itself.

The second largest pyramid is that of King Aspelta, Taharqa's great-grandson. Excavated at the same time as Taharqa's tomb, it contained a large granite sarcophagus and a collection of gold vessels, perfume jars, and another small army of *shawabti* figures.

The remainder of the pyramids are in various states of decay, their lime render long gone and their sandstone blocks long since used for local building.

Further off-site are the remains of the pyramids of the queens. Smaller and even more ruined, they represent the final resting place for 53 queens.

A permit is needed to visit Nuri. Although the site is quite open, the *ghaffir* will appear out of nowhere to collect your permit – and to turn away those without one. He takes his job very seriously indeed so turning up without the requisite piece of paper is no guarantee of entry, although it's worth a try if you've arrived from the north rather than from Khartoum.

Getting there and away

If you're based in Karima, you'll need to take a ferry to get to the pyramids. Foot ferries do the crossing throughout the day from a landing on the northeastern edge of town. It's not immediately obvious – follow the train tracks for 500m out of Karima by the river; the boats are tied up near the large petrol storage tanks. Fares are 50SD each way.

Taking the boat here you're struck by the dynamic nature of the Nile – the Karima bank is a steep shelf showing the change in the river level throughout the year; on the Nuri side is a wide beach of rich alluvial silt. Sandbanks appear and recede with the seasons, showing the dangers of navigation for large boats.

Once you've landed, rickshaws can take you directly to the pyramids. Alternatively, walk out through Nuri village for 200m, then turn north and follow the track along the irrigation canal for 1km before turning east for the pyramids, about an hour's walk away. If you can find someone to lend or hire you a bicycle this would be a lovely ride, through green fields and palm groves.

A second choice is to cross the Nile on the vehicle ferry to Merowe from Barkal village just southwest of Karima. From here, take a local minibus or *boksi* direct to Nuri along a mercifully smooth tarmac road built to service the construction of the dam upstream.

EL KURRU

The royal cemetery at El Kurru is thought to be the only Kushite site of its kind. Situated on the northern edge of a small Nile village, there are plenty of tumuli and mounds to excite archaeologists, but even those with a more casual interest will still enjoy the charming and well-preserved wall paintings of the tombs that are open to visitors.

El Kurru gives a good indication of the huge gaps in our knowledge of Kush. The earliest tombs discovered date from the 9th century BC and for want of proper names are simply attributed to Lords A, B, C and D. It is supposed that the presence of a royal cemetery indicates an early capital of Kush, before the culture became centred on Jebel Barkal. Little evidence of royal palaces or settlements has been found, however.

Pyramid building at El Kurru began with the 25th dynasty king Piye (or Piankhy). Prior to him, graves were covered with a tumulus or stone mastaba. Piye's pyramid has long since disappeared; it stood around 8m high, and had a chapel and enclosure wall surrounding the tomb. Kings were frequently buried with sacrificial animals and a cemetery with the graves of 24 horses has been uncovered at the site.

THE MEROWE DAM

The huge dam being built near Merowe just below the Fourth Cataract is Sudan's biggest construction project and will be the largest hydro-electric dam in the country. It will generate 1,250MW of power, doubling the current capacity of a country that is currently suffering from chronic electricity shortages. Over 1,700km of power cables will distribute the electricity to Khartoum, Port Sudan, Dongola and Atbara. Chinese construction firms are overseeing the project, which has a price tag of US$1.1billion.

All this power comes at more than just a financial cost. The dam will cause the Nile to flood 170km upstream, creating a lake up to 4km wide. Around 50,000 people will have to be resettled as a result, potentially causing massive social disruption on the scale experienced by the Nubians during the flooding caused by the Aswan Dam in the 1960s.

The towns and villages won't be the only loss recorded by the rising waters. The National Corporation for Antiquities and Museums has launched the Merowe Dam Archaeological Salvage Project in an attempt to record and rescue important sites along the Nile. While none of these have the glamour of the Egyptian temples rescued 40 years ago from Lake Nasser, there are myriad smaller sites – mainly belonging to the little known Post-Meroitic period of Sudan's history, as well as forts and burial sites from the medieval Christian kingdoms, Kerma culture remains, and important prehistoric sites. The survey work is currently one of the most intensive projects of its kind in the world and travellers in the area are just as likely to find Sudanese asking them if they are archaeologists as tourists. Construction of the dam is expected to be completed in 2008.

Two tombs are accessible to visitors; both are entered down a flight of stairs cut out of the rock. The tomb nearest the entrance gate belonged to Tanwetamani, nephew and successor of Taharqa, who died around 653BC. Tanwetamani moved the royal cemetery back to El Kurru from his uncle's chosen site at Nuri. This may have been an attempt to dissociate himself from Taharqa who had lost Egypt to the Assyrians, and with it the Napatan dream of resurrecting the glories of old Egyptian kingdoms. Tanwetamani's tomb is empty, but the two plastered chambers are covered in wonderful wall paintings. The king is painted with dark red skin wearing the Kushite cap with *ureaus* (royal cobra), being led to his burial; the entrance to the inner chamber is flanked by the protective goddesses Isis and Nepthys. The style of the paintings is entirely Egyptian, with hieroglyphic texts.

The second tomb is that of Tanwetamani's mother, Qalhata. If anything, the wall paintings are even better preserved here, with scenes describing the queen's path to the afterlife. The ceiling is painted with a delicate star field. A plinth for the sarcophagus is all that remains of the tomb's contents.

A permit is needed to visit the cemeteries at El Kurru, which are kept locked. Take a torch when visiting as there is no electric light in the tombs, although the *ghaffir* often has a lantern. On the outskirts of the village there is a small petrified forest which is worth a quick detour.

Getting there and away

Local minibuses run the 12km between Karima and El Kurru. The tombs are on the northern edge of the village. From the mosque on the Nile side of the main road, turn left and walk past the shop with the green front painted with Japanese cartoon characters. Take the next right and walk 200m to reach the tombs. You'll need to find the *ghaffir* to get him to unlock the tombs. There is a vehicle ferry at El Kurru, crossing the Nile to Tangazi.

Ghazali

The ruined monastery of Ghazali sits on a rise 20km east of Merowe, on the edge of the seasonal Wadi Abu Domm. The walls are well preserved, with some in excess of 3m in height.

Monasticism was very popular in the medieval church in the Near East in the Middle Ages, often following the ascetic example of St Anthony who

FOLLOWING THE NILE BEND

The most straightforward way of getting between Karima and Dongola (or Karima and Atbara) is to take an exhilaratingly bumpy *boksi* across the desert, cutting the corners off the Nile's great s-bend. An alternative is to go the long way around and village hop along the river.

If you plan on sticking to the Nile, it's definitely worth picking up a detailed map of the area from the Sudan Survey Department in Khartoum, as most of the commercially available maps of Sudan are lacking in fine detail. Sheet NE36 gives good coverage of this entire stretch of the river, from Dongola as far south as Shendi. Many of the roads are out of date, but the topographical details and locations of villages are still largely accurate.

If you take one of these routes, you should be prepared to rough it. Only the larger villages with a lot of passing traffic will have any formal accommodation like a *lokanda*. Instead, you're more likely to bed down in a teahouse or cafeteria as rope beds are conjured from nowhere. It's quite common on longer bus trips for the driver to break at a teahouse for the night. The men stretch out on the floor while women are expected to sleep in the vehicle. I've even had the village shopkeeper let me sleep on the floor while he curled up on the other side of the counter. The traditions of Sudanese hospitality mean that you'll often be offered a place in someone's house. Never abuse this. Bear in mind that you're off the beaten track and the villagers are likely to be very poor. Gifts of fruit, sugar and coffee are good ways to show your appreciation, although your hosts are likely to be offended if you offer them money outright.

walked into the Egyptian Desert to be closer to God. Indeed, it is possible that Ghazali may have resembled a smaller version of the still-functioning 4th century Monastery of St Anthony in Egypt. The monastery was close to an old trade route across the Bayuda Desert, but the number of documents written in Coptic excavated at Ghazali also hint at close ties with the Church in Alexandria.

The monastery was surrounded by protective walls a metre thick, to ward against raiders from the desert. Ghazali was abandoned in the 11th century. Inside, up to 48 monks lived in cells, with a church and refectory meeting their spiritual and material needs.

Out in the desert, you'll need your own vehicle – or one hired from Merowe – to reach Ghazali.

OLD DONGOLA

The remains of the medieval city of Old Dongola sit on a hill overlooking the east bank of the Nile. From the 7th to the 14th centuries the city prospered as the capital of the Christian kingdom of Makuria, controlling the river from the First Cataract south along the Dongola Reach, possibly even as far as Atbara. As an urban centre, Old Dongola's location was well chosen. The land was

Transport can be erratic, so grab whatever is going and be prepared to chip in extra if you want the vehicle to leave before it is full. Many villages along this stretch are set far back from the road, making hitching difficult.

Heading to Atbara, there is a good road on the southern bank of the Nile that services the Merowe Dam just above the Fourth Cataract. This road won't be extended, as the banks will be flooded when the dam becomes operational in 2008. For the time being there are little more than tracks following either side of the Nile in this direction, linking a series of hamlets and villages. The Fourth Cataract itself is still worth a visit, with good views over the rocky straits, although you'll almost certainly need your own vehicle to get there; it's most accessible from the northern bank. The railway tracks can be followed partway, before you need to cut in to the village of Hamdab. Be warned that this route is very sandy and it is easy to get bogged down.

West from Karima, there is plenty of transport along the southern bank to the junction at Abu Dom. Merowe and Tangazi (with their ferry crossings) are the best places to pick up vehicles, but there are fewer options after Korti. The teahouses at Abu Dom are the best option for picking up onward connections, possibly as far as Dongola. At Ed Debba, there is a weekly livestock market on Mondays – with people congregating to sell camels, goats, sheep and donkeys – and improved transport connections. Slightly further north is El Ghaba, where there is a vehicle ferry which is ideal for reaching the ruins of Old Dongola.

agriculturally rich, the walled city easily defensible and trade along the Nile (as well desert caravans from Darfur) easily controlled.

Old Dongola was a medieval boomtown. Throughout its history there was a seemingly unending period of church building. Churches were typically monolithic affairs, visually unimpressive from the outside with narrow windows and doors, and flat roofs. Inside, the basilica formed a long axis, with columns separating aisles on each side. Cruciform plans were also adopted, as were domes, although such churches only now survive in frescos. Remains of at least a dozen churches have been excavated at Old Dongola.

The site of the city covers around 3km², but only suggestions of its former glory remain. Since the collapse of the kingdom, houses and churches have been plundered for building materials. The most prominent surviving building is the so-called **Throne Hall**, a massive two-storey edifice with metre-thick walls.

The Throne Hall was built between the 9th and 10th century. Its exact purpose is unknown, but the best guess is that it served some royal purpose. The downstairs features a series of narrow, barrel-vaulted chambers, totally without windows and possibly used as a storage area. There is a separate door for the stairs to the upper level, which is completely distinct from the ground floor. Here, several columns remain surrounding a square throne hall or audience room. On the walls there are traces of a painted floral band and the figures of Christ and a Nubian bishop.

Towards the end of the 13th century, Makuria was riven with continuous struggles for the throne, with kings and princes alternately invoking the support of, or provoking the army of, the Egyptian sultan beyond the First Cataract. The Egyptians repeatedly came south to fight their neighbours, eventually playing the role of kingmakers to the Nubians. In 1323, the Muslim Kanz ed-Dawla was placed on the throne of Old Dongola, effectively marking the end of Christian rule. The Throne Hall was converted into a mosque. Its frescos were whitewashed over and a plaque mounted in the wall of the upstairs hall to proclaim the glory of Allah – it is still *in situ*. The mosque was in regular use as recently as 1969.

Near the Throne Hall is the **Church of the Granite Columns**. This was a cathedral, and as such the seat of Old Dongola's bishops. The cruciform design of the building, dating to the 7th century, has been excavated, with nearly a dozen columns indicating the interior. The remains of several red-brick piers – a later addition to support the ceiling – can also be seen, giving the building its alternative name, the Church of the Brick Pillars.

Close to the walled city are the ruins of the Monastery of the Holy Trinity. This is an active dig site being excavated by Polish archaeologists and only part of the complex has so far been uncovered. You may need to ask to be shown around – if this is possible, you can see dozens of well-preserved wall paintings in their original state.

Getting there and away

Old Dongola is best reached with your own vehicle; there is no direct transport. The village of El Ghaba on the west bank has a vehicle ferry across to the northern end of the site, so it should be possible to hire a *boksi* (or even a *caro*) to take you there. El Ghaba can be reached by any vehicle travelling between Dongola and Khartoum, or by boksi from Ed Debba. Otherwise you're looking at some expensive vehicle hire – a full day's trip from Dongola won't leave you with much change from 20,000SD, using a *boksi* along the east bank.

DONGOLA

The capital of Sudan's Northern State, Dongola sits in a burst of greenery on the Nile. It's the largest town in the region and the heart of Nubia proper. The place has a real oasis-in-the-desert feeling to it – there are tarmac roads, well-stocked shops, and ice cream to cool you down. The air of prosperity comes from agricultural wealth. Well-irrigated fields send plenty of cereals, fruit and vegetables to market, but Dongola's real riches are its groves of date palms. Dates are everywhere in this town, and the harvest in September and October is a time of celebration and weddings. Whatever time of year you arrive, the easy-going atmosphere makes Dongola a good place to settle in for a few days.

Modern (or New) Dongola has Mameluke as well as Nubian origins. When Mohammed Ali came to power in Egypt at the start of the 19th century he expelled its Mameluke rulers, who fled south. They made their base at the walled town of New Dongola and clung on to a diminishing power base before Mohammed Ali's invasion of Sudan in the 1820s pushed them into history. Dongola's most famous son took his revenge on the Egyptians 60 years later – Mohammed Ahmed, the Mahdi, had his roots here. Jaafar Nimeiri, Sudan's president in the 1970s, was also a Dongolawi. Today the town has a mixed Nubian and Shaqiya Arab population.

Along with dates, buzzing and biting insects also seem to be found in profusion here. One Dongolawi even joked to me that in the 1940s, when the British were trying to find a solution to the Jewish/Palestinian question, they thought about turning the land around Dongola into the Jewish homeland, but that they turned it down because of the bugs and settled on Israel instead! Even without this very Sudanese aside, some insect repellent is a good idea here.

All foreign visitors must register with the security police on arrival. You have to do this *before* you can check into a hotel, which is a real pain after a long bus trip, especially since the office is on the opposite side of town, a 10-minute rickshaw ride away. Ask for *maktub amn al watany wahdat amni Dongola* if you need to direct the driver! At the office, you'll be asked how long you plan to stay and where, and your details will be entered in a ledger. Make sure they give you a signed chit to give to your hotel when you check in.

For travellers, Dongola is mainly a place to relax; there is little to see in the town itself. Its gentle charms are best enjoyed after a spell on the desert tracks of the north. The town can then feel like a metropolis, its tidy shops stacked with goods seeming like supermarkets and its palm groves like the slices of Eden they really are. A very enjoyable pastime is to sit at one of the teashops by the ferry crossing and watch the tide of river traffic – people, animals and vehicles – pass by.

Getting there and away

By air

Two flights a week with Sudan Airways link Dongola to Khartoum. As always, schedules are a moveable feast; while I was there the route had been temporarily suspended. Sudan Airways also operate a weekly flight to Jeddah, and rumours persist of an occasional service to Cairo. The airport is 10km west of the town.

By road

Dongola is 500km from Khartoum and is the best place to arrange transport to the north. With the exception of services to Khartoum, public transport is scarce on Fridays. There are several departure points depending on your destination.

Transport to Khartoum, as well as north along the west bank of the Nile, leaves from the Souq es-Shabi. Buses to Omdurman Souq es-Shabi and Khartoum's Sajana bus terminal cost from 4,000SD and take around 11 hours. A tarmac road extends 40km south of Dongola before reverting to sand and gravel. At Abu Dom junction, the tarmac reappears and leads all the way to the capital. Heading north on the west bank, there is a weekly bus from Omdurman as far north as the villages of Ghobba Salim and Hamid, near the ruins of Soleb and Sedeinga, which usually passes through Dongola on Thursdays.

Transport north along the east bank is more plentiful and departs from the Dongola ferry station. There is a small booth next to the teashops by the ferry on the west bank that sells bus tickets to Wadi Halfa (24 hours) and Abri (12 hours). Direct Wadi Halfa buses (24 hours) tend to leave on Mondays to connect with the ferry to Aswan. On the east bank of the ferry crossing (actually the village of Selim) there is a large *boksi* stand, offering services running north to Kerma (several daily, two hours, 600SD), Delgo (five hours), and Abri (nine hours). *Bokasi* to Karima (four hours, 2,000SD) also leave from here on most days, but they can take a long time to fill.

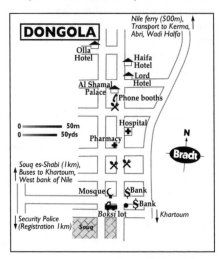

If you have your own transport, it's worth noting that the last vehicle ferry north of Dongola is at Delgo. Road surfaces – while still sand and gravel – are slightly better on the east bank of the Nile heading north, with a lot more villages and passing traffic if you run into difficulties. The exception is the relatively short section between Dongola and Kerma, which is probably the sandiest stretch along the Nile until you get close to Wadi Halfa.

Where to stay and eat

Hotels in Dongola insist that you register with security *before* allowing you to check in, a real pain if you've come off a long bus trip. All are located on or just off the main street.

Olla Hotel (tel: 0241 12848) pegs itself as Dongola's most upscale hotel. Rooms face onto a pleasantly green and shady courtyard with tables and chairs. The en-suite bathrooms don't quite run to hot water, but the rooms are clean. A small restaurant can rustle up some breakfast if you try hard enough, but it doesn't really get going until later in the day. It's a nice enough place to stay, but at 2,750/5,150SD for a single/double, it can be hard to see what you're paying extra for.

The **Lord Hotel** confusingly has entrances on two streets, marked with large red and yellow oil drums. It's a good budget option if a little dusty – rooms with shower and up to three beds cost 500SD per person. Beds in a room with shared bathroom cost 300SD. English is spoken and there is a small cafeteria attached. The feta cheese sandwiches are a treat.

Across the main street is the **Al Shamal Palace**. Most rooms have a small bathroom and jostle for space around a tiny courtyard. Inside they have a slightly dark air – whether this makes it gloomy or a cool respite from the baking Sudanese sun is a matter of taste. All rooms are doubles, available at a flat price of 1,300SD/1,600SD with or without a shower.

The **Haifa Hotel** used to have a crocodile's head above the door. It must have been scaring off customers because these days the hotel seems to be packed to capacity. I visited several times but was always told it was full, and no-one would let me look around. If you fare better, expect *lokanda*-style accommodation with shared bathrooms. Prices are 500SD per bed.

Most of the eating-places also lie along the main street and around the local *boksi* lot by the market. The **Al Madina Restaurant** lives up to its billing of 'All nice food and drink'. To my mind, Dongola has the tastiest *taamiya* I've found in Sudan; there's also some great fish on offer. The unmarked **cafeteria** opposite the **purple sweet shop** does delicious Nile perch, while *baklawa* and ice cream are served just across the road.

Kawa

The Kushite centre of Kawa is 3km south of Dongola on the east bank of the Nile. The site covers 40ha and includes remains from the Kerma culture and New Kingdom Egypt as well as Kush. Tutankhamun built a temple here in the 14th century BC. Kush's greatest builder, Taharqa, erected a Temple of Amun next to it, filling it with gold and roofing it with cedarwood from Lebanon. A particularly beautiful granite sphinx with the king's head was recovered from Kawa and is now in the British Museum. Kawa was a regional capital, linked to Jebel Barkal by a road through the desert. The city was abandoned in the 4th century AD with the final collapse of Kush and the sandy winds of the *haboub* eventually reclaimed Kawa for the desert.

Kawa was excavated by the British in the 1930s but has been covered again with wind-blown sand. As a result, there is little to see of the Temple of Amun

THE DATE PALM

Phoenix dactylifera, the date palm, is central to the Nubian economy and culture. Palm groves form a continuous strip of green along the Nile, a vital sign of life and community. Palms are a symbol of continuity and harmony as well as a cash crop.

One reason for the palm's special status lies in the Koran. A palm tree provided shade for Mary as she gave birth to Jesus and its fruit gave her strength. Dates are traditionally the first food to be taken when breaking the fast at dusk during Ramadan. Recognising the palm's importance, the Prophet Mohammed even declared 'I entrust to thy care and attention your aunt, the date palm'. Palms do indeed become part of the family, well looked after as property and provider of food and raw materials.

The palm is not actually a tree but a type of grass. A single bud at the top of the plant stretches ever upwards; the bark is the remains of dead leaf growth. A well-tended palm can live for over a hundred years, fruiting every year. Palms have genders – in the spring farmers will collect flowers from the male trees and hang them from the fronds of the female palms to pollinate them. The fruit is harvested from September to November. Women process the dates and fronds, and men pack and sell them.

Date palms aren't just a source of fruit. Its fronds can be woven into baskets, its fibres made into rope and its trunk used as roofing beams. The living palm also provides essential shade to allow other plants to be grown beneath it, its roots binding the sandy soil against erosion. At the end of the day, some Nubians like to relax with a glass of *araki*, a strong spirit distilled from dates.

You'll find dates on sale everywhere in north Sudan, with the stickiest and best found during harvest time. Dried dates are great for long bus trips – they're packed with energy, and passing a handful through the bus is the perfect Sudanese ice-breaker.

The last word on the centrality of the date palm to Nubians comes from a man who lost his home to the Aswan Dam inundation in the 1960s. Relocated to the east he still remembered: 'We left some good dates, my son, and I miss them'.

itself, except a scattering of potsherds of indeterminate age and the tops of the columns, which are slowly being eaten away by the wind and sand into weird sculptural forms. British archaeologists are excavating the town and cemeteries elsewhere on the site and continue to make important discoveries.

No permit is needed to visit Kawa, which is really best looked at as a pleasant walk along the Nile. Take the ferry from Dongola and walk south from Selim along the river. It's difficult to get lost, but villagers along the way will point you in the right direction if needs be, probably assuming you're an archaeologist. Early morning is best; remember to carry plenty of water.

Dongola to Wadi Halfa

This chapter deals with Sudan's far north, along the
stretch of the Nile running through Nubia from
Dongola to the port town of Wadi Halfa. With its
landscape of sandy and rocky desert it's known locally
as 'the Belly of Stones'. It's a part of Sudan
frequently rushed through in transit or overlooked
altogether, but a trip here is worth anyone's time.
Isolated ruins continue to attest to Sudan's ancient past
– temples left behind by Egyptian conquerors, and the
mysterious Deffufas, the oldest standing buildings in sub-
Saharan Africa. Many more sites were lost with the flooding of
the Nile by the Aswan High Dam. The real attraction, however, is simply in
the landscape itself – the desert bluffs and green palm groves strung out along
the river. The incomparable hospitality of the Nubians makes this part of
Sudan one of the most rewarding to travel in.

TRAVEL ALONG THE NILE

It is quite possible to travel from Dongola to Wadi Halfa in a single
concentrated burst – roughly 24 hours by bus. It's far more pleasurable,
however, to take your time and village-hop along this route. That way you can
get a sense of the gentle pace of life in this part of Sudan. Nothing much seems
to happen here, but somehow that's part of the charm; nothing is ever rushed
when life is governed by the easy flow of the Nile.

Transport connections are some of the most rugged in Sudan. After
Dongola, tarmac becomes just a memory. Instead, sand is the order of the day,
with the road surfaces continually switching from hard gravel to fine dust and
all conditions in between. To make up for this, the views are always changing.
The cool blue and brown waters of the Nile appear and disappear amid swathes
of palm threes and carefully tended fields. Villages pass by with their men in
gleaming white jallabiyas riding donkeys and women in bright billowing *tobes*.
Away from the river there are rocky scarps, golden sand dunes and great piles
of basalt boulders that lie strewn in the desert. It's spectacular country.

Transport is by desert bus or *boksi*. The buses are the true classics of
Sudanese motoring, engineered for the most demanding conditions, with the
most basic of bus bodies bolted onto the back of a truck chassis. The slatted
sides are open, to allow some precious fresh air to circulate, as the interior is

often overloaded with passengers, produce
going to market, and half the worldly
possessions of Nubia, or so it can
seem. They are certainly not
built for comfort and the
cramped   seats   and
struggling suspension are
some of the best arguments
for taking things slowly along
this part of the Nile. It's simply too uncomfortable to travel for extended
periods! Buses stop frequently along the way, so you needn't worry about
taking too many food supplies, although water for the trip is an obvious
necessity.

There is little or no public transport on Fridays along the Nile. The main
transport hubs are the small towns of Kerma and Abri, with buses and *bokasi*
busiest on Sunday and Monday respectively, as these are the town's weekly
market days.

For the most part, the road north closely follows the Nile, and you are never
more than a few kilometres from the nearest village – good news for those
with their own vehicle in the event of mechanical problems. Traffic is also
frequent along this road, at least as far north as Abri, so if you do encounter
difficulties you shouldn't have to wait too long for someone to pass by. From
Abri to Wadi Halfa there is less traffic; or rather the traffic is more
concentrated around the arrival and departure of the Aswan ferry, in port on
Tuesdays and Wednesdays.

From Dongola to Kerma is the sandiest stretch of road in the north,
although it sticks close to the river. After Kerma, the road veers out into the
desert to cut a bend off the Nile, rejoining it near Delgo, and is quite stony.
There are no villages on this part of the route. From Delgo the road regularly
switches from gravel to sand but sticks close to the cultivated strip of land by
the Nile, passing through villages every few kilometres before arriving at Abri.
This pattern continues until the tracks reach the hamlet of Akasha, where you
look down on huge palm groves and the ever-widening river, its flow slowed
by the dam at Aswan. The road then heads back into the desert, along the most
inhospitable part of the route since Dongola. The gravel tracks are well worn,
so navigation shouldn't be a problem here if you have your own vehicle, but
you should always treat the environment with respect and carry as much spare
water and fuel as you can.

After Dongola, there are only two vehicle ferries along this northern
stretch of the Nile, at Kerma and Delgo. Small boats cross the river
wherever there's a settlement – reason enough for the adventurous to cross
to the opposite bank for more exploring. The west bank is less populated
than the east, with fewer transport options. A bus runs intermittently from
Dongola to Ghobba Salim and Hamid, and *bokasi* run between most
villages, although you may find yourself hiring one complete if you really
want to explore the west bank.

DESERT DUST

Whichever way you approach it, travel in northern Sudan is a dusty proposition. A bandana to cover the mouth is highly recommended for any sort of trip here. Travel writer Philip Marsden definitely gets to the essence of the area in his story *The Nubian Desert*:

> At midday the expedition left Dongola and pushed north into the desert. For more than a week we drove in convoy on roads that were sometimes narrow and rutted, sometimes multi-stranded tracks and sometimes not roads at all but just the wide-open desert. Our world was sand – soft sand, impacted sand, pebbly sand, wind-blown sand that gathered in drifts or rose into dunes, sand that browned the waters of the Nile, that turned to mud in neat riparian plots, that seeped into every corner of our lives so that when hands were pushed into pockets they found pools of fine, egg-timer sand and when we closed our eyes at night we saw nothing but the bouncing plains of sand ahead, stretching out to a sandy horizon.

The farther you travel from Dongola, the more expensive many goods become. Small markets and poor transport infrastructure have an inflationary effect, in particular on items such as bottled water. To a Nubian villager this is a luxury item and is priced accordingly; it can be up to three times the Khartoum price in a village between Abri and Kerma – if it's on sale at all.

KERMA

Sitting just south of the Third Cataract, Kerma is the largest settlement between Dongola and Abri, and the local market town for this stretch of the Nile. Kerma itself doesn't feel very big, but it extends along the riverbank, blurring into neighbouring villages for several kilometres. There's a definite feeling of business about the place and slightly more prosperity than elsewhere – there are more fired (rather than mud) brick buildings here, more livestock, and the fields seem particularly productive.

For small-town Nubia, Kerma has illustrious roots, being the seat of the first independent kingdom of Kush. An early culture sprang up here in around 2400BC – evidence of the oldest urban settlements in sub-Saharan Africa. Kerma sits in rich agricultural land, but prospered as a way station for the trade between the tropical south and Egypt. Kerma was a densely packed walled city and a political power in its own right. Its heyday was from 1750 to 1600BC, when the Egyptian kingdom was in turmoil and Kerma's rulers pushed far north to extend their rule to Aswan. There is no local written record of Kerma's history, and our knowledge is mainly derived from archaeological digs. Kerma was particularly known for its high quality pottery, many fine examples of which can be seen in the National Museum in Khartoum. In the

THE NUBIANS

Nubia comprises the land along the Nile reaching from just south of Dongola to Aswan in Egypt. Its inhabitants are neither Arab nor black – the Nubians have a distinct ethnic and cultural identity, they speak their own language with its own script, and they have a history that reaches back well before the Kingdom of Kush. At times in their history, the Nubians have followed the Pharaonic religions, had an indigenous Christian culture, and now follow Islam.

It's a history that Nubians are proud of, although they complain that the central government has neglected the long pre-Islamic history of their region in favour of a standard Islamist narrative of Sudanese culture. Nubia remains as neglected as any part of Sudan away from Khartoum.

Modern Nubians are divided into three main groups – the Danaqla around the Dongola Reach, the Mahas from the Third Cataract to south of Wadi Halfa, and the Sikurta around Aswan. Each group speak slightly different dialects of the Nubia tongue. In Sudan, the groups also practise facial scarring. Mahas men and women often display three wide scars on each cheek. With the Danaqla the same scars are found around the temple. Scarification, however, is becoming less and less popular with younger generations.

Nubian architecture is very distinct. Houses sit in a large courtyard surrounded by a high wall. The most notable feature of the building is the gateway. The threshold to the property is often of an exaggerated size and highly decorated with stucco and bright colours. Geometric patterns are popular, but also pictures and symbols that may relate to the family inside – vehicles are popular, as are stars and palm trees. Scorpions and eyes ward off the evil eye, while a book (representing the Koran) and the Holy Ka'aba in Mecca may indicate that the owner has performed the Haj Pilgrimage.

15th century BC, New Kingdom Egypt marched south to Nubia to conquer the region, ending Kerma's rule for good.

Just north of Kerma is Tombos, a New Kingdom Egyptian cemetery, with some polished but broken granite statuary lying lonely in the sand and some inscriptions left by Thutmose I to commemorate his conquest of Kerma. The site was an important ancient granite quarry.

Kerma is at its busiest on Mondays with its large, lively and very photogenic weekly market. Onions are grown in great quantities here, and the *souq* bulges with huge piles of them, while the other fresh produce jostles for space.

Getting there and away

Most transport arriving in Kerma drops you in the main town square 500m north of the *souq*. A *boksi* is the most convenient form of transport out of Kerma, as buses mostly just pass through here rather than start their journeys from the town. The exception is the bus to Wadi Halfa, which leaves on

Where possible, the gate always faces the Nile. Inside the compound a flat-roofed area provides a sitting area facing the courtyard, with separate entrances for the family and guest to maintain privacy. Houses are typically roofed using split palm trunks, but richer owners may roof their properties with mud brick domes to help keep the inside cool during the day.

Music is important in Nubian culture. Unlike Arabic music it's based on the pentatonic scale, and so is more immediately accessible to western ears. Traditional music features a *kisir* (five-stringed lyre) and a *tar* (drum). Nubian 'pop' music is highly synthesised and often introduces horns to weave further melodies into a heady jazz mix. Whichever style is played, the themes remain the same – call-and-response chants, love songs and songs in praise of the land. The latter have become increasingly popular in the last 40 years with the flooding of Nubia's heartland and the urban drift of Nubians to Khartoum and Cairo.

The best place to hear Nubian music is at a wedding. If you're lucky enough to get invited to one it will be one of the highlights of your trip. A big wedding can last several days. The groom's family holds an open house, building up to a large wedding feast. After eating, the music and dancing begins. Men and women dance separately but opposite each other in a highly charged and sensual atmosphere.

The bride is prepared with smoke baths, then elaborately dressed, bedecked with jewellery, and painted with henna. On the wedding night, the bride and groom go to the Nile to wash to ensure their prosperity. The groom will have paid a bride-price to the bride's father, which is one reason why first-cousin marriages are popular, as this keeps wealth in the family. Weddings are an expensive business, and the wages of Nubian expats working in the Gulf have greatly inflated bride-prices, causing problems for poor young men at home.

Sundays and takes up to 24 hours to reach its destination (3,000SD). Dongola is a two-hour *boksi* ride to the south (600SD) or it's seven hours north to Abri (1,500SD). The *boksi* lot is just south of the *souq*, with offices and auto workshops lining the streets.

There is a modern bridge from Kerma to Argo and the west bank of the Nile. A sandy piste leads south to Dongola and north on the west bank as far as Ghobba Salim.

Where to stay and eat

There is only one place to stay in Kerma: the **Hotel Karma** (sic), 200m north of the main *boksi* lot. It's a mix of modern red brick with a traditional open veranda at the front. There is no running water in the toilets, and they can get a bit grim if the place is busy. Four large rooms are packed with beds, each costing 300SD per person.

The main town square has several lively *ful* and *taamiya*-style joints. The side streets of the main *souq* are also good places to eat, and start frying up *kibda* from mid-morning, or *zalabia* for the sweet-toothed.

Deffufa

The word *deffufa* is a Nubian term meaning mud-brick building and there are two such monumental structures in Kerma dating from the earliest Kushite period, which are over 3,500 years old. The larger Western Deffufa is 5km south of the town centre.

The Western Deffufa is a huge building, measuring 50m by 25m and standing over 18m tall. It is the largest and possibly the oldest man-made structure in sub-Saharan Africa, another example of Sudan's early history being overshadowed by that of its its Egyptian neighbours. Ancient and weather-beaten, the structure is almost organic, as if it just grew out of the ground, and its antiquity can seem hard to fathom. The Deffufa once stood at the centre of the city of Kerma and the area immediately surrounding it was open and paved. A single staircase leads to the roof where there would probably have been a shrine.

There is a low boundary wall surrounding the Deffufa, and a permit is required to enter. Some travellers have visited and found the *ghaffir* absent altogether and simply walked in through the open gate, although the building can clearly be examined from behind the boundary wall should he appear and refuse entry to those without permits.

The Eastern Deffufa is 2km east of this site, located on the edge of the desert in the huge eastern cemeteries of ancient Kerma. The building is of a similar size but is shorter, and due to its location it is associated with funerary

THE DROWNING OF NUBIA

The building of the High Dam at Aswan in the early 1960s is most often depicted as a triumph for Egypt, thanks to the taming of the Nile floods and the stupendous rescue of ancient temples such as Abu Simbel. The story of its effects on Sudan, however, is less well known.

The High Dam created Lake Nasser (known in Sudan as 'the Nubian Lake'), flooding the Nile far south of the Second Cataract. The old town of Wadi Halfa disappeared, along with nearly 30 villages – the heart of Nubia.

In total, around 50,000 Sudanese Nubians were relocated as a result of the flooding. The scheme was ill planned and the compensation package agreed between the Egyptian and Sudanese governments was inadequate. The old town of Wadi Halfa succumbed to the rising waters of Lake Nasser in September 1963. Mosques, houses and palm groves all met a watery end. Most of the town's inhabitants were forcibly moved to a new settlement at Khasm el Girba on the Atbara River near Kassala. Having lost their livelihoods once, disaster befell the population here a second time, again because of a dam. A small dam built downstream on the seasonally flowing Atbara succeeded in altering its course, causing massive erosion and ceremonies. The cemeteries contain an estimated 30,000 graves and have been the main source of our knowledge of the Kerma cultures. The Eastern Deffufa is surrounded by the massive grave *tumuli* of Kerma's kings.

Bodies, along with the owner's possessions and food offerings for the afterlife, were buried in oval pits and covered with a low *tumulus*. The body was always laid with its right side aligned east–west, with the head to the east looking north and the hands covering the face, and the whole under a shroud of cowhide. Royal tombs were more elaborate, with a corridor leading to a vaulted burial chamber, all lined in brick and sometimes covered in paintings. A large marble slab covered the grave mound. Sacrifices were common, with royal bodyguards, servants, wives and even children being buried along with the ruler. When excavated, one royal tomb contained over 300 sacrificial victims accompanying the king to the afterlife. Cattle were also sacrificed in large numbers; it seems that Kerma was a fantastically bloody culture when it came to giving their rulers a proper send-off.

WEST BANK TEMPLES

There are the remains of several ancient Egyptian temples between Kerma and Abri, all on the west bank of the Nile. This is the region that the Egyptians regarded as Middle Nubia, and was traditionally the buffer between their border at the First and Second Cataracts and their unruly neighbours in Kush. During the reign of all-conquering Thutmose I in the 16th century BC, the Egyptians invaded Nubia, pentrating Kush as far as Kurgus, north of Atbara. Permanent settlements and temples were built, invariably with large fortresses attached to them to protect the all-important Nile trade.

the loss of farmland. Large numbers of Nubians upped sticks again, this time following the urban drift to Khartoum. This second dam also had serious knock-on effects on the local Beja pastoralist population and their herds.

A similar relocation scheme in Egypt met with marginally more success, with a similar number of Nubians relocated to Kom Ombo and Edfu (sites that were at least on the Nile), although compensation remained negligible.

The Bishariyyin nomads either side of the border that lost large amounts of summer grazing along the Nile received no compensation whatsoever, as they were not regarded as having any formal claim on the land.

As in Egypt, there was an archaeological rescue package which succeeded in saving the temples of Buhen and Semna, as well as the Nubian Christian frescoes of Faras, all now in the National Museum in Khartoum. Many more undiscovered sites now lie underwater.

The High Dam at Aswan and the botched resettlement package tore the heart out of Nubian culture, and its reverberations are still felt today. New Wadi Halfa does not even benefit from the electricity generated by the dam that flooded the original. Many fear that the new Merowe Dam at the Fourth Cataract may soon repeat the failings of its predecessor downstream.

The remains of many Egyptian towns in northern Sudan were lost to the construction of the High Dam in Aswan – the important Middle Kingdom garrison town of Buhen near the Second Cataract for example. Its temple, along with two from Semna further south, was rescued from the rising waters and can be seen reconstructed in the grounds of the National Museum in Khartoum.

What's left is a mixed bag. By any measure, the sites are greatly ruined and a keen interest in archaeology is needed to get the most out of them. Those with only a passing fancy are likely to be disappointed. Archaeological permits from Khartoum are technically required, but in practice the sites are so rarely visited that the *ghaffirs* are not likely to insist on them for entry, if they are on site at all. The west bank of the Nile is less densely populated than the east, and has fewer transport connections. In many ways, that is one of the greatest attractions of these temples – while the Kerma to Abri road could hardly be described as the beaten track, exploring the west bank is a different ballgame altogether. With its uncertainties of transport and accommodation, getting to sites is as much of the adventure as the temples themselves. It's you, the Nile, the desert and not much else.

Sesibi

The ruins of the New Kingdom Egyptian town of Sesibi are on the west bank of the Nile, across from Delgo. It was founded during the 18th Dynasty in the 14th century BC, the southernmost of the fortified towns founded by the Egyptians in Upper Nubia. The town contained several temples built by the heretical king Akhenaten, who abandoned the pantheon of Egyptian gods in favour of the worship of the sun disk Aten – the world's earliest recorded monotheistic religion. Three columns stand proud in the tumbled blocks of the temple, the sole remains of this brief chapter in the saga of the Egyptian gods.

Of the town itself, little more than the eroded walls of the buildings remain, although the layout of the original settlement is clearly visible. Just to the north of Sesibi is the craggy hill of Jebel Sesi, which has commanding views along the Nile. The area was a thriving agricultural centre in the late Meroitic and medieval period, and on the top of the hill are the remains of a hill fort from the 5th century AD.

Jebel Sesi is worth the detour for the climb; a vehicle ferry links Delgo to the west-bank village of Kedurma. From the ferry it's a few minutes' walk to Jebel Sesi, or a walk of prehaps 25 minutes to Sesibi village. Local children may offer their services as guides, hiring out their donkeys for the ride.

Soleb

The Temple of Soleb is probably the best preserved Egyptian temple standing on the Sudanese Nile; if you're going to travel along the west bank, this is the one to see. Soleb was built by Amenhotep III in the 14th century BC and was dedicated to Amun and Nebmatre (the lord of Nubia, a representation of the pharaoh himself).

The temple is very close to the banks of the Nile, with a processional way leading from the river to the main halls. It has the scattered blocks of two pylons, a hypostyle hall, a court and a sanctuary. Four massive columns, originally 14m high carved as stylised palms, make up part of a kiosk by the standing walls of the first pylon. Through this are several columns that formed part of the temple court, this time carved as papyrus. When complete, the temple would have been around 130m in length, contained behind an enclosure wall double that size. The temple layout is very similar to the Temple of Luxor in Egypt, which was also built by Amenhotep. Two red granite lion statues were moved in antiquity to the Temple of Amun at Jebel Barkal and now reside in the British Museum.

Soleb temple has relief carvings showing the *sed* festival of Amenhotep. The *sed* was a celebration of renewal, first enacted in the 30th year of a pharaoh's rule, and then every three years thereafter. It was the most important ritual in a pharaoh's reign, regenerating his rule and assuring his reign in the afterlife. The exact procedure of the ceremony is unknown, but representations of the solar eye (the ruling god Amun) and the lunar eye (a lioness goddess Tefnutmehit) are shown as integral. The fact that the *sed* festival may have been celebrated here on the Egyptian-Nubian frontier is intriguing, as the lunar eye is also associated with Horus, the falcon-headed god and protector of the pharaoh. Horus lost his eye in battle with his brother Seth, a fight that was said to have taken place in Nubia. Reliefs on the southern wall of the hypostyle hall show conquered Nubians, as if to ram the symbolism home.

Soleb is opposite the east bank village of Wawa, 40km south of Abri, where a foot ferry crosses the river. In Soleb, Mohammed Hamid has a house where you may find accommodation, but it is best to be self-sufficient if you intend to stay.

Sedeinga

The temple of Sedeinga is 12km north of Soleb. As with Soleb, it was built by Amenhotep III, but while the former may have been built to mark both the pharaoh's jubilee and his victories over the Nubians, Sedeinga was dedicated to his favourite wife Tiye, deifying her in the process.

Very little remains of the temple: just a single column with an elaborately carved capital, surrounded by a few fallen blocks. As with the other west bank sites, the ruins face the empty desert and there is a real feeling of emptiness here. Perhaps it's the revenge of the ancient gods – Tiye was the mother of Akhenaten, who tried to consign them all to history in his monotheistic fervour.

To get to Sedeinga there are foot ferries from Sawarda on the east bank to the nearby village of Ghobba Salim. There is a bus roughly once a week running down the west bank to Dongola, taking anywhere from 12 to 24 hours to make the trip. Ghobba Salim is the site of the large tomb (*ghobba*) of a 19th-century local sheikh. It's possible to continue slightly farther north on the west bank to Sai Island, 30km away; halfway between the two is the village of Hamid, with a foot ferry across to Oshamatu.

ABRI

A market centre on the east bank of the Nile, Abri feels like the archetypal Nubian town. It's a sleepy, good-natured place that's worth catching your breath in; sit in its teahouses, potter around its small *souq*, or simply watch the Nile pass by. The town is edged by green fields and palm groves that make for pleasant walks and a foot ferry on the edge of town can take you to the small village on Arnata Island in the middle of the river. Archaeology buffs can head south out of Abri and over to Sai Island, with its ancient and medieval ruins.

Getting there and away

Abri has good onward transport connections, with several bus and *bokasi* offices running services to Wadi Halfa, Dongola and all points in between on the east bank. The Monday market day has the most transport options. Wadi Halfa buses (1,500SD) take around ten hours, mostly departing on Sunday and Monday to link with the Aswan ferry. Buses to Dongola (1,500SD) depart most days except Friday and take around twelve hours. If you want to get off halfway at somewhere like Kerma you'll most likely have to pay the full fare. The Abri-Kerma run is the busiest *boksi* route, taking seven hours (1,500SD), and stopping at Delgo, with some *bokasi* continuing on to Dongola.

THE DESERT RAILWAY

If you're rattling through the Nubian Desert on the Wadi Halfa train, spare a thought for the men who laid it. Much more than just two tracks stretching to the horizon, it is one of the great achievements of Victorian engineering.

The track was laid as a supply line for the Anglo-Egyptian Conquest of Sudan. Without it, the advancing army was dependent on camels and carts, or a Nile whose cataracts made navigation difficult and expensive. The train was the key to Kitchener's campaign.

The challenge was considerable. The track had to be laid across 360km of unsurveyed and waterless desert, advancing into enemy territory. Furthermore, the track was to be laid during the stifling heat of summer. Kitchener consulted widely with the railway experts of the day as to his plan, only to find that many dismissed it as both crazy and impossible. He pressed on anyway.

By the turn of 1897, the small town of Wadi Halfa was transformed into a bustling railhead and Sudan's first industrial centre. Engineering plants, ironworks and machine shops sprang up, all under the direction of the newly formed Railway Battalion. Egyptian and Sudanese were trained as rail-spikers and telegraph operators, engines were shipped from Britain and coal was brought from Alexandria. Captured enemies were pressed into service as labourers and the great advance began.

Work began in May 1897. Survey teams rode ahead of the working

Where to stay and eat

Abri has just one hotel, the **El Fagre Hotel**. Half a dozen rooms face into a central courtyard, with reasonably decent toilets and showers. The hotel's satellite dish attracts a good crowd for football matches – a good reason to turn on the electricity. Rooms have four or five beds, each costing 500SD.

If you want to experience some traditional Nubian hospitality, Mugzoub Hassan keeps an open house for travellers. He speaks good English and can help arrange transport. His mother is also an excellent cook and her *maashi* (stuffed aubergines and peppers) is worth the stop in Abri alone. There's no phone, but Mugzoub can be found in the *souq*, where he also runs a newspaper kiosk. The cost is 1,000SD a night, with a further charge for meals.

Small cafeterias form the highlight of Abri's dining experience, with *ful* top of the menu. Meat dishes are thin on the ground. In the morning, teahouses serve up delicious sugary *zalabia* for breakfast, best enjoyed with milky tea. Abri's small *souq* is well-stocked for fresh produce including fruit, but a large bottle of mineral water will set you back 300SD.

Sai Island

Two kilometres south of the ferry landing are the remains of a mud brick Ottoman fort, built in the 16th century when the region formed the boundary

party, who were divided into four teams. The first laid the plates, the second the sleepers. A third team followed to fix the rails and the final team levelled the line. The line advanced by an average of 2km a day, occasionally covering an incredible 5km under the desert sun.

The advance party was kept supplied daily by two trains. The first brought the rails and sleepers. The second brought supplies for the workers, with a few trappings of civilisation – according to Churchill, 'the letters, newspapers, sausages, jam, whisky, soda-water, and cigarettes which enable the Briton to conquer the world without discomfort'.

A telegraph followed the line and a station with passing sidings was built roughly every 30km. Water was found at Stations 4 and 6 by digging deep wells – the latter is still an important stop for today's train service. While water worries were eased in this way, the engineers also had to overcome the rising and unexpected rise in the gradient of the line. Work slowed as the line approached the northern bend of the Nile, to wait for punitive operations against the Mahdist forces there. The railway reached Abu Hamed in October 1897, just five months after the first rail was laid. With it, the fate of the Khalifa was sealed. Men and munitions were rapidly brought forward in an unstoppable advance. Within six months, the Khalifa's army had been smashed at Atbara, and the line extended there. Omdurman fell in September 1898, and the railway was finally brought to the capital. More than anything else, it was the train that won the war.

between Egypt and the rising power of the Funj kingdom from Sennar far to the south. As an illustration of the role Nubia has played as a frontier, the fort is constructed on the stone remains of a New Kingdom Egyptian town built nearly three thousand years earlier.

The site is currently being excavated by French archaeologists, and is difficult to interpret by the non-specialist. The ruined fort has great views of Jebel Abri rising out of the desert opposite and peregrine falcons are a common site here.

There are four villages on Sai Island. If you walk inland from the ferry towards them you pass four upright granite columns of a medieval church. Crosses can clearly be seen carved on the capitals which are all that remain to mark this outpost of the Nobatian kingdom.

The crossing to Sai Island is 10km south of Abri by the village of Tabaj, which is situated in the middle of a palm grove. The ferry is large enough to take two cars. It only makes the crossing four times a day, roughly at 08.00, 10.00, 12.00 and 16.00, so make sure you don't get stranded overnight (unless that's your purpose).

WADI HALFA

At the northernmost tip of Sudan, Wadi Halfa can feel like the end of the world. The only real reason to visit is to use it as a transit point to or from Egypt and the place has a real waiting room air to it. Beyond the port, the town sprawls out away from the shore, a motley collection of low buildings and sandy expanses. As a place to either leave or enter Sudan, Wadi Halfa is undoubtedly a disappointment.

It wasn't always like this. Until the start of the 1960s Wadi Halfa was a lively, thriving Nubian town. Shaded, tree-lined streets stretched along a corniche facing the Nile and there were well-tended fields and palm groves, and old houses built in the traditional Nubian style with massive gates and painted walls. The end came for old Wadi Halfa with the raising of the High Dam across the border at Aswan. The flooding of the Nile sent the town to a watery grave in 1963. Many of Wadi Halfa's inhabitants were relocated, but a small population remained to rebuild their homes.

The result looks nothing more than temporary, as if the spirit of the place was drowned along with the houses and fields. New Wadi Halfa is a forlorn place. The town is set back from the lake as floods are not uncommon as the water level rises and falls. As a result there is little agriculture here, and barely a scrap of the bright green colour that enlivens towns and villages further south along the Nile. A Chinese-built fishing plant has attempted to create a new industry here, but if it wasn't for the weekly ferry, you get the impression that Wadi Halfa would disappear altogether. The contrast between the few days when the ferry docks and the torpid atmosphere for the rest of the week is striking.

There are no 'attractions' in Wadi Halfa, although the rocky hill in the centre of town has good views over Lake Nasser. The markets are full of imported Egyptian foods but low on fresh produce. A bottle of mineral water costs almost twice as much as it does in Khartoum.

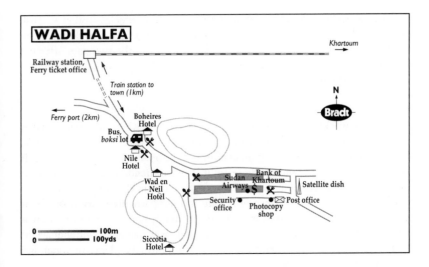

Those newly arrived from Egypt must register with security on arrival. You need a copy of your passport and one photo; the cost is 5,700SD. There is a photocopy shop a few yards west of the security compound – when they have electricity they charge a steep 50SD per copy. Across the street is the incongruous four-storey Sudan Airways building, which has a branch of the Bank of Khartoum on the first floor.

Wadi Halfa has a fleet of *bokasi*, mostly beaten-up Land Rovers that look as if they were left behind by the British after independence. On the day of the ferry they trawl around the hotels and market places to pick up passengers for the 3km drive to the port.

Getting there and away

All transport connections in and out of Wadi Halfa are designed to link up with the ferry service to Aswan in Egypt, which arrives in port on Tuesdays and departs the following day. There is a Sudan Air flight linking Wadi Halfa to Khartoum every Wednesday, but it is prone to cancellation.

By boat

By far the best way to enter or leave Sudan is by boat. For more information on this trip, see the box *The Wadi Halfa-Aswan ferry* below.

By bus

Rugged desert buses make the run south along the Nile to Abri (15 hours), Dongola (24 hours) and all points in between. There is no service all the way to Khartoum, presumably because the trip would be too much of an endurance test for even the most desert-hardened Sudanese. The road is made of sand and gravel, although after a few hours you might imagine it's just made of dust and ruts.

There's no bus station in Wadi Halfa, but most transport tends to leave from the open area in front of the Nile and Boheires Hotels. For those who read

Arabic, the destinations are painted on the side of the vehicles – otherwise ask around. There is very little *bokasi* traffic out of Wadi Halfa. Check departure times as soon as you arrive – most transport leaves in the two days after the ferry docks, so if you miss a connection you'll probably have to wait another five days for the next bus.

By train

There is a weekly train between Wadi Halfa and Khartoum which takes around 36 hours, but with mechanical failures or sandstorms, trips of over 50 hours aren't unknown. The train station is 1km north of the town centre. If you have arrived in town on the ferry, it is recommended that you buy your tickets as soon as possible. Second class sells out quickly; first class seats are also at a premium. The train ride is long and not particularly comfortable. If you need to get to Khartoum in a hurry, a better option is to take the train as far as Atbara (around 24 hours), and then swap over to a bus along the tarmac highway. There is a restaurant car on the train, but take plenty of water and

THE WADI HALFA-ASWAN FERRY

The weekly ferry between Wadi Halfa and Aswan is currently the only way to cross into Egypt. The voyage takes around 18 hours, and leaves Wadi Halfa every Wednesday. It's a supremely relaxing way to travel between the two countries.

The Wadi Halfa ticket office is at the train station. First class tickets (in a two-bed cabin) cost 10,900SD; second class (no allocated seating) is 6,300SD. Tickets include one meal on the boat. You can also buy ferry tickets in Khartoum from the train station in Bahri, but they don't include the meal. The latter is recommended if you want a cabin in first class, which can sell out quickly.

You are allowed to take bicycles and motorbikes on the ferry, which cost 1,100SD and 10,600SD respectively. There is a barge that attaches to the ferry that can carry cars if you need to ship a larger vehicle. The cost is around US$530. You should arrive in Wadi Halfa several days before planning to sail to arrange this. A cargo boat that can take up to six cars can be hired, but this is based in Aswan and must be booked well in advance. The fee is US$1,800 for the whole boat, so costs vary depending on how many vehicles want to make the voyage. The cargo boat takes four days to cross the lake. Bring you own ratchet straps or ropes to help secure your vehicle.

Immigration procedures take place in the security office in Wadi Halfa town rather than the ferry terminal. First you have to pay a port tax of 1,550SD (keep the receipt) at the small window at the front of the security office. Inside the compound, the Alien Office (signed in English) then checks the registration stamp in your passport and gives you a chit before sending you to the Passport Office. Everything is then re-checked and entered into a ledger, and you are given an exit form (for which you must pay 200SD).

snacks. The only major stop through the desert is at Station 6 where there are food stalls and teashops but not much else. The desert night can be as cold as the days are hot, so also take some warm clothes.

If you arrive in Wadi Halfa by train, most of your fellow passengers will be going to Egypt. If there are delays on the line, the ferry to Aswan will be held up to make the connection.

For cyclists, it's possible to put your bike on the train, but turn up early at the station so that it can be weighed and charged accordingly. If you arrive late at night, the station master may insist that you wait until morning to collect it, as the freight cars remain locked until they can be unloaded with supervision.

Where to stay and eat

If you have arrived by train, remember that the vast majority of passengers will also be heading for the hotels, so get into town as soon as possible to avoid the crush of people trying to check in. The arrival of the train and ferry is the big

Note that if you bought your ticket in Khartoum you'll need to go to the ticket office in Wadi Halfa to get it revalidated, and buy a meal ticket for a steep 800SD. Without this you won't be allowed through immigration! This accomplished, you can now proceed to the ferry terminal.

At the terminal, getting stamped out of Sudan is now a formality. Egyptian officials are also on hand to check your visa and yellow fever certificate.

During the voyage, there's little to do but watch the landscape go by. The land south of Aswan is characterised by rocky hills, which have formed a weird coastline of creeks and islands rising out of the lake. Second class seating below decks consists of rows of benches. It can get pretty stuffy inside, so if you've got a sleeping bag try sleeping under the stars. During the day, the spaces under the lifeboats are good place to keep out of the sun. Your meal ticket can be redeemed in the restaurant (also used as passport control), and there's a separate cafeteria for tea and snacks.

If the ferry leaves Wadi Halfa by early afternoon, you have a good chance of passing the temple of Abu Simbel in daylight. This magnificent site, built by Ramses II in the 13th century BC, was relocated at great effort to save it from the rising waters of Lake Nasser, and it's a rare treat to be able to see it from the water.

If you are sailing from Egypt to Sudan, tickets can be bought from the Nile Navigation Company in Aswan, or from the port on the day of departure. Fees in Egyptian pounds (E£) are: first class (E£200), second class (E£130), motorbike (E£270), car on barge (E£1,800). The ferry sails on Mondays and is the busier leg, as it's full of Sudanese traders laden down with merchandise. Again, passport control takes place on the boat, but you will need to register with security on arrival in Wadi Halfa.

weekly event for Wadi Halfa's hoteliers, so even if you turn up after the crowds, they'll still find somewhere for you to sleep.

Wadi Halfa has four hotels, all cut from the same template. Rooms are simple mud-brick structures with sandy floors and rope beds. Electricity is intermittent. Water is a problem in Wadi Halfa so each hotel has water tanks with standpipes, long drop toilets and (quite literally) bucket showers. There is a flat rate of 300SD per bed wherever you stay, and with nothing to choose between the hotels you pay your money and take your choice. The **Nile Hotel** and **Boheires Hotel** are opposite each other, near where the buses congregate. The **Wadi En Neil Hotel** is closer to the market, and the **Siccotia Hotel** is on the opposite side of the low hill.

There is a busy restaurant between the Nile and Boheires Hotels that serves a good selection of *ful*, *fasuliya*, kebabs and stews. In the market, there are several small cafeterias – try hunting out the delicious fried fish, enlivened with a squeeze of lime juice. Stalls run by tea ladies on most corners offer liquid refreshment. Fresh produce is more expensive than in the rest of northern Sudan.

Nubian Christian frescos

Khartoum to Kassala

The road out of Khartoum heads southeast along the Blue Nile to Wad Medani before turning away from the river to reach Gedaref. This flat and featureless area is Sudan's agricultural heartland. Sorghum and millet are the main crops here, along with cotton, sesame and sunflowers. North of Gedaref, the highway runs close to the Ethiopian and Eritrean borders. The land is harsher and drier here and better suited to the nomadic pastoral lifestyles of the Rashaida and Beja peoples. You'll often see their tented camps, along with large herds of cattle and camels being driven to waterholes.

Kassala sits at the base of the Taka Mountains, a giant granite escarpment that rises improbably out of the plain and that's great for scrambling. The town is famous for its fruit and has one of Sudan's best markets, but security is tight due to periodic instability on the Eritrean border.

WAD MEDANI

The city of Wad Medani is the capital of Gezira State and the centre of the region's cotton farms. Wad Medani first rose to prominence in 1821, when it was used by the Turco-Egyptians as the base from which to conquer the fading powers of the Funj Kingdom at Sennar. Nearly a hundred years later it was chosen by the British as the headquarters of the ambitious Gezira Project to revolutionise Sudanese agriculture. Today the city still prospers from the surrounding fertile lands and has the bustle of a thriving business centre.

Wad Medani is located just off the Khartoum–Port Sudan highway in a pleasant location on the Blue Nile. Its proximity to the capital and relaxed air has made it a popular destination for honeymooners, who you can see walking together on the Nile Avenue in newly wedded bliss. The beaches on the opposite bank of the Nile look inviting and it might be worth trying to find a boat that can take you there; the alternative is a very long diversion back to the main road and over the Blue Nile bridge. There's little else to do in Wad Medani, but as a break on a longer journey it has good facilities – well-stocked shops, a good choice of hotels, internet access and a number of decent open-air restaurants along the banks of the Nile.

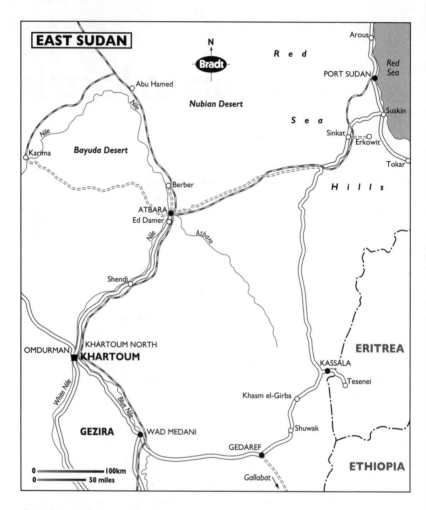

Getting there and away

Transport in and out of Wad Medani is quick and easy, due to its location on the Khartoum-Port Sudan highway (the town itself is 5km off the main road). Buses and minibuses leave throughout the day from the Souq es-Shabi on the east side of town. It's just two hours to Khartoum (700SD) by minibus and three to Gedaref (800SD). Buses to Port Sudan leave early in the morning and take around 15 hours, stopping at Kassala on the way. Most days it's also possible to catch a bus to Kosti via Sennar (1,000SD).

Wad Medani has Sudan's newest and shiniest fleet of bright red taxis, with minibuses plying the main routes and to the Souq es-Shabi.

Where to stay and eat

It's possibly a mark of Wad Medani's popularity as a honeymoon destination that in just about every hotel I visited the twin rooms had their beds pushed together. There's a flat room rate for single or double occupancy which is good for the just-married crowd, but less good for the sadly single.

In the centre of town is the slightly cavernous **Wad Medani International Hotel** (tel: 051 42240). All rooms are en suite with air conditioning and a balcony, but are otherwise a little uninspiring. Make sure you get a clean room – I was shown several where the open balcony was providing a pigeon roost and was covered in droppings and feathers. Rooms are 5,500SD for either a single or twin.

The aptly named **Nile Hotel** (tel: 051 45739) faces the river. The en-suite rooms are clean and simple, and there's a large pleasant garden in front, ideal for cold drinks in the day or smoking a *shisha* in the evening. Single/twin rooms are 6,000SD a night.

The **Continental Hotel** (tel: 051 345345) is 200m east of the Nile Hotel. It has a certain air of better-remembered days, and is in need of a slight spring clean. Rooms have air conditioning and the bathrooms have genuine baths (5,000SD single/twin). Outside there are plenty of trees and flowers and a dovecote on the veranda providing a calm, relaxed atmosphere.

Unsigned in English but next to the tall building on a corner, the **Namarg Hotel** has Wad Medani's best budget accommodation. Private rooms are spotlessly clean, as are the showers and toilets, and the place was gleaming with a new coat of paint when I dropped in. Rooms have one or two beds, at a flat rate of 1,200SD.

Just around the corner is the **Central Hotel**, which feels a lot more tired in comparison. The place is a bit grubby and the management grumpy, but it's a cheap option for those who prefer a courtyard *lokanda*. Beds are 500SD a night.

The **Continental Hotel** has a restaurant that's open in the evenings. Across the road there is a series of riverside restaurants stretching east for nearly a kilometre. These offer a great change from the standard cafeteria

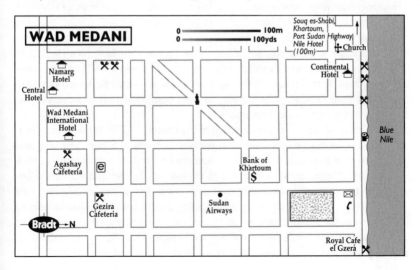

experience of Sudanese food, and if you've been in the country for a while the sudden appearance of a knife and fork feels like a genuine novelty. There's not much to choose between the different restaurants, but the **Royal Cafe El Gzeera** (sic) is typical of the bunch with tables on green lawns, fairy lights in the foliage and really good fish with bread and salad for 1,000SD. Dine late – most restaurants don't get going (or even open their doors) until at least 19.00.

There are plenty of more traditional Sudanese eateries in the centre of Wad Medani offering *ful*, *taamiya*, *kibda* and the like. Lots of places also sell *agashay*, where meat is pounded flat, breaded and cooked over hot grills. *Agashay* is a West African dish brought to Sudan by Fellata immigrants, many of whom originally settled around Wad Medani for seasonal farm work. It's a definite improvement on the standard kebab and a serving should cost you no more than 70SD.

GEDAREF

The agricultural town of Gedaref takes its name from *al-qadarif*, the wide flat plains of the area that are watered by seasonal rains, making them ideal for cultivation. Sorghum is the main crop, along with great quantities of sesame.

Gedaref's population are primarily Shukriya Arabs, a branch of the Juhayna. They were originally camel-herding nomads, but settled in the area in the late

COTTON FIELDS AND BREADBASKETS

The great clay plains of Gezira, the region sitting between the Blue and White Nile, are some of the richest agricultural lands in Sudan, and the most intensively farmed. The main crop is cotton for export, the result of a massive experiment carried out by the British in the early days of the Condominium.

The foundation of the British Empire was commerce – access to cheap raw materials and markets for exported goods. In Sudan, large-scale agriculture was developed to provide raw cotton for the mills of northern England. To this end, the Gezira Project was conceived, a vast irrigation scheme that would ultimately bring a million hectares of land under cultivation. It was the largest development project the British carried out in Sudan, at a cost of £3 million. The project, conceived in 1911, nearly went bankrupt at the outbreak of World War I and had to be bailed out with loans from London. When it was officially opened in 1926 the project was nearly five times over budget.

Cotton exports led to a doubling of the country's GDP in just a few years, but the Gezira Project also revolutionised land use in Sudan. The land was given over to tenant farmers, and absentee landlordism largely eradicated. A quarter of each tenant's land was cultivated with cotton, half was left fallow and the remainder sown with local grain crops. Irrigation was provided free of charge, and a light railway crisscrossing Gezira provided quick access to markets. Cotton profits were split equally between the state and the farmer; whatever else the farmer grew was for himself.

18th century and rose to some degree of influence in the fading years of the Funj Kingdom. The Turco-Egyptian invasion in 1821 led many farmers to flee the Nile to escape the harsh new regime, and many settled around Gedaref, helping to transform the settlement, which was originally just a marketplace for nomads. Gedaref still continues to attract people from the whole of Sudan who are looking for work on the area's many farms.

Modern Gedaref is quite a compact town, with a built-up centre surrounded by clusters of villages of round, thatched mud-brick houses, or *jutiya*.

The main reason to stop in Gedaref is if you are travelling overland between Sudan and Ethiopia. Between here and the first big Ethiopian town of Gonder there are several days worth of rutted tracks through the middle of nowhere, so make use of the trappings of civilisation while you're here. If you've arrived in Gedaref from Ethiopia, a tear of joy at reaching the asphalt road to Khartoum can easily be forgiven.

Getting there and away

Gedaref's bus station – the Souq es-Shabi – is right on the main road between Khartoum and Port Sudan. From here it's a 2km walk or *boksi* ride into the

To aid irrigation a dam was constructed at Roseires on the Blue Nile, a point of some concern to newly independent Egypt, which was completely reliant on the Nile's waters. The Gezira Project led directly to the signing of the Anglo-Egyptian Nile Waters Agreement of 1929, a treaty that is still the basis of water sharing agreements throughout the Nile Basin, and that remains a source of some discomfort to those at the Nile's headwaters.

Over-reliance on one export crop ultimately brought problems. Fluctuating cotton prices and periodic disease and locust outbreaks forced a change of tactic after independence. In the 1970s, President Nimeiri tried to create some massive infrastructural projects of his own. He aimed to turn Sudan into 'the breadbasket of Africa' and to do this he borrowed massively from the World Bank and the Gulf States, flush with money from the oil boom. The biggest schemes were the diversion of the White Nile through the Jonglei Canal for irrigation, and the Kenana Sugar Project south of Gezira.

It was a disaster. Investment was ill directed and plans were mismanaged and prone to corruption. The Jonglei Canal alienated the southern peoples and provided another grievance for the resumption of civil war. The Kenana Sugar Project was completed so late and over budget that its sugar cost more to produce than it did to buy. Nimeiri managed to turn Sudan from one of Africa's great prospects to a basket case saddled with crippling debts and barely enough money to maintain an infrastructure on the slide. By the time he was overthrown in the 1985 coup, Sudan's agricultural output had shrunk by 50%.

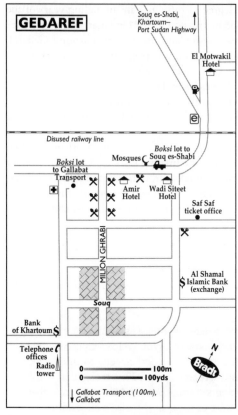

centre of the town. There is a *boksi* lot next to the mosque across from the railway line for transport running in the opposite direction. There are plenty of minibuses linking Gedaref to Kassala and Wad Medani (roughly three hours and 800SD in either direction). Khartoum buses take seven hours, with prices starting from 1,200SD. There is a Saf Saf office in the centre of Gedaref selling tickets for long-distance coaches.

Connections to the Ethiopian border at Gallabat are intermittent, but there is usually public transport running most days – this is usually a mish-mash of trucks and *bokasi*, so take whatever is going, and arrange things the day before travel if possible. Vehicles leave from the area outside the whitewashed Coptic church, although you'll need to ask around to find someone making the trip. Fares start at around 1,200SD depending on the mode of transport. (See the boxed text *Crossing the Ethiopian border*, page 176.)

Where to stay and eat

El Motwakil Hotel (tel: 0441 43232) features Gedaref's best accommodation, offering pleasant en suite rooms with satellite television catering mainly to Sudanese businessmen. The lobby is large and cool with plenty of comfy seats to sink into, and the restaurant looks large enough to hold an ice-rink. Rooms are 8812/13,113SD for a single/twin, with breakfast included.

Gedaref's budget hotels seem to have a problem with their water supply. Bucket showers and hand-flushed toilets are the order of the day here. The **Amir Hotel** is marginally the better option. Clean, adequate rooms with up to three beds are a flat rate of 2000SD. There are a few 'luxury' rooms at 3000SD that have a sink and toilet that the manager is keen to promote to prosperous *khawajas*.

The **Wadi Siteet Hotel** is the alternative to the Amir. The rooms are a bit basic, but in an attempt to recreate the *lokanda* experience, most guests haul their beds out onto the balconies. Beds cost 800SD per night, and if the place isn't too busy you'll get the room to yourself. Most of the toilets are kept locked, leaving just one to serve the hotel and overflow in the process. The others are perfectly clean and the manager likes to keep them this way 'because if I unlock them, people will use them'. If you can't accept his logic it's worth asking the manager to lend you a private key for the duration of your stay.

There is a restaurant at **El Motawakil Hotel** if you're craving a meal eaten with Western cutlery. Otherwise, head for **Milion Ghrabi** around the corner from the Amir Hotel. This street is a hive of activity and is lined with restaurants, cafeterias and snack stalls. Milion Ghrabi roughly translates as 'a million fools', possibly a reference to the throngs of people in your path as you try to navigate from one end to another. You can find all the Sudanese standards here – various stews and *ful*, fried fish, and some great roast chicken and *agashay*. There are several ice cream and pastry shops for dessert.

At the end of Milion Ghrabi is the covered *souq* selling fruit, vegetables and meat.

KASSALA

You can see Kassala long before you reach it. The strange sugarloaf Taka Mountains rise suddenly out of the pancake flat surroundings, totally dominating the city. Today, Kassala is best known as a destination for Sudanese honeymooners, for the fertility of its fruit orchards and for its lively *souqs*, but it is also the spiritual home of one of Sudan's most important Sufi orders.

The Khatmiyah Sufi order and its ruling al-Mirghani family have been at the heart of Kassala since the early 19th century. During the Turkiya, they forged close ties with Egypt and rejected the rise of the Mahdi and the city had to be taken by force. The Italians (the colonial power in Eritrea) recaptured Kassala from the Khalifa in 1894 with the encouragement of the British, fully four years before the Battle of Omdurman. The British were less pleased in 1940 when the Italians briefly occupied the city again, and quickly sought to restore their 'proper' rule.

Kassala has a very mixed population. The dominant group are the Beja, easily identified by curly hair, and their habit of wearing waistcoats over their short jallabiyas. The colourfully dressed Rashaida live outside the city but visit the markets from their nomad's camps. Fellata – originally migrants from West Africa – are also well represented. More recently arrived is the large population of Eritreans. Many of these settled in Kassala during the Ethiopian civil war, with others arriving during the war between Eritrea and Ethiopia in the late 1990s. It's not uncommon to see signs written in the distinctive Eritrean Tigrinya script as well as in Arabic.

As you enter Kassala you pass over the wide gravel bed of the Gash River. From September to June the river is as dry as a bone and you're more likely find to kids playing football here than any signs of water. It's a misleading impression. As soon as the rains come, the Gash turns into a powerful river. Flash floods happen frequently. In August 2003 the river burst its banks and flooded Kassala almost completely. Thirty people lost their lives and tens of thousands were made homeless. The after effects are still clearly visible, and parts of Kassala have yet to fully recover.

You'll see a lot of soldiers and armed police in Kassala. The city is in a sensitive area close to the Eritrean border, where there has been low-level insurgency since the mid-1990s, albeit on a scale unlikely to affect travellers (see boxed text *The Troubled East*, page 182). For this reason, travel permits are required to stay in Kassala and are rigorously checked by the authorities. Without one you probably won't be allowed off the bus. Once inside Kassala, you are free to wander as you will, but producing a camera near soldiers or loudly questioning the political situation is ill advised.

Getting there and away
Kassala's Souq es-Shabi is 1km off the main road into the city, and has ticket offices for all the main bus companies. On arrival, some buses may just drop you off at the teahouses on the Kassala junction. It's a further 3km into town,

CROSSING THE ETHIOPIAN BORDER
The Sudanese–Ethiopian border at Gallabat offers one of the most straightforward ways of entering or leaving Sudan overland but this involves a couple of days of rough and dusty travelling.

Gallabat is a dusty one-horse outpost (the word town is far too grand) but it once played an important role in Sudanese history. It was here in March 1889 that the Mahdist army fought and beat the Ethiopian forces of Yohannes IV. Over 15,000 men are thought to have been killed, and so many captives taken back to the markets of Omdurman it caused the price of slaves to collapse. It was a pyrrhic victory – the Ethiopian king was killed, but the cream of the Mahdist army was destroyed and the battle essentially marked the end of the expansionist dreams of the Khalifa.

Trucks and *bokasi* travel on an ad hoc basis between Gedaref and Gallabat. The road is a rutted earth track and the journey can take as little as six hours or as many as twelve. In the rainy season the ground turns to thick black mud, making the route difficult for all but the most determined drivers. A trade agreement signed between Sudan and land-locked Ethiopia includes plans to upgrade the road, eventually creating a paved highway that will stretch from Port Sudan to Addis Ababa, but how long this will take is anyone's guess. Many vehicles stop at the halfway village of Doka, where there is both *ful* and fuel.

Immigration procedures on the Sudanese side are quick and easy, although if you are entering you need to register at the same time as being stamped in at a cost of 5,500SD. This must be paid for in local currency and as there are no formal money change facilities, officials are usually happy to let you wander around the *souq* looking for someone willing to sell you dinars. When I crossed this border, I was somewhat improbably told that it was the money changer's holiday that day! The *souq* also has several places with *bokaski* running to the main lot in the centre of Kassala, as well as what may well be the most decrepit taxis in Sudan. Kassala is roughly equidistant from Khartoum and Port Sudan, and all manner of buses and coaches make the run both ways in the early morning, taking about seven hours and costing from 2,000–4,000SD depending on the style of travel. Minibuses leave throughout the day to Gedaref.

The main *boksi* and minibus lot also provides local transport to the village of Khatmiyah at the base of the Taka Mountains. *Bokasi* to Lafa next to the Eritrean border (if it's open) leave on demand from outside the Riyad Hotel – check well in advance if there are any vehicles running. There is no direct transport into Eritrea itself. It's wise to have the actual border listed on your travel permit to reduce potential problems – these are more likely to arise with the periodic closure of the border.

Kassala has an airport 5km out of town on the road from Khartoum, although at the time of going to press Sudan Airways services linking Kassala to the capital were suspended.

serving food and drink. In the event of getting stuck on this side of the border, there is nowhere to stay, but Sudanese hospitality can almost be guaranteed to magic a bed from somewhere.

The border is the small stream separating Gallabat from the Ethiopian border post of Metemma. Immigration procedures are carried out in a thatched mud hut set back from the actual border. From Metemma, it's a 90-minute bus trip to the town of Shihedi, from where you can arrange transport to Gonder. Ethiopian buses have the peculiar habit of always leaving at around 06.00 no matter what the destination is, so you'll end up spending a night in one of Shihedi's cheap hotels next to the bus station. It takes around seven hours to reach Gonder and as the road rises into the Ethiopian highlands you can feel the temperature drop significantly. Those who have found Sudan a little too dry will rejoice when the bus passes the Dashen Brewery as it pulls into Gonder. There is plenty of accommodation in Gonder for all budgets, but if you fancy a treat after some dusty roads, the Circle Hotel has comfy carpeted rooms with hot showers for US$11/14 for a single or twin, and a roof terrace that's ideal for a cold beer. Gonder is two days from Addis Ababa by bus and is also well located for reaching the towns of Bahir Dar, Axum and Lalibela – highlights of any trip to Ethiopia. Ethiopian Airways also runs an extensive domestic schedule connecting Gonder to the rest of the country.

Whichever way you are travelling it is essential to obtain a visa in advance. Until recently the Ethiopian embassy in Khartoum had a frustrating rule that they would only issue visas for travel by air, but this has thankfully been abolished. If you're entering Sudan, Addis Ababa is one of the most agreeable places to get a Sudanese visa, with the necessary stamp issued without hassle in less than 48 hours. A yellow fever certificate is also mandatory.

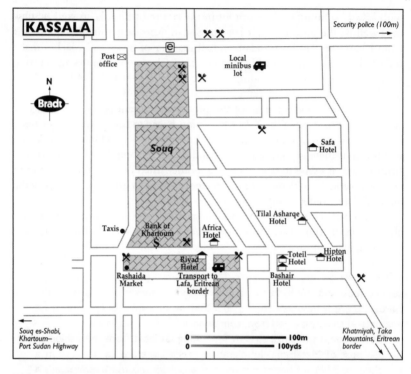

Where to stay and eat

When you're checking in, most hotels will ask to check your travel permit as well as your passport. It's unlikely that you'll actually be asked to register with the security police; at most an officer may arrive at your hotel to take your details. On the last night of my stay in Kassala the manager of the hotel where I was staying decided that he hadn't quite followed procedure and woke me up at midnight to ask me to go and register with the police that instant! After much grumbling, a security officer was summoned who seemed equally confused and aggrieved at being taken from his bed, and he had to be persuaded to note down my details.

The **Hipton Hotel** (tel: 041 22357) is Kassala's best. The lobby is positively plush, marred only by the disconcerting optical illusion painted on the wall opposite the front desk. The rooms are good and clean with satellite TV, and the en suites have water heaters for the shower. There are good views of Kassala and the Taka Mountains from the rooftop restaurant. Rooms are 5,700SD irrespective of single or double occupancy.

A decent mid-range option is the **Safa Hotel** (tel: 041 22711). Rooms here are a little spartan, but there is a choice between en suite and shared bathroom. Rooms start at 3,000SD with shared facilities, or 3,500SD en suite.

If the Safa Hotel is full, there's more of the same at the **Tilal Asharqe Hotel** (tel: 0122 18076); there's precious little to choose between the two.

The cheaper end of the spectrum starts with the **Bashair Hotel**. The rooms are a bit shabby, but shutters keep them cool against the sun. The first floor has a large open area for sitting, next to clean communal showers and toilets. The hotel is a Sudanese rarity in offering genuine singles at 700SD, or 1,200SD for a twin. The **Toteil Hotel** next door offers similar rates.

The **Africa Hotel** is the largest of the *lokanda*-style places, and rooms have wide balconies overlooking the main street. The bathroom facilities are immaculate, and rooms have up to four beds, each costing 1,000SD. The hotel had lots of Eritreans staying there when I visited, possibly attracted by the paint scheme matching their national colours.

The **Riyad Hotel** is just south of the Africa Hotel, next to the stop for buses to the border. The rooms are big and airy and overlook part of the *souq*, but the number of oil drums by the bathrooms may point to a problem with the water supply. Singles and doubles cost 1,000SD and 2,000SD respectively.

The **Hipton Hotel** has a small restaurant on its roof, serving kebabs and the like. There are plenty of the usual *ful* places dotted around town, with several cafeterias lined up along the minibus lot. A nameless but brightly neon-lit restaurant around the corner from the Safa Hotel has good soup and *sheya*.

The tea ladies that are such a common feature of Sudanese towns are less prevalent in Kassala, where men take their turn to serve up the drinks instead. The best stalls are in the heart of the action near the main minibus lot, where a plate of sugary *zalabia* makes the perfect breakfast. There are several rooftop cafés by the lot, serving *jebana* with a *shisha* pipe for a mellow evening. Juice stands line the street along the west side of the lot.

Kassala Souq

The *souqs* of Kassala are some of the most interesting in Sudan. There are several markets throughout the town, selling everything from grapefruit to firewood. One of the main souvenirs that can be picked up here are Beja knives – short scary daggers in leather sheaths. Older Beja men occasionally offer swords for sale as well – they're a metre long with a wide point at the tip of the scabbard. Rashaida jewellery can also be found, and there is a section in the souq catering mainly to Rashaida nomads, with yards of bright material being sold for the manufacture of dresses and shawls.

Kassala is particularly famous for its fruit, and at different times of year stalls almost groan with local produce. Grapefruit, oranges and mangoes are the best of the region, and there are plenty of juice stands offering up thirst-quenching drinks.

Taka Mountains

The granite domes of the Taka Mountains loom large in Kassala, a huge massif seemingly placed at random on the plain, with no consideration for the usual conventions of mountain geography. The shapes are weird, almost unearthly, as if they have been half melted before being set in stone. There are no foothills, just giant boulders and whalebacks of rock – it's ideal for scrambling, and a great place to watch the sunset over Kassala. From such vantage points the hidden greenery of Kassala reveals itself, with its palm trees and fruit orchards. There are four main peaks running from north to south: Mukram, Taka, Toteil and Aweitila.

Several villages are strung out along the foot of the mountains – among them are Khatmiyah, with its mosque (see below), and Toteil, at the southern end of the range. At Toteil there are a number of cafés serving coffee and popcorn. A little higher up there is a well fed by a spring. It's a popular place for Kassala's honeymooners to visit, as the water is said to encourage bridal fertility.

There are baboons in the mountains and several villagers warned me against hyenas, although I'm not sure how likely that is. Snakes may be more of a concern, as the rocks are ideal for basking reptiles; lizards are very common.

From the centre of Kassala, allow a good hour to walk all the way to Toteil, or simply flag down one of the many minibuses heading that way.

Khatmiyah Mosque

This delightful old mosque sits at the base of the Taka Mountains and is the most important centre for the Khatmiyah sufi *tariqa* in Sudan. Mohammed Osman al-Khatm founded the order at the end of the 18th century, bringing it to Sudan from Arabia. The mosque is dedicated to his son, Hassan al al-Mirghani, who did much to spread the Khatmiyah's teachings until his death in 1869. It is believed to have been built on soil brought by al-Khatm from Mecca, making it even more holy. Hassan al-Mirghani's tomb stood on the

THE RASHAIDA

The low goat hair and canvas tents of the Rashaida are a common sight around Kassala. The Rashaida are relative newcomers to Sudan, being an Arab tribe that migrated to the region in the middle of the 19th century. They make their living herding camels, moving their camps and livestock twice a year along the seasonal pastures between Kassala and Gedaref.

The delicate Arab features of the Rashaida immediately mark them out against other Sudanese, but it is their dress that really makes them distinct. The men never wear white *jallabiyas*, preferring pale greys, blues and greens, topped off with a coloured headscarf or *keffiyeh*, and they often wear a curved sword by their side. The swords are more for decoration than anything else, but are wielded with scary vigour during the Rashaida sword dance often performed at weddings. Even small children pick up the blade to take part in this musical duel and if you get the opportunity to see it, don't pass it up.

Rashaida women wear long black dresses enlivened with bright patterns in red and green and covered with a heavy shawl or *burga*. All Rashaida women wear a veil covering their nose and mouth, often edged with fine beadwork. Girls start to wear this covering from the age of eight to protect their modesty at the onset of puberty; it's quite literally a 'virgin's veil' (*mungab*). Facial tattoos are common among Rashaida women. Silver jewellery is both a status symbol and portable wealth for Rashaida women. It can be very fine, and can often be found in Kassala's *souqs*.

site of the original mosque, which was destroyed by the Mahdist Ansar in the 1880s. Visitors come to pray to receive *baraka* (blessings) from the tomb of Hassan, who has been elevated to the position of a *wali* - the closest that Islam comes to a saint.

The mosque is of plain brick, with a pointed octagonal minaret. The main prayer hall is open to the elements, with its arcades of columns. Attached is the domed *ghobba* (tomb) of Hassan. The drum of the dome is similarly open and local tradition has it that when it rains the tomb remains dry.

There is a very peaceful air around the mosque. Women sit at the threshold selling dates and seeds, boys read the Koran in the attached school and there is a regular stream of people arriving to pray, against the low Sufi chant of 'La illaha illallah' ('There is no God but Allah'). During Eid al-Adha, the mosque is packed with people bringing sheep for the ritual sacrifice. Non-Muslim visitors are welcome, but it is polite to ask before entering or taking photos. A more relaxed example of the traditions of Sudanese Islam is hard to imagine.

Behind the mosque, the huge boulders of the mountains are a fine place to watch the proceedings, with their views of Khatmiyah and Kassala. It takes nearly an hour to walk to Khatmiyah from the centre of Kassala following the main road southeast. The minaret is clearly visible from the road – any minibus to the village will also be able to drop you off.

The average Rashaida household owns between 50 and 70 camels. Most are raised for milk, with a smaller number of finer racing camels sold to the Gulf States. Male camels are sent to the Egyptian meat markets. The Rashaida camel (a breed of its own) produces a lot of milk, which, along with sorghum, is central to the Rashaida diet. The milk is converted into butter and a type of dried cheese (*madhur*) that forms a staple in the dry season when milk yields are low. This processing of camel milk is highly unusual in nomads.

The nomadic lifestyle has precluded access to formal education, and the Rashaida are largely illiterate. Unsurprisingly they have a strong oral culture and take great pride in recounting the lineage and pedigrees of their herds over many generations. Illiteracy hasn't harmed the Rashaida's business savvy, either: the Rashaida also live across the Eritrean border, and there is a brisk profit to be made in smuggling, as well as in keeping on the move to avoid taxation. Many Rashaida families have also maintained close links with Saudi Arabia, providing further markets for their livestock.

Regional instability has also benefited the Rashaida. During the Ethiopian civil war they greatly profited from smuggling arms to the Eritrean resistance movement and were able to increase their herds accordingly, further taking advantage of the declining fortunes of the Beja to increase their pasturage. For nomads, the Rashaida are a relatively affluent people.

THE TROUBLED EAST

Security is tight in eastern Sudan and you'll notice a heavy army presence, particularly in Kassala. While the civil war in the south and troubled Darfur are well reported, the political disaffection in the east has been less publicised. As with the other areas, the root of the instability is lack of development and political representation.

The Beja Congress, formed in the 1960s to represent the Beja, was banned in 1989 after the Islamic coup, and took up arms in the early 1990s. They complained about the political marginalisation of the east and an almost complete lack of investment or infrastructure in the area. In 1995 the Beja Congress joined the National Democratic Alliance, an umbrella organisation of opposition groups that includes the SPLA and the Democratic Unionist Party. They received military training at camps in Eritrea and a formal 'eastern front' was opened in 1997.

The NDA/Beja Congress has met with some military successes and has captured and held a 40km strip of land along the Eritrean border 100km north of Kassala. This is sometimes referred to as the Hameshkoreb Area, after the town that has switched between government and rebel control. Lightning raids have even been made on Kassala itself. The rebels insist that they are not interested in independence, but that their grievances be handled with the same vigour as the government negotiations over the south. The fact that the NDA was largely excluded from this peace process has only increased their grievances.

The activity of the NDA/Beja Congress has been a continuing source of rancour between Khartoum and Asmara, as the Eritreans host the headquarters of the NDA (at one time even giving them offices in the closed Sudanese embassy).

For its part, the Sudanese government has provided support for the Eritrean Islamic Jihad Movement, which has carried out a series of attacks in western Eritrea. The irony is that previous Sudanese governments gave logistical support to the now-ruling Eritrean People's Liberation Front in their struggle for independence from Ethiopia.

A small Rashaida rebel group, the Free Lions Forces, has periodically operated independently along the border south of Kassala, but has had little impact on the political process.

In September 2004 the NDA announced that it would disband its military wing to enter into negotiations with the government. At the same time, the Free Lions Forces signed a memorandum of support for the rebel Justice & Equality Movement in Darfur. It is very unlikely, however, that rebel or army activity will impact on your trip, let alone place you in any danger. At most, you are likely to have your travel permits checked rigorously, although it should be noted that periods of instability can lead to closure of the Eritrean border that may force changes in your travel itinerary.

Above Nomads on migration near Tokar, eastern Sudan (MP)

Below Beja nomads, Red Sea Hills, eastern Sudan (MP)

Above Royal Cemetery of Nuri, with Taharqa's Pyramid (PC)

Right Crocodile warning sign on the Nile, Sai Island (PC)

Below Halaib village, eastern Sudan (MP)

Camel racing

The nomadic tribes of Kassala have long held camel races to celebrate weddings and festivals. In recent years there has been some attempt to organise formal competitions around Wadi al-Lasoub, west of Kassala. Gulf Arabs have put up prize money and pick-up trucks for the winners, and use the occasions to buy the best racing camels – the Anafi breed of the Rashaida and the Bisharin of the Beja. The races, which take place on the plains west of Kassala, have become large nomad gatherings, with music and markets.

Getting hold of information about the racing festivals is hard and the dates appear to change frequently. In 2003 a large racing festival was held in June; in 2004 it was in September. If you do manage to get to one of these races, let us know how it went.

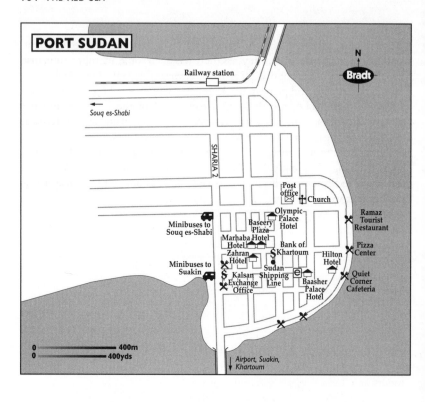

The Red Sea

Sudan has 853km of coastline, stretching along the Red
Sea from Egypt to Eritrea. The land is dry and bare,
isolated by the spine of the Red Sea Hills that run the
length of the coast. It is inhabited mainly by the
nomadic Beja. The country's most important
connection with the outside world – Port Sudan – is
a busy modern port that's barely a hundred years old.
A little further down the coast is the much older port of
Suakin, which has been an important staging point for
traders and pilgrims travelling to Arabia for centuries, and
which is now a crumbling ruin of coral houses.

The reefs and wrecks along the coast offer some of the best scuba diving in
the Red Sea, including the site of Jacques Cousteau's experiment in
underwater living. Sudan's recent isolation means that diving is only now
starting to take off here, and at the moment it's still possible to enjoy many
dive sites virtually to yourself.

A travel permit is required to travel along the highway from Khartoum to
Port Sudan; flying presents no such bureaucratic obstacles.

PORT SUDAN

Sudan's most important sea port is a young upstart compared to ancient
Suakin a little further down the coast. The British founded Port Sudan in 1905
as a replacement for its neighbour. Its deep-water harbour was better suited for
the larger ocean-going vessels cutting through the Suez Canal on the route to
the east.

Port Sudan is hot and humid in the main, with an occasional sea breeze
freshening the air. The town planners built according to the climate and the
majority of older buildings have wide balcony terraces to catch the wind as
much as possible. Even so, the climate is not suited to strenuous activity.
There's a certain torpid air here, and even by Sudanese standards people don't
like to rush about their business.

Scuba diving and the ruins of Suakin are the main draws in Port Sudan.
There's not much in the city itself, but it has an easygoing, relaxing vibe,
and the central market and wide streets of colonial buildings are worth
exploring.

Getting there and away
By air
Port Sudan's airport is 25km out of town on the main road south. There is a daily Sudan Airways flight to Khartoum, and a useful weekly connection to and from Cairo on Saturdays.

By bus
Port Sudan's Souq es-Shabi is 3km out of town and is served by minibuses running from a lot in the centre of the city. Most of the long distance bus companies have offices in the town, between the Zahran Hotel and Sharia 2. It's a good idea to buy tickets in advance as long-distance buses can leave as early as 05.00. The fastest luxury coaches take 14 hours to get to Khartoum (7,800SD) and seven to Kassala (3,900SD), with times increasing as the price and quality lower. Slow buses to Khartoum normally stop overnight at a truck stop – you'll be greeted by people hiring out rope beds for the night for 100SD to sleep under the stars. Buses also run to Atbara on most days (3,500SD).

Minibuses to Suakin leave as soon as they fill up from just outside the Al-Hilal Sports Club on Sharia 2.

By train
There is a weekly train from Port Sudan to Atbara taking roughly 24 hours before it continues on to Khartoum. The service currently leaves Port Sudan on Wednesdays and returns the following Tuesday.

By boat
There are no passenger services out of Port Sudan's docks, which handle freight only. The Sudan Shipping Line has an office selling tickets for the ferry to Jeddah, but this sticks to the time-honoured tradition of sailing from Suakin. For more on this ferry see the boxed text *Sailing to Saudi Arabia* on page 196.

Where to stay
The **Hilton** (tel: 31 39800/39801, fax: 31183; email: reservation.portsudan@ hilton.com) is deservedly Port Sudan's grandest hotel. For a chain hotel it feels surprisingly compact, and the lobby is crowned by a painted glass dome showing the marvels of the Red Sea. Rooms are as comfortable as you would expect, with satellite TV, (non-alcoholic) minibar and internet connections. Prices start at US$125/145 plus 13% tax for a single or twin. The energetic can take advantage of the tennis court, burning off the calories gained at the pâtisserie. There are two further restaurants. The hotel has frequent weekend package offers promoted by its sister hotel in Khartoum.

The **Baasher Palace Hotel** (tel: 031 2334) is an excellent mid-range choice. Rooms come in two categories, normal and luxury, with the only difference between the two being the hot water heater in the bathroom of the luxury rooms. Singles/twins cost 9200/11,000SD or 16,100/17,200SD

THE SUDANESE RED SEA

Formed over five million years ago, the Red Sea is a huge basin running along the fault line between the African and Arabian tectonic plates that's been flooded by the waters of the Indian Ocean. The plates started to move apart around 25 million years ago and the basin has been flooded and dried up several times, resulting in large deposits of salt on the sea bed. Combined with the negligible flushing of water through the Straits of Bab al-Mandab at Yemen, this gives the Red Sea much higher salinity levels than the Indian Ocean (divers will want to compensate for buoyancy when diving). As Africa and Arabia continue to drift apart, the Red Sea is slowly growing, widening by over 1cm per year.

The Red Sea's warm waters and comparative isolation have resulted in a spectacular array of marine fauna. Soft and hard corals thrive to produce wondrous reefs, giving a home to innumerable crustaceans, molluscs, echinoderms, and fish. Blennies, triggerfish, butterflyfish and angelfish live among the coral, with snappers and jacks also forming large schools. Hawkbill and green turtles are often spotted, along with dolphins in open water. Sharks are common in Sudanese waters, with white tip, hammerhead, grey reef and nurse sharks regularly seen.

Along the Sudanese coast, water temperatures average 27–28°C. This is hot enough to reduce the planktonic and algal blooms that are so common further north. As a result the sea is generally clear with visibility of up to 30m not uncommon.

respectively. The hotel has a lovely quiet garden to relax in, with a juice bar and attached restaurant, and it also has its own internet café next door.

The **Baseery Plaza Hotel** (tel: 031 21999) falls halfway between the mid-range and budget categories. Rooms with shower and toilet are 3500SD for single or double occupancy. There's a restaurant attached that's open in the evenings, and wide open balconies to catch any passing breeze.

The **Zahran Hotel** is a popular budget option. The decent-sized rooms are a little basic, but for an en suite they are good value at 1500/2500SD for a single or twin. At ground level there is a terrace that's a popular spot for tea and a *shisha*.

Across the road, the **Marhaba Hotel** is another good choice. Bathroom facilities are shared but clean. A room with three beds costs a flat 2100SD. There are a couple of singles at 1000SD, but as these don't have an overhead fan, you might find the atmosphere a bit stifling when the hot weather sets in.

The **Olympic Palace Hotel** has had good reports from several travellers, but there was no-one there over the several visits I made to the place. It was probably a glorious place 50 years ago but time hasn't been kind and it is now very battered around the edges. A bed with shared bathroom shouldn't cost more than 800SD a head.

Where to eat

If you're after good seafood in Port Sudan, your choices are limited. The **Red Sea Café** at the Hilton is the best option with a variety of freshly caught fish and shellfish starting from US$6 a head. The hotel's **Suakin Restaurant** has an open buffet at US$17.50, or à la carte menu.

The **Baasher Palace Hotel Restaurant** has an eclectic choice of dishes where you can order anything from a club sandwich (1,000SD) to chicken chow mein or jalfrezi (1,750SD), all brought to you by immaculately liveried waiters. The juice bar in the garden is a pleasant place to while away an hour.

The **Baseery Plaza Hotel** also has a restaurant, offering local dishes such as kebabs for a couple of hundred SD. Alternatively, head down to the waterfront near the Hilton where there are several restaurants offering fish dishes, chicken, soup, kebabs and the like. Try the **Ramaz Tourism Restaurant** or the **Quiet Corner Cafeteria**. For a Sudanese take on a western standard, there's **Pizza Center** ('East or West, Center is best').

In the centre of town, there are plenty of *ful* joints near the souq and around the Marhaba Hotel area. On Sharia 2 near the Suakin bus stand there are several open-air barbeque places doing great half chickens with bread and salad for 800SD.

THE BEJA

Living in an arc of land stretching from Kassala along the Red Sea coast to Egypt and out to the Atbara River, the Beja make up around 5% of Sudan's population. They are a Hamitic people, one of Sudan's oldest groups. Their language, Ta Bedawiye, is said to be spoken from the chest (heart) rather than the lips, apparently giving them a more sincere form of communication than their neighbours. There are three main tribal groupings: the Hadendowa, Amarar and Bishariyyin. Across the Eritrean border are the related Beni-Amer.

The Beja were known in antiquity as the Blemmyes, who harried the Kushite kingdom, and as the Bugas, who troubled the borders of Ethiopia's Axum. At the end of the 19th century, the British came up against the Hadendowa – many of whom supported the Mahdi – led by the celebrated leader Osman Digna. Their tenacity and warrior spirit greatly impressed the British soldiers. Rudyard Kipling celebrated them in poetry, christening them the 'Fuzzy-Wuzzies' for their shocks of curly hair, a compliment that sounds decidedly back-handed today. During the Condominium, British officials later complained that the Beja wouldn't turn their hands to work on the railway, declaring that they 'preferred brigandage or robbery to manual labour'.

Small wonder – the Beja are a nomadic people, proud of their camel herds and the open desert. Their tents, shaped like up-turned rowing boats, can be seen along the highway between Kassala and Port Sudan. Family groups are the basic unit of society, forming larger clans of several lineages. As with many nomads, the Beja are religiously influenced by Sufism, in particular the Khatmiyah order in Kassala.

SCUBA DIVING FROM PORT SUDAN

As a dive destination, the Sudanese Red Sea is virtually untouched. At a popular dive site in Egypt you can find yourself sharing the water with up to a hundred other divers; in Sudan there are probably barely that number along the entire coast.

There are two big draws for divers. The first is the chance to follow in the footsteps (or fins) of diving's pioneers. Hans Hass made his name here in the 1950s, and a decade later Jacques Cousteau led his maiden voyage of the *Calypso* here, and carried out his experiments in undersea living near Port Sudan.

The second major attraction is the fish. Nowhere else in the Red Sea can offer the range of big species or fish in such large schools. The numbers are staggering – schools of up to a dozen manta rays, 50 barracuda or over a hundred hammerhead sharks are not uncommon

The only thing that Sudan lacks as a diving destination is a great wreck. In every other respect, the Sudanese Red Sea offers truly world-class diving.

Organised diving in Sudan is still in its infancy. Most dives are carried out from all-inclusive and European-run liveaboard boats, which must generally be booked in advance. A new development is the onshore dive

In recent decades there has been an increased drift toward urbanisation among the Beja. The Bishariyyin, famed for their riding camels, came under pressure from the loss of pasture caused by the Aswan High Dam, and the resulting removal of 50,000 Nubians to Beja land impacted further on pastoral lifestyles. Droughts in the 1980s led to a catastrophic loss of up to 80% of the Beja livestock, and the massive influx of refugees from the Ethiopian civil war merely added to the problems. Further pressure on the Beja has come from the expanding camel herds of the Rashaida, and where they co-exist the Beja now primarily herd cattle and sheep. Many Hadendowa – the proudest of the nomads – have switched to cultivating crops, as they're no longer able to range over the pastures with their herds.

Beja relations with Khartoum have always been prickly. The Beja Congress was formed in 1964 and has variously held seats in parliament or been suppressed by the ruling party. Since the early 1990s the situation has greatly deteriorated. The ruling Islamists banned the Beja Congress and sold swathes of rich agricultural land near Kassala to Gulf Arabs, including a sizeable chunk to Osama Bin Laden, further depriving the Beja of land for grazing and cultivation. Since 1997 the Beja Congress has been involved in low intensity military operations against the Khartoum government.

Despite this, the Beja remember their nomadic heritage. Even where pressures have forced Beja to the towns and cities, you can often see tents set up on their plots of land, making the mud bricks houses look all the more temporary. Don't be surprised if you bump into a Beja in Port Sudan, wearing his sword as he shops in the *souq*.

centre at the Hilton in Port Sudan, run by Emperor Divers and offering dive courses, equipment hire and trips on its day boat. Excessively hot weather means that neither liveaboards or dayboats operate out of Port Sudan in July or August.

With such a pristine environment, divers have a particular responsibility to minimise the impact of their visit, while still enjoying the delights on view. View is the operative word here – never touch anything on the reef or feed the fish. Violent strokes of your fins can damage coral directly, or kick up sand and smother it. Carefully controlling your buoyancy can help reduce the chance of accidentally crashing into the reef. Coral is slow growing and can take years to recover from damage. Your liveaboard should take particular care when anchoring or discharging oil or sewage near a reef.

Operators

Most companies can book connections from Cairo to Port Sudan on the weekly Egypt Air flight and can also arrange your visa, which is generally collected on arrival in Port Sudan (for more information see *Visas* on page 42). When booking, be clear how many dives you expect from the trip – two or three dives a day and a couple of night dives in a week are pretty standard. Liveaboard prices generally start at around US$950 for a seven-day diving trip starting in Port Sudan. Most prices do not include a US$10 tourist tax and marine park fee of US$7 per day for liveaboards.

JACQUES COUSTEAU'S UNDERWATER EXPERIMENT

The reef at Sha'ab Rumi is the site of one of the most intriguing projects carried out under the sea. Jacques Cousteau, pioneer of scuba diving, chose the site for his Conshelf II experiment in underwater living, made famous in his award-winning film, *World Without Sun*.

Naval officer Jacques Cousteau developed the aqualung during the Second World War when he was part of the French Resistance. A devoted spearfisherman, he went on to become a pioneering marine conservationist and advocate of the oceans. As the producer of hugely successful films in the 1960s and '70s, he brought the world beneath the waves to millions from his ship *Calypso*.

Cousteau was fascinated by the possibilities of living underwater. In 1962 he teamed up with George Bond, an American naval doctor who had unsuccessfully been trying to convince the US Navy to fund the building of underwater modules to allow divers to stay beneath the waves for weeks at a time. These would allow greater exploration of the deep as dive times could be extended and the problems of decompression reduced. From this, Conshelf (Continental Shelf Station) was born, 10m down on the Marseilles coast. Its success led to a more ambitious follow up, Conshelf II, sited at the Sha'ab Rumi reef lagoon in the Sudanese Red Sea.

In 1963, the main unit, dubbed the 'starfish house' for its shape, was sunk

If the boat is in harbour it may be possible to join a trip, but don't rely on this. If you do get lucky, you'll still need to have your dive certification and logbook (PADI or equivalent) to join. There are several main liveaboard vessels operating out of Port Sudan and one dayboat, the *Empress Isa*.

MSY *Elegante* Beautiful British registered ketch taking 12 divers.
MV *Baron Noir* French-owned, 22m boat, up to 10 guests.
MV *Freedom* Owner-operated luxury 22m motor yacht, taking 8 guests.
MV *Don Questo* Italian-owned converted research vessel. Takes up to 19 divers, with the only onboard recompression chamber in Sudan.

A list of diving tour operators can be found in the *Planning and Preparation* chapter. **Emperor Divers** (tel/fax: 0311 24815; email: reservations.sudan@ emperordivers.com) operate Sudan's only onshore dive centre in the grounds of the Hilton hotel. They offer full equipment hire and day dives starting from €65/day.

Dive safety
With additional information by Liz Bomford
While Sudan has some truly wonderful underwater opportunities, diving is still in its infancy so some caution is advised. The only hyperbaric chamber in the country is on the Don Questo liveaboard; otherwise the nearest decompression facilities are at Marsa Alam in southern Egypt.

at a depth of 9m, and occupied by five divers for up to a month. A second unit for two people was 27m deep, allowing Cousteau's aquanauts to dive below 100m. The resulting film caught the imagination of a public wrapped up in the space race; here man was exploring a quite different frontier.

Cousteau was never short on ideas for his undersea habitat. At the same time as building Conshelf II he was imagining *Homo aquaticus* – people with surgically grafted artificial gills to allow them to breathe underwater. Conshelf's modules had a helium-rich atmosphere that altered the voice; to compensate for this, he proposed that future 'aquanauts' would speak a type of undersea Esperanto.

Conshelf threw up some interesting discoveries about human physiology. Hair growth was slowed, but wound healing was accelerated. Divers also complained about appetite loss, and perhaps predictably the lack of privacy.

At the end of the experiment, the living quarters were removed and only the submarine garage left behind. Its airtight dome is probably the closest thing to a Holy Grail for modern divers.

While the Conshelf site has been long abandoned to the fish, it has had a huge influence on the diving world and beyond. Its spiritual successor, *Aquarius*, is used by Nasa to train astronauts to help them understand long-term space travel.

If you are going to dive in Sudan you should be an experienced diver, taking responsibility for your own dives. Most dives in Sudan are not suitable for newly qualified PADI open-water divers. It is essential to dive within guidelines and take your own computer so you do not depend blindly on your dive leaders. Do not dive with any outfit that does not carry oxygen on the boat. Make sure you ask about this; your life may depend on it.

Diving in Sudan is not regulated to international standards and operators are not obliged to provide good quality octopus rigs, or to service equipment regularly – or indeed to carry out any of the 'housekeeping' that is required to provide safe diving. Dive operators working from Port Sudan are generally European-run and have good safety records, but you should discuss equipment before booking your dive and, if you can manage it, bring your own equipment. Also make sure that you are conservative with your dive profiles and take an extra long safety stop on ascending.

Dive sites
Abington Reef
Accessible only by liveaboard boat, Abington Reef is known for its manta rays, which congregate in September and October each year. The reef has a so-called 'Christmas cake' formation, with a series of flat shelves on top of a plateau. The top layer of the 'cake' is exposed to the air, making weather conditions critical for a dive here. Most reef species are represented, including large numbers of silvertip sharks.

Sha'ab Rumi South
The reef here is considered to be one of the best in the world. At a depth of 20-30m a wall of coral slopes to the edge of the reef before dropping off to 700m. Just about every species of Red Sea fish and invertebrate can be found here in a crazy profusion of life. Shark sightings are almost guaranteed. Large schools of hammerhead sharks and barracuda are common.

Sha'ab Rumi West – Conshelf II
Less rich in sealife than its southern neighbour, Sha'ab Rumi west makes up for this with its history. A lagoon behind the reef contains the remnants of Jacque Cousteau's Conshelf II (see boxed text *Jacques Cousteau's Underwater Experiment*, page 190). A dive here lets you get in touch with scuba history. The 'starfish' living quarters were removed in 1963, but the submarine garage remains, now totally covered with soft corals. It's still airtight and you can even surface inside the dome's upper section. Also covered with corals are three fish pens nearby, and a shark pen at a depth of 27m.

Sanganeb
The reef at Sanganeb is divided into four main sectors. The north sector attracts huge schools of whitetip and grey reef sharks, hammerheads, barracuda and manta rays, but anchoring on the reef is difficult and it is less frequently visited than Sanganeb East and South. The south has a profusion of

fish to rival Sha'ab Rumi, even surpassing it with its coral. The reef is a sea plateau rising from 800m and carpeted with coral. In the open water, sharks and manta rays abound. Sanganeb also boasts an attractive, British-built lighthouse in grey stone, now manned by the Sudanese navy.

Wingate Reef
The Italian ship *Umbria* sank here in 1940 and it lies on its port side at a maximum depth of 36m (the shallowest point can be explored by snorkel). She was sabotaged by her crew to prevent her being captured by the British; when she went down she was carrying over 300,000 artillery rounds and bombs destined for the Abyssinian campaign, as well as many vehicles. It's Sudan's best wreck. Diving here was pioneered here in 1949 by Hans Hass.

Sha'ab Suadi
Another wreck site, this time enlivened by a spilled cargo of Toyota cars. The *Blue Bell* ran aground in December 1977, and was then pulled over by the tugs sent to rescue her. She lies upside down, making most of the ship inaccessible, but the cars she was carrying have been scattered over the sandy bed at a depth of 15m. Oil leaks have killed of much of the coral, but there are plenty of fish.

SUAKIN
The harbour at Suakin is Sudan's oldest port. Connected to caravan routes from the Nile and deep into west Africa, it owed its prosperity to carrying both heavenly and base cargoes: pilgrims to Mecca and slaves. The town is divided into two sections – the mainland settlement of El Gerf, and the island port of Suakin proper, now linked to the mainland by a causeway. On the island are the remains of a once thriving port, with its houses made of blocks of coral.

Suakin was first used as a port by the New Kingdom Egyptians, who were attracted to the idea of a coastal trade route that sidelined the quarrelsome Nubians along the Nile. For unknown reasons, the port was abandoned by the time of the Romans, and was used little until the process of Arabisation of north Sudan was firmly under way in the Middle Ages. By the time of the Funj in the 16th century Suakin was booming once more, the final African terminus for slaves and pilgrims. As such it was kept firmly under the control of the Ottoman sultans and was ruled from Jeddah. Mohammed Ali wrested it for himself in the 1840s and Egypt formally annexed it in 1865.

During the rise of the Mahdi, Suakin was one of the few places to remain under Egyptian control; it was kept under siege, but was readily garrisoned and supplied by sea by the British. That it held out was no mean feat given that Suakin's most famous son was Osman Digna, a Hadendowa and one-time slave trader who was the most implacable and cunning of the Mahdi's generals.

With the construction of Port Sudan at the start of the 20th century Suakin was largely abandoned. The last government offices were moved out in 1922 and the town has been on the slide ever since.

SUAKIN AND THE HAJ

Before it became a slave port, Suakin was the embarkation point for Muslim pilgrims making the Hajj to Mecca. The caravan routes to Suakin ran along the Atbara river and west from the Nile, increasing in importance with the large scale Muslim conversions in the Funj Kingdom and Darfur Sultanate. This helped tie Sudan into transcontinental trade routes stretching across the southern edge of the Sahara to West Africa.

The pilgrims were called *takarir*. They were mostly poor but devout, and had to work their passage to reach Mecca. During the Condominium there was a shortage of labour on Britain's large-scale agricultural projects, so many pilgrims were encouraged to settle in Sudan. The Fellata, mainly of Hausa and Fulani origin, are among those who settled here.

As it was an important staging post, the Ottomans were keen to keep Suakin under their control. It had two rulers – an Emir appointed by Jeddah helped oversee spiritual matters, while an Aga directly answerable to the Sublime Porte in Istanbul looked after trade and tax. This cosy relationship only came to an end with the rise of Mohammed Ali in Cairo, who went on to threaten Istanbul as well as conquer Sudan, and snatched Suakin for himself.

Despite the abandonment of Suakin for Port Sudan, sailing to Jeddah is still popular in Suakin. Billboards on the edge of town advertise regular sailings; tickets are sold from one-room offices with nothing more than a desk and phone. The town is busiest during the Haj, but a large number of Sudanese travel to Saudi Arabia for work, sending home their remittances. The quarantine and clearing houses on Suakin Island are now in ruins, but this age-old sea passage continues as strongly as ever.

Suakin is mainly a Beja town, although historically many traders from southern Arabia have also settled here. Aside from the ruins on the island, the *souq* is worth exploring. It's an open area of tin and wood shacks that's full of blacksmiths, laundries, teashops, hobbled camels and goats wandering everywhere you look.

Getting there and away

There is a host of minibuses running between Suakin and Port Sudan, costing 250SD and taking little over 30 minutes. Halfway between the two, the Bashair Marine terminal, the head of the pipeline bringing oil from the south of Sudan for export, is clearly visible from the road. Long-distance buses are liable to drop you at the junction of the main highway; it's another 2km to the centre of Suakin.

For more information on the Suakin-Jeddah ferry, see the boxed text *Sailing to Saudi Arabia*, page 196.

Where to stay and eat

For some reason, the authorities don't seem keen on allowing foreigners to stay in Suakin. In spite of my travel permit stating I had permission to be in town, all the hotels I visited were reluctant to show me rooms, and insisted I must sleep in Port Sudan.

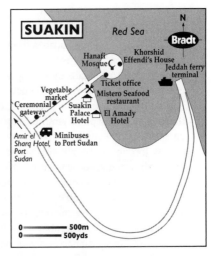

If you have more luck, you might want to try your hand at the **El Amady Hotel** or **Suakin Palace** by the harbour. Both looked a bit scuffed around the edges, fitting into the *lokanda* bracket – expect to pay around 500SD a head. The slightly more upscale **Amir el Sharq** hotel sits at the Suakin junction of the main highway.

The **Amir el Sharq** has a reasonable restaurant offering kebabs and the like, alongside several other cafeterias at the Suakin junction. Next to the causeway leading to Suakin Island is the **Mistero Seafood Restaurant**, where the catch of the day is grilled and served up with bread and a bit of salad. It really gets going later in the day, so if you're hungry for lunch you'll need to eat at the teashops in the *souq – ful* and *adis* is about as exciting as it gets.

Suakin Island

Legend has it that Suakin was once the home of magical spirits: King Solomon imprisoned a djinn on the island. A ship full of Ethiopian maidens was on its way to visit the Queen of Sheba when a storm blew it off course to Suakin. When it finally set sail again, the virginal girls were astonished to discover themselves pregnant, carrying the seed of the supernatural host.

Most of Suakin's visitors were the victims of other, worldlier transgressions. Slaves raided from the southern fringes of the Sudanese state – Bahr al-Ghazal and along the White Nile – were brought here to be shipped to the markets of Jeddah and Cairo. The Funj, Ottomans and Egyptians all prospered from the trade. The first European to record his impressions of Suakin was the explorer John Lewis Burckhardt, who in 1814 found it a place of 'ill-faith, avarice, drunkenness and debauchery'. Around 3,000 slaves annually passed through Suakin, including Burkhardt's own slave whom he sold at the market.

Suakin owed its success to its lagoon location, which was ideal for the shallow draught of Arab ships. A 3km channel was eventually cut through the surrounding reef to improve access. The coral that was dredged up was cut into blocks and used in the construction of the island's buildings. These were then bolstered with wooden pillars and covered with plaster. A causeway was built in 1880 under the orders of General Gordon to link the island to the

SAILING TO SAUDI ARABIA

A novel way of leaving Sudan is to take a ferry to Saudi Arabia to travel on through the Middle East. Ferries run by the Sudan Shipping Line sail from Suakin to Jeddah. By taking one you'll be following the path of countless pilgrims over the centuries.

Getting the paperwork to enter Saudi is easier than it used to be, but there are still hoops to jump through. To apply for a transit visa your passport must contain a visa for onward travel – in most cases this means Jordan. Visas are not issued to females under the age of 40 unless they are accompanied by their husband or brother. If you are married, you'll need your marriage certificate to prove this; if you can't fulfil these criteria you'll need to make other travel plans. In the immediate run-up to the Haj pilgrimage (at Eid al-Adha, currently around the end of December), the Saudi embassy often stops issuing transit visas altogether to concentrate on the needs of pilgrims.

The frequency of ferries varies according to the time of year. For most of the year there is a weekly sailing to Jeddah, but in the two months leading to the Haj ferries run three times a week. The trip takes around 14 hours and the Red Sea is hot and humid.

There are plenty of travel agencies in Khartoum, Port Sudan and along the main road into Suakin that can arrange tickets. The Sudan Shipping Line Travel Agency in Khartoum (Sharia al-Qasr; tel: 779180) has been recommended as particularly helpful. First class cabins cost 26,000SD; second class unreserved is 17,500SD. The ferries can take vehicles, which typically cost around 35,000SD for a car.

Port procedures in Suakin are straightforward. At the gates of the port your tickets and registration stamp are checked. There is a departure tax payable of 1,000SD, with an extra fee of up to 4,000SD if you have a vehicle. Paperwork for the vehicle can take some time before it is put on the manifest. Finally, you complete immigration forms in triplicate and are stamped out of Sudan.

At the end of his trip to Sudan, the traveller Peter Strong enjoyed watching Africa disappear off the stern of the ship and writes: 'There they basked in the fading light, the coral ruins of Suakin with their minarets still standing amid the crumbling stonework. The sun, low in the sky and obscured by the rising dust of a coming storm, was kind to the decaying old city. It could almost have been Venice, sinking slowly into the sea.'

mainland. The town's gate, 1km inland in a straight line from the causeway (and conveniently next to the minibus stand) also dates from this period.

Since the abandonment of the port a hundred years ago, Suakin has been decaying rapidly. The island itself is deserted, and you can have the place pretty much to yourself. Most of the buildings are in terrible shape. One of the best-preserved buildings is Khorshid Effendi's house, on the northeastern side of the island, which was occupied by Kitchener in the run up to his campaign against the Khalifa. The fine wooden *mashrabiya* screens that covered the windows and allowed the female occupants to look out without being observed are long gone, but there is still evidence of the building's fine decorative stucco. The best-preserved buildings are the Hanafi and Shafai Mosques, with their distinctive stubby minarets. They were restored during the Turkiya, but probably date from at least the 16th century. Along the western side of the island is the skeleton of a huge warehouse, a clearing house for both goods and people. Opposite the northern tip is the modern ferry terminal, still re-enacting the pilgrim route to Arabia.

This is one historical site in Sudan that doesn't require a permit to enter, although the authorities manage to make up for this by charging a steep 1,000SD to visit the island. There is a small office at the end of the causeway where you will be asked to buy a ticket.

Erkowit

The hill resort of Erkowit was a popular retreat with the British. Situated high in the Red Sea Hills, it is exposed to the south-east monsoon, giving it a much greener nature than the plains. The vegetation is a mix of Mediterranean and Afro-montaine, with cacti and the spiky-leaved *Draecana* tree being common. At an altitude of around 1,100m, it is pleasantly cool and makes for a good escape from the humidity of the coast; the British dubbed it a 'mist-oasis' for its dominant atmospheric conditions. In December and January rains are frequent. If you are self-sufficient, there are some tempting opportunities for hiking here, with good views over the crumpled hills. Away from Erkowit it is occasionally still possible to see Nubian ibex on the hillsides.

Erkowit isn't as green as it once was, however, and the region has suffered greatly from soil erosion in recent years. Increased agricultural pressure from the resident Hadendowa tribe has degraded the land, with the topsoil frequently washed away in the seasonal rains.

There is no direct transport from Port Sudan to Erkowit. To get there you need to take an hour-long minibus to Sinkat and change there; *bokasi* then run the 30km to Erkowit. Alongside the remains of British bungalows, there is a small **hotel** at Erkowit (catering mainly to honeymooners from Port Sudan) and a small *souq* where it is possible to get food.

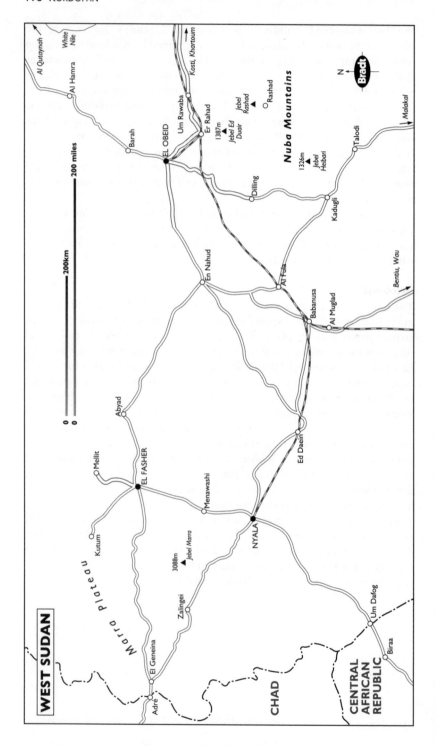

Kordofan

Divided into three provinces – North, South and West – Kordofan is mostly dry and flat, and covered with thorny *heskanit* grass, acacia and baobab trees. It's ideal country for raising camels, and Kordofan is home to many nomadic Arab groups doing just that – the Hamar, Kababish and Rizayqat. The regional centre of El Obeid sits in the middle of this arid land. It was an early rallying point for the Mahdi in the 1880s and still carries those political sympathies. Nowadays it is equally known for its *souq* and the quantities of gum arabic produced in the area.

In South Kordofan is the fertile, hilly country of the Nuba Mountains. The Nuba Mountains also straddle the dividing line between North and South Sudan and many of the political and cultural fault lines between the two have been exposed here during civil war. Culturally diverse, the Nuba were made famous in the West through the photographs of Leni Riefenstahl in the 1960s. It is an area that has been isolated in recent years and is only now beginning to open up to outside visitors. Travel permits are required to visit the Nuba Mountains, but not to visit El Obeid.

EL OBEID

The capital of north Kordofan, El Obeid is a dry and dusty place, and essentially marks the western limit of the tarmac road from Khartoum. After this it's all tracks.

In the 18th century, El Obeid was in the hinterland between the Funj Kingdom and the Darfur Sultanate. As relatively neutral ground it prospered as a market place, and sent great caravans north through Kordofan to Shendi. Slaves were a major export. In 1821 it was incorporated into the Turkiyah and grew to be Sudan's second largest town.

In the early 1880s the Mahdi came to El Obeid to gather support for his revolution. With his star in the ascendant he was able to spark a series of local uprisings against the Turco-Egyptian regime, sapping its strength until he could raise an army. The Ansar laid siege to El Obeid using soldiers actually captured in battle, and in January 1883 El Obeid surrendered, its garrisons throwing their lot in with the Mahdi.

The fall of El Obeid outraged the British, who were pulling the strings of

Egyptian policy from London. An expeditionary army, led by a retired colonel, William Hicks Pasha, was sent to recapture the town. It was an unmitigated disaster. The soldiers were ill provisioned and harried by tribal attacks, and by the time they reached Sheikan, just south of El Obeid, they were out of water and food. The Mahdi's army fell upon them and wiped out the entire column of 10,000 men. Nothing now stood between the Mahdi and the capture of Khartoum.

El Obeid is a good place to stop if you are planning on travelling to the Nuba Mountains or are able to head farther west, but it also has a couple of good attractions itself – a small museum and a slightly incongruous Roman Catholic cathedral. The centre of town is dominated by a sprawling *souq*. Gum arabic is a major regional export, and the huge headquarters of the Gum Arabic Company sit next to the Souq es-Shabi; raw gum is sold just outside.

GUM ARABIC

El Obeid is regularly called 'the gum arabic capital of the world'. This sticky resin is little known, but is an essential ingredient in the manufacture of anything from fizzy drinks to shampoo.

Chemically speaking, gum arabic is a complex mix of water-soluble sugars and glycoproteins. It is produced by the *Acacia senegal* tree as a defence mechanism, and is exuded to reseal the tree's bark after it's been damaged, a process called gummosis. The chemical makeup of the gum makes it an ideal binding agent. It was originally used mainly in ink production, but is now widely incorporated into a variety of confectionery. The sticky foam of marshmallows is created with gum arabic's binding properties, and the syrups of soft drinks use it to stabilize their flavourings. Gum arabic is also used by the pharmaceutical industry as a binder of tablets and pastilles, while herbalists have also used the gum in syrup form to treat coughs and sore throats.

Sudan produces 80% of the world's gum arabic, which is produced primarily in Kordofan and sold through the state monopoly Gum Arabic Company. Gum harvesting usually starts in October. Farmers harvest the acacia trees by slashing the bark to tap the resin. It takes around six weeks for enough resin to be produced, with further collections made every subsequent three weeks. The resin is dried and sold at market or sorted for export. It's graded from 'clean amber' to 'dust' before processing.

After the events of September 11, Sudan's old links to Osama Bin Laden in the 1990s let to a widely circulated rumour that the terrorist had cornered the world gum arabic market, therefore profiting every time a can of cola was sold. During his residence in Sudan, Bin Laden had owned several acacia estates in Blue Nile province but not the production company itself, and he fully divested himself of these when he was expelled from Sudan in 1996.

Although a travel permit isn't required to visit El Obeid, the security police still insist that you register with them on arrival. The unmarked office sits opposite the cathedral. Make sure they give you a chit to give to the manager of the hotel where you're staying.

Getting there and away
By air
El Obeid's airport is 4km from the centre of town and is clearly visible from the main highway to Khartoum. Sudan Airways' erratic schedulers usually plan two flights a week to and from the capital. This service carries on to Nyala but you will need a travel permit to fly to Darfur, an unlikely event at the time of going to press.

By road
A good tarmac road links El Obeid to Khartoum. El Obeid's main bus station is the Souq es-Shabi just north of the town centre, which serves destinations to the east (primarily Kosti and Khartoum). Coaches leave in the early morning to Khartoum's Souq es-Shabi, topping out at 3,900SD for a Saf Saf coach or similar and taking eight hours. All the main bus companies have offices at the station. Buses stop halfway for refreshments at the closest thing Sudan has got to a western-style motorway service station, with decent food and gleaming toilets. (If you have your own vehicle and wish to enjoy these delights, look for the Gadrah petrol station at the Kosti turn-off on the main road. The service station is plastered with Coca Cola adverts.) Minibuses to Kosti leave when they're full; the three-hour trip costs 1,250SD.

For transport to the Nuba Mountains, take a minibus to Salahin Station on the southern outskirts of El Obeid. A mixture of buses and minibuses make the eight-hour trip to the central town of Kadugli at a cost of 2,000SD. Roughly halfway is Dilling, on the edge of the hills (800SD). The road quality deteriorates the further south you travel.

If the situation in Darfur improves, transport to El Fasher and Nyala departs from Nahud Station on the western edge of El Obeid. The tarmac road continues west for around 100km before petering out into sandy tracks. Hardy desert buses and lorries are the order of the day, taking two or three days to reach El Fasher, and up to five to get to Nyala.

If you have your own vehicle and are driving to El Obeid from Khartoum, it's important to follow the left hand road that crosses the train tracks as soon as you pass the airport to take you into the centre of town.

By train
The decrepit train station in El Obeid doesn't see much action these days. There is a branch line in theory linking El Obeid to the line between Nyala and Khartoum. Railway staff couldn't tell me when they thought the next train would arrive or depart; given the situation in Darfur this line is unlikely to be burdened by heavy demand in the near future.

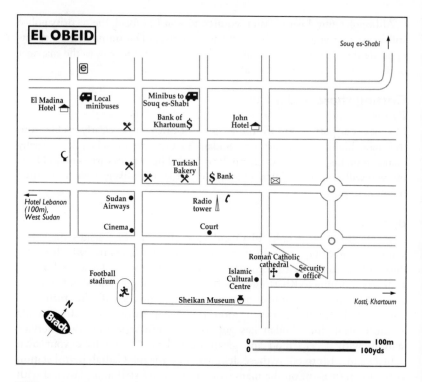

Where to stay and eat

The bright pink exterior of the **John Hotel** (tel: 0611 22282) is an obvious landmark and the inside is just as cheery, with its new paint job and plastic flowers everywhere. The rooms are tidy and the shared showers and toilets are spotless. Singles/twins cost 2,000/3,000SD.

El Madina Hotel is on the opposite side of the central *souq*. Rooms are a little more tatty but still perfectly decent; showers and toilets are bucket-operated. A room with one or two beds costs a flat 1500SD. The hotel is above a courtyard off the main street, which is good for parking if you have a vehicle.

There are several *lokandas* dotted around the side streets to the west of the *souq*; all are equally uninspiring and several are downright dire. The **Hotel Lebanon** is the best of a poor selection, with dreary beds costing 350SD.

For food, the restaurant at the **John Hotel** is the pick of the bunch with its clean tablecloths and places set neatly for dinner. The menu offers a mix of Sudanese and European food, with half a chicken setting you back 1,000SD. Check out its claim to be open 24 hours. If you're not fussed about using cutlery, the central *souq* and its side streets offer a host of cheap eating places. The *batatas* (potatoes with broth) seem particularly tasty here, but all the usual suspects are on offer, with plenty of fresh fruit available on the market stalls. For sticky sweets, head for the **Turkish Bakery** near the Bank of Sudan.

There are quite a lot of Chinese in El Obeid, passing through en route to the oil fields in the south. This may account for the fact that many food shops are unusually well stocked with instant noodles.

What to see
Sheikan Museum
This little museum is tucked away between the football stadium and the cathedral and is well worth a visit. Two large rooms give a general overview of Sudanese history from the Neolithic era to the close of the 19th century.

The first room starts with prehistoric stone tools and offers a handy primer on early Nile culture with a collection of pottery predating Kerma. There are some very Egyptian-inspired *shawabti* figures from Nuri and El Kurru, as well as Napatan amulets.

The second room sees Christian Nubia represented with pots from Faras and Ghazali and has a reproduction of a Faras fresco of the Virgin Mary, but it is more concerned with the Mahdi and the Battle of Sheikan that gives the museum its name. There is a host of weaponry, from spears and flintlocks to a captured machine gun, as well as a lovely patchwork *jibbeh* (Ansar robe) and banner. The real treat, however, has to be the Mahdi's own hairdressing set – comb, razor and mirror – donated by the son of his barber! There is also a small ethnographic exhibition which includes a fine, two-necked wine jar from Kadugli, and some scary Nuba throwing sticks.

Outside in the garden is a series of friezes (made from what looks to be cement moulds) commemorating the Battle of Sheikan. The Madhi's men are impressively resolute and the Egyptians suitably feckless. In the final panel, Hicks Pasha comes to a very sticky end at the point of a Mahdist spear.

The museum is open from 08.00 to 13.00 (closed Fridays). There is no entrance charge.

Roman Catholic cathedral
The cool interior of El Obeid's cathedral provides a stark contrast to the heat and dust outside. After spending any length of time in Sudan, crossing the threshold into somewhere so apparently, well, European, can come as something of a shock.

The cathedral was completed in 1971; El Obeid only received its first bishop nine years earlier. It isn't the biggest cathedral in Sudan (that's said to be in Wau), but it claims to be the most beautiful.

Above the chancel is a painting of the Virgin and Child. It's a very Sudanese scene – the Virgin sits in a desert landscape and is attended by Bishop Daniel Comboni and Sister Josephine Bakhita, both important figures for the Catholic Church in Sudan, and both now elevated to sainthood. Above the Virgin, the four Evangelists are depicted writing the Gospels. The ceiling of the church is brightly painted, with the columns lining the aisle displaying the words 'Hail Mary' in a dozen languages. Above the main door is a beautiful stained glass window.

Visitors are welcomed at the cathedral. The entrance is on the side street; you

ST BAKHITA

In the year 2000, Sister Josephine Bakhita was canonised by Pope John Paul II, becoming Sudan's first saint.

Much of St Bakhita's early life is unknown, including the name given to her at birth. She was born in Darfur, probably in 1869. Aged nine, she was abducted from her village by slavers and taken to the markets of El Obeid. Here she was given the Arabic name Bakhita, meaning 'lucky one'. She was sold to a succession of owners, before being taken to Khartoum and undergoing scarification to underline her status. At the age of 13 she was sold for the fifth and final time, to an Italian trader, Callisto Leganani. In 1884, Leganani fled Khartoum in the face of the Mahdist approach and returned to Italy.

Arriving in Genoa, Bakhita was given to a friend, August Michieli, and she served as a nanny to the family's daughter. She was treated well and accepted as a member of the family. When the family moved to Suakin in 1888, she was given permission to remain in Italy and be schooled by the Canossa Sisters in Venice. It was here that for the first time she heard the word of God, and was baptised as Josephine. When Mrs Michieli returned from Suakin to take Bakhita back to Sudan, she discovered that her slave had been declared free by the authorities, and wanted to join the Sisters as a nun.

Josephine Bakhita never returned to Sudan. She taught and gave lectures, and was renowned for her care of the poor. 'If I was to meet those slave raiders that abducted me and those who tortured me,' she wrote in her biography, 'I'd kneel down to them to kiss their hands, because, if it had not have been for them, I would not have become a Christian and religious woman.' Having served as a nun for fifty years, she died in 1947. Thousands came to pay their respects.

Josephine Bakhita was beatified in 1992 and canonised eight years later. Her saint day is February 8.

may need to knock to get someone to open up. There are two services on Sunday, in the early morning and evening. A building near the gate houses the Justice and Peace offices, which runs political and civil rights workshops and seminars. In the 1990s, the Saudis built a huge Islamic centre opposite the cathedral, its tall minarets making a strong statement to the skyline across the street.

THE NUBA MOUNTAINS

Heading south from El Obeid, the flat plains of Kordofan are suddenly and startlingly interrupted by the broken hilltops of the Nuba Mountains. It's some of the most fertile and picturesque land in the whole of the country, inhabited by the Nuba, a conglomeration of proud, culturally diverse black African farmers. The Nuba Mountains cover around 50,000km², and have an estimated population of 1.5 million people – mostly Nuba but with a significant minority population of Baggara (cattle-raising Arabs). At the geographical centre of Sudan, the Nuba sit neither fully in North or South Sudan, which has made their land a major battleground in the civil war, and as such it has been largely inaccessible for the best part of two decades. As part of the recent moves towards a comprehensive peace agreement, the Nuba Mountains were chosen for a pioneering international monitoring mission to oversee the ceasefire between the government and SPLM/A, a model for the proposed UN monitoring missions throughout southern Sudan.

The Nuba

If Sudan is one of the most ethnically diverse countries in Africa, the Nuba are a reflection of that in microcosm. The Nuba aren't one people as popularly supposed, but many. In the confined area of the 'ninety-nine hills' of the Nuba territory, there are around fifty tribes with their own identity, speaking nearly as many languages. Depending on the tribe, Nuba may variously follow Muslim, Christian or traditional religions, and the social structure may be matrilineal or patrilineal. Despite this Babel of culture, however, it is still possible to point to the common strands that bind together Nuba identity.

Given this diversity it is unsurprising that there is no common history to the origins of the Nuba. Many claim their origins from the remnants of the Nubian kingdoms that broke up with the arrival of Islam in the 14th century. Several Nuba languages belong to the Nubian family (the terms Nuba and Nubia are confusing in the this context, and many Arabs often use the words interchangeably), but linguistic research suggests that the Nuba settlement of the hills probably predates Islam at least in part. Linguistic analysis has been a key tool in unravelling the history of the Nuba. In total there are ten language groups in the mountains. Along with Nubian, other language groups include Daju, originating in the Darfur region, and Kordofanian, the most diverse (and therefore oldest) language group spoken by the Nuba.

It is likely that the Nuba Mountains historically served as an area of retreat for a variety of tribes. The rich agricultural land was attractive to people displaced by larger pastoral groups. From the north, Baggara Arabs pushed black tribes out of the plains to the hills, starting from around the 14th century. To the south, the expansion of the Dink and Nuer since the 18th century probably drove smaller tribes from the Bahr el Ghazal region into the Nuba Mountains. Nuba society has been accordingly fragmented, with society ordered at little more than village level. The one exception to this was the Tegali Kingdom that arose in the northeast Nuba Mountains in the 16th century, converted to Islam, and had relations with the Funj Kingdom. The Tegali Kingdom ended with the invasion of the Nuba Mountains by the Mahdist armies in the 1880s.

As a result, the otherwise disparate Nuba identity has been as much about defining who they are not as who they are. Firstly, the Nuba are defined by their affiliation to their village and tribe and their agricultural lifestyle. Secondly, they define themselves against their neighbours – the arrival of the

Baggara in the Nuba region 200 years ago and their interaction with the Nuba has done much to shape local culture.

The Nuba are primarily farmers. The main crops are sorghum (*dura*), sesame and beans grown in hillside terraces (near farms) or in the clay plains below (far farms). The sorghum is made into a type of porridge, and is also brewed to make *merissa*, a type of beer. Many Nuba also work as labourers on the cotton plantations introduced by the British.

A major figure in Nuba communities is the *Kujur*, or rainmaker, a figure of some importance given the Nubians' dependency on the rains for agriculture. The *Kujur* leads rituals to encourage the rains, which fall between May and September, and plays a prime role in the festivities that accompany the harvest. These festivals (*Sibir*) are celebrated by all the Nuba tribes and are accompanied by music, feasts and wrestling (see boxed text *Sibir*, opposite).

Above anything else, wrestling is central to Nuba identity, a facet most famously shown in George Rodgers' famous 1955 black and white photo of a Nuba wrestler, naked and covered in ash, carried triumphantly on the shoulders of his brother. Together with Leni Reifenstahl's photo studies of the Nuba in the 1960s and 1970s, it has done much to shape perceptions of the Nuba (modern interpretations of the photos are more problematic, suggesting an idealisation of 'the noble savage'). Wrestling matches are held from harvest time until the middle of spring, with villages competing against each other. Messengers are sent out to summon competitors, who arrive decorated with skins and ashes in the wake of the village flag. Praise singers celebrate the wrestlers and taunt their rivals. Wrestlers aim to throw their opponents on their backs under the supervision of a referee. Prizes and money are often given to the victor. Matches are usually held in the afternoons and if there is a good harvest, wrestling bouts may be held daily.

It is often possible to see Nuba wrestling on Fridays in the Haj Yusef district of Khartoum North (see Khartoum chapter, *Nuba wrestling*, page 124).

Less common nowadays is stick fighting, which mainly practised by the Moro Nuba between Kadugli and Talodi. Potentially lethal, the fight is a ritual duel with stick and shield, but is now usually restricted to demonstrations.

Recent history

Geography has lain at the heart of the recent history of the Nuba Mountains, since they sit at the geographical centre of the country, neither in North or South Sudan. For a short while the Nuba Mountains formed a separate province, with its capital at Talodi, and the British even toyed with including it in the South before Arab pressure placed it inside Kordofan. The area was governed by Native Administration, the British method of providing a degree of self-governance while also shielding the area from Arab encroachment. At the same time the British tried to bring the Nuba down from the hills to work on their cotton plantations.

When Native Administration was abolished in the 1970s, the Nuba Mountains came under immediate Arab pressure. Land was sold off to Arab traders and mechanised farmers. As a result, land disputes with the cattle-

SIBIR

Festivals are very important in Nuba culture, and are given the generic name of *Sibir*, which roughly translates as joy or celebration. *Sibirs* can take places at different times throughout the year, but most are held after the harvest is collected in November, as an occasion for villagers to gather together and enjoy the fruits of their labours.

The most popular festival is Sibir al-Nahr, or the Fire *Sibir*, which takes place at harvest time and at the burning of stubble to clear the fields. The *Sibir* is directed by the *Kujur*, or rainmaker, of the village. The start is often announced by the *Kujur* climbing a hill above the village and burning a bundle of sorghum for all to see. Food is prepared in advance, and women brew *merissa*, a beer made from sorghum, to be drunk in great quantities. Goats and cattle are often killed to provide food for guests. The *Kujur* calls the people of the village together to bless their livestock, and provides food at his house for visitors. In the centre of the village a fire is built and green grass burned to ward off the evil eye.

Wrestling and dancing follow the ceremonies. Young women may dance in front of the men of a neighbouring village to taunt them into providing a wrestler to face their champion, and the wrestlers dance to show their prowess before the bout. Music continues into the night.

Each village may hold its own *Sibir*, which is generally used as a gathering for their neighbours. In larger villages, the *Sibir* is also used as a local market, with stalls and food, and loudspeakers for announcements. In the event of a bad harvest, the *Sibir* may be cancelled altogether.

Given the diversity of the Nuba, there are many variations on the *Sibir*. Around Dilling, the Ajunk Nuba hold the Sibir al-Khail (Horse *Sibir*) in September; horses are decorated, fed on milk and porridge, and raced for the pride of the village. Sibir al-Bukhosa, performed north of Kadugli, is named for the dried gourd made into a musical instrument that accompanies the frenzied dancing.

If you are able to visit a village during its *Sibir*, it should be the highlight of any trip to the Nuba Mountains.

---

herding Baggara became more common. Muslim proselytising also increased, convincing many Nuba that the government was set on eradicating their 'backward' culture. Chronically under-developed, the Nuba struggled to organise themselves politically to counter such moves.

The Nuba and the civil war

Disaffection grew into resistance. In the mid-1980s, the government of Sadiq al-Mahdi started arming Arab militias (*murahilin*) to raid Nuba land and confiscate property. As a result, the Nuba reached out to the southern rebels for support. Nuba were recruited by the SPLA and sent to training camps in Ethiopia, igniting a new front in the civil war.

The SPLA quickly took large swathes of the southern and western mountains, and a pattern was set of rainy season offensives against the government forces, with the army replying in the dry season, and destroying entire villages in retaliation. The *murahilin* came on horses to loot, and carried off Nuba children into slavery. Government forces also regularly called in their Antonov bombers for support, which bombed whole areas indiscriminately.

In 1992, the government called a *jihad* in the Nuba Mountains. Despite many Nuba being Muslim they were declared apostates, giving the army a free hand to target the civilian population and even desecrate mosques. The entire region was blockaded and access was denied to the UN's Operation Lifeline Sudan. Many Nuba were moved into government 'Peace Camps', while captured land was sold off to the Khartoum elite. Africa Watch declared the assault, which was largely hidden from the eyes of the world, genocide.

By the late 1990s, the SPLA had recovered much of their lost territory, and the situation on the ground had reached a stalemate. In January 2002, the Burgenstock Agreement was signed in Switzerland between the government and SPLM/A, announcing a ceasefire in the Nuba Mountains – a test case for confidence-building between the two sides in attempts to broker a comprehensive peace deal in Sudan. The agreement set up the internationally run Joint Military Commission, with observers from the government and SPLM/A. The ceasefire has subsequently been renewed every six months, and led to the free movement of people and some semblance of normality in the area. It did not, however, address the Nuba grievances of marginalisation, and the region's status as one of the contested 'Three Areas' caused a major sticking point in the peace talks in Kenya. For the Nuba, not naturally secessionist, the main goal continues to be strong self-rule, whether in the north or south of the country. The peace protocols signed in May 2004 called for significant autonomy for the Nuba Mountains.

Travel in the Nuba Mountains

The Nuba Mountains are just beginning to open up to outside visitors. Permits are required, and at the time of going to press were being issued for Dilling and Kadugli (the provincial capital). Permits are checked rigorously on arrival in the Nuba Mountains area and without one you will be put on the next bus back to El Obeid. You must register in Dilling and Kadugli on arrival. These permits allow some exploration of the villages close by. An alternative route into the mountains may be south from Er-Rahad to Karling, or from Umm Ruwaba to Rashad. No permits were being issued for Kauda, which lies in the SPLM/A-administered zone, although everything can change with political developments.

The Nuba Mountains are green and lush in many places, a mix of hills and rocky crags rising out of the plain. The landscape seems ideal for trekking and scrambling, but there is a clear landmine risk in many parts of the regions. The

UN Mine Action Service has made road-clearing a priority and is being assisted by government and SPLA forces. The banks of irrigation channels, unused paths, and the areas around abandoned garrisons are all strong contenders for being unsafe areas. Stick to well-worn paths where the locals walk and always remember that mines are laid to be invisible.

Travel as far as Kadugli is straightforward, but transport options seriously decrease once you head into the mountains, with only occasional buses and *souq* lorries running between the villages. It's simply a case of taking whatever is heading in your direction. From June to September, rains make travel a lot harder. The whole region would be a joy to travel by bicycle, and indeed bikes are the primary mode of transport once you get off the main road. In Dilling and Kadugli it's not hard to find someone willing to rent a bike for the day for a couple of hundred dinars. With a larger budget you can hire a motorbike for the day (riding pillion) for around 13,000SD.

Nuba villages, with their neatly tended fields and thatched mud huts (*jutiya*), are very picturesque, but they are also poor. Sudanese hospitality means that you may be offered tea or food, so make sure you do not take advantage of your hosts. Small gifts of coffee or sugar are appropriate as practical tokens of your gratitude. Visitors to an area that has been isolated for so long have a special responsibility to ensure that they treat their hosts with particular respect and leave good impressions behind them.

Accommodation options are limited, with a couple of *lokandas* in Dilling and Kadugli. In the villages there is no formal accommodation, although you may be offered space for the night in a *jutiya*. The Nuba Mountains are one place in Sudan where I'd venture that having a tent might be a worthwhile investment.

In theory, a comprehensive peace deal may eventually open the road south from Kadugli, allowing travel through Talodi to Malakal, and possibly even to Bentiu and on to Wau. Travel on both of these roads would certainly only be feasible in the dry season.

Dilling

The quickest way into the Nuba Mountains is through Dilling. The town is surrounded by the craggy hills that mark the start of the Nuba Mountains. It's well watered and, if you have come from El Obeid, surprisingly green. Dilling isn't a big town but it has a small university, and students may approach you to practice their English. There's not much else in the town, which is best used as a base to explore neighbouring Nuba villages.

The **Lokanda Ar-Rahman** has beds for 300SD a night. Several buses a day leave for El Obeid (three hours away, 800SD), and to Kadugli (four hours, 1,000SD).

Kadugli

South Kordofan's capital is a medium-sized town, and the base for many aid agencies working with the Nuba. Kadugli has a lively traditional *souq*, but much of the town is still showing the scars of civil war. The hills above the football stadium give good views of the town and surrounding area.

The headquarters of the JMC are in the village of Tillo just outside Kadugli. They run a small café as a community project that's open to visitors.

The **South Kordofan Lokanda** offers simple accommodation for 300SD a night. Kadugli is eight hours from El Obeid, with a mix of minibuses and rickety coaches costing around 2000SD. The road between Kadugli and Dilling is poor but particularly scenic, with plenty of trees and greenery before it crosses the plains of Kordofan proper. Three times a week there is a early morning bus to Khartoum which takes around 17 hours.

BABANUSA

Sat virtually inside Darfur, Babanusa is a sandy, medium-sized railway town. Originally a small Arab market, it grew in the 1960s with the opening of a branch line to Wau in Bahr al Ghazal. Meant to open access to South Sudan, the line was repeatedly attacked by the SPLM/A during the civil war, suspending the train service. Throughout the 1990s, the only trains running on this line carried military supplies to the government garrison in Wau. These trains gained a terrible reputation as they were often accompanied by *murahilin* outriders of the Popular Defence Force, who raided Dinka villages along the way, abducting women and children into slavery.

The end of the war in the south has finally brought calm, potentially reopening old transport routes, although it will be some time before these are fully viable. The railway line for the old 'Wau Express' has been damaged beyond repair – a survey in 2004 reported destroyed bridges and over 140km of missing track. A few trucks reportedly use this route, although there is a landmine threat along stretches of the line. Even if cleared, this route would be flooded and thus impassable by vehicle in the wet summer months.

Darfur

13

In Sudan's far west, Darfur is an area roughly the size of France, covering three provinces and touching Libya in the north and stretching south along the borders of Chad and Central African Republic. It is a region of staggering emptiness, of sahel and *qoz* (rolling sand dunes) – a harsh environment in which to make a living. The exception is the central Jebel Marra region, a volcanic mountain range which is well watered and fertile. Despite this, Darfur is no less ethnically diverse than the rest of Sudan. Exclusively Muslim, it is a mixed population of Arabs and Black Africans, although these definitions are often more fluid than is often supposed. Arab nomads such as the Hamar, Rizayqat and Kababish herd camels, others herd cattle, and African tribes including the Fur and Masalit are sedentary farmers.

In 2004, Darfur became less known for its deserts and people than for its appalling war, carried out across its wide plains, with killings, refugee flight and depopulation occurring on a massive scale, and accusations of ethnic cleansing and even genocide being thrown at the Sudanese government. Just at the point of the signing of a historic peace deal between the government and SPLM/A to end the war in the south, Darfur became the biggest humanitarian crisis in Africa. Typically described as a straightforward Arab-Black conflict, the reality (as is often the case in Sudan) was invariably far more complex. At the time of going to press, there was no immediate prospect of a solution to the Darfur crisis, and its people were continuing to suffer.

A WARNING

Due to the ongoing Darfur crisis, it was impossible to visit the region in the course of researching this book. Simply put, the area is presently a war zone, where even humanitarian access for the UN has been restricted. The Chad border, a traditional entry point to Sudan for overlanders, is not only closed but also host to nearly 200,000 refugees who have fled the fighting. In the current climate, attempting to travel to Darfur would be foolish in the extreme. At the very least, travel permits are not being issued, and any foreigners found in the area without permission are likely to be expelled or arrested.

In the hope of a resolution to the crisis, some basic travel information is presented below. If, during the lifetime of this edition, it becomes possible to visit Darfur, it should be borne in mind that reconstruction rather than tourism is likely to be the first priority for the region. Even if appropriate action is taken by the Sudanese government, reigning in the mobile and independent-minded *janjawid* is likely to be difficult, so banditry, a perennial Darfurian problem even before the current war, will probably continue in some form, making overland travel risky. With the region having undergone rapid depopulation and destruction, infrastructure is likely to be over-stretched in the towns and non-existent outside them.

BACKGROUND

The history of Darfur is essentially that of the struggle between the settled farmer and the nomad. At the beginning of the 17th century Suleiman Solongdungo founded a Fur kingdom around Jebel Marra. The non-Arab Fur were primarily farmers, but they were also known as powerful horsemen. Adopting Islam as their state religion, their power base grew rapidly. The Keira Dynasty – more usually referred to as the Fur Sultanate – was not ethnically exclusive, and the ruling elite was drawn from all of Darfur's major tribes. From their capital at El Fasher they controlled the lucrative slave trade, raiding the non-Muslim black tribes to the south and sending them north to Egypt along the Forty Days Road. The major threat to the Fur Sultanate was the constant encroachment of nomads, such as the camel herding Zaghawa and the cattle herding Arab tribes of the Baggara, as well as the Funj Kingdom on the fringes of Kordofan to the east.

The Fur Sultanate continued to hold sway even after the arrival of the Turco-Egyptians. It wasn't until 1874 that the infamous slaver Zubeir Pasha sent an army into Darfur and overthrew the sultan, presenting the territory to the Egyptian Khedive. Seven years later, Darfur was invaded again, this time to be 'pacified' by the armies of the Mahdi. Darfur's governor, the Austrian Rudolf Slatin Pasha, became the most celebrated of the Mahdi's European hostages.

After the Battle of Omdurman, Ali Dinar restored the sultanate and with tacit British approval ruled from El Fasher, from where he proved adept at controlling nomad raids and maintaining order. At the outbreak of World War I, however, Ali Dinar raised his standard in support of the Ottomans and the British were forced to act. An expeditionary force was sent against him, and in November 1916 he was run to ground by two planes from the proto-Royal Air Force. Ali Dinar was shot from the air and his body recovered with a bullet hole 'neatly drilled through his forehead', or at least that's the way the British told the story.

Under the Condominium, Darfur was run by Native Administration with the help of just a handful of British officials. Things didn't improve much at independence, with the region looked on from Khartoum as too distant to be invested in or developed.

Roots of conflict

To understand the current crisis we need to go back to the 1970s. On the edge of the Libyan Desert, northern Darfur has been undergoing a slow process of desertification for generations. In the 1970s and early 1980s a series of repeated droughts and localised famines caused the nomadic tribes of the north, primarily Arab, but also the black Zaghawa, to move south to seek water and pasture for their herds. This brought them into inevitable conflict with the Fur and Masalit farmers in Darfur's fertile central zone.

In many ways, this was merely another chapter in the long history of discord between the nomadic and settled communities. It also happened to coincide with the abolition of Native Administration in Sudan, which removed the traditional forms of conflict resolution. As a result, simple disputes turned into full-blown fights over resources. As drought continued it became clear the nomads' move south was becoming permanent.

From the start of the 1980s, successive governments became increasingly Islamist in outlook. The Fur had traditionally been supporters of the Mahdist strand of Sudanese politics, but Khartoum began to associate Islamism with Arabism. Having dominated Darfur since the days of the Sultanate, the Fur found themselves politically marginalised in favour of the minority Arab tribes. For the first time, disputes began to take on an ethnic dimension.

Sadiq al-Mahdi's government threw its lot in with the nomadic Arabs. In 1987 a group of Darfurian leaders calling themselves the Arab Gathering demanded an increased Arab hand in ruling Darfur and played a part in encouraging disputes between the non-Arab tribes (given the dismissive title *zurq*, or black) to keep them politically weak. To hide their own ambitions, it was even claimed that the African farmers were planning to expand into nomad territory, threatening the Arab camel and cattle herds. Sadiq responded by arming the Arab nomads and the Baggara in southern Darfur, encouraging them to raid farms and villages.

Ironically, at the same time the Sudanese government was shipping arms to Chad in support of the Zaghawa-dominated government, then in the throes of a civil war of its own – against Arab tribes funded by Libya. This war frequently spilled across the border into Darfur, adding another layer of confusion to the political situation there, and another level of suffering for its people.

From 1987-89, a low-intensity war raged between the Arabs and the Fur. The Fur raised their own militia to fight against the horse and camel-mounted Arab raiders, generically called the *janjawid*. Over 2500 Fur and 500 Arabs were killed, with tens of thousands of head of livestock lost and hundreds of villages burned. The conflict was almost completely ignored by the West.

The seizure of power by the National Islamic Front in 1989 did nothing to change the situation in Darfur. The arming of Arab militia was legitimised through the Popular Defence Force Act and the government increased its reliance on these proxies throughout the west as well as in the civil war to the south. The SPLA made a short-lived attempt to open a new front in Darfur in 1991, but was hampered by long supply lines and internal division.

Division was also on the cards in Darfur. In a move to further undermine the Fur, their heartland around Jebel Marra was parcelled up and split between the newly formed provinces of North, South and West Darfur in 1994. A year

DARFUR'S ETHNIC MIX

The human map of Darfur is a complex one. It has three main ethnic zones, but contains over 30 tribes or groups in its population of four million. At the simplest level, groups can be divided into nomad and sedentary farmers, Arab and non-Arab. The majority of non-Arabs are Nilo-Saharan, with the most prominent groups being the Fur, Masalit and Zaghawa. The communal labels of 'African' or 'black' which they use to describe themselves are relatively recent innovations, and these labels are promoted by the SLA and JEM.

Lifestyle has traditionally played as important a part in identity as ethnicity. For example, a Masalit who accumulated a large number of cattle would effectively become a Baggara, and in just a few generations would be classed as an Arab, even gaining an Arab lineage to back it up. As a result, it can often be hard to physically distinguish between someone describing themselves as 'Arab' or 'African'.

Darfur is wholly Muslim, but the area's isolation has also meant the retention of many traditional religious beliefs, such as witchcraft and the importance of the evil eye.

The largest and traditionally the most powerful group in the region are the Fur. Their homeland, or Dar, is based in the fertile Jebel Marra mountain range, which gave rise to the Fur Sultanate and which gave its name to the entire region. The Fur are farmers, growing millet and potatoes. The Mediterranean climate around Jebel Marra lends itself well to cash crops such as sugar cane and tobacco, as well as a wide variety of fruit. The lowland Fur also raise cattle and until recently have maintained close relations with their Baggara Arab neighbours.

later, the Masalit homeland was similarly broken up, with the plum administrative positions given to Arabs. This provoked the three-year Arab-Masalit war, another dirty guerrilla fight that resulted in hundreds of deaths, torched villages and streams of refugees fleeing into neighbouring Chad. Like the Fur-Arab conflagration before it, this little corner of anarchy went largely unnoticed in the West.

Arab-Masalit fighting broke out again in 1999, and over 125 Masalit villages were burned before a peace conference agreed compensation and placed safeguards on nomad herd movements and water access. Set against these gains was a continued government programme to harass and disenfranchise Darfur's black African population.

Darfur in crisis

The picture began to change in early 2003 with the appearance of two Darfurian rebel groups, the Sudan Liberation Army (SLA) and the Justice and Equality Movement (JEM). Their platforms reflected the grievances of the populations they were drawn from – primarily Fur, Masalit and Zaghawa –

The Masalit are also farmers, on both sides of the Darfur–Chad border, with their Dar centred on the border town of El Geneina, the site of their historic sultanate. The Masalit have often sought to expand into Fur territory, leading to violent clashes between the groups. Polygamy is common among the Masalit but women maintain a strong degree of freedom. Wives own and maintain their own fields, giving them economic independence. After marriage, the husband lives with his bride's family and tends his mother-in-law's fields, only moving out after the birth of the first child. Divorces are common.

The Zaghawa are non-Arab semi-nomads, probably originating from the Tibesti Mountain region of Chad and Libya. Dar Zaghawa is the plateau straddling the border between North Darfur and Chad. Their herds are a mixture of camels, cattle and sheep, with the women cultivating millet and other crops. Wild grains and tubers are also gathered where conditions restrict agriculture. The Zaghawa have traditionally raided Arab tribes for camels.

Darfur's Arabs are overwhelmingly nomadic, and are found on either side of Darfur's central agricultural belt. Arabs are collectively known as either *abbala* (camel-raising) or *baggara* (cattle-raising). The Baggara are the original Arab expansionists, having spread from the Nile bringing Islam to the region. Their herds mark the southern borders of the Arab world, with further progression halted by tsetse flies and (to the east) the boundaries of the Sudd. In South Darfur, the Arab tribes comprise the Rizayqat and Messeriyya. In the North they comprise the Kababish, Bani Halba and Bani Hussein.

Other groups in Darfur include the sedentary Jabal and Tungur, and the nomadic Berti and Bedayat.

and the need for political representation, development and security. The SLA took a more secular approach, with the JEM espousing moderately Islamist credentials, including the guiding hand of a defecting government minister. As with other marginalised groups, they felt excluded from the government's peace process with the SPLM/A, which ignored other deeply rooted problems across Sudan. Armed rebellion was their response.

Initially the SLA was the most active group. Mainly Fur and Masalit, it launched well-co-ordinated attacks in February 2003, followed by an audacious assault on El Fasher, North Darfur's largest town, two months later, occupying the airport and capturing a government armoury. In May it briefly occupied Mellit, an important town on the trade route to Libya. The largely Zaghawa JEM joined in these later attacks.

The early military successes of the rebels reaped a whirlwind of retribution from the Sudanese government. For the first time the Sudanese army was fully deployed in the region. As well as the regular army, the government used helicopter gunships and Antonov bombers in North Darfur, with no attempt to discriminate between rebels and civilians.

The *janjawid* were also given free reign to ride against the civilian population. Their ranks were swelled by criminals specially released from jail for the purpose – the *ta'ibeen*, or 'those who have repented'. Food stocks were looted, women systematically raped, even mosques and Korans burned. With fighting also disrupting the planting season, subsequent food insecurity became inevitable. The first signs of mass population flight were visible by June. The phrase 'ethnic cleansing' began to rear its head.

Chad has played a muddled role in the escalation of the crisis, as it shares

JEBEL MARRA

Written with contributions from David Else

The Marra plateau in central Darfur covers an area of over 12,000km², reaching from the Tabago Hills north of El Fasher to the Tebella Plateau south of Zalingei, near the Chad border. The heart of the plateau is between Nyala and Zalingei, at the 3,088m peak of Jebel Marra, Sudan's second highest mountain. Surrounded by rolling hills, it's the homeland of the Fur, who keep terraced farms and orchards, and raise their herds here. In happier times, Jebel Marra could offer the best trekking in Sudan.

The plateau is classified as Montane Woodland, with dry woods surrounded by Sahel. Jebel Marra itself is well watered, receiving up to 1,000mm of rain a year, most of it falling between May and September. The lower slopes are secondary grassland, with terraces as high as 2,600m. There has been much deforestation to clear land for farming and fuel, but the upper slopes are more heavily wooded.

Until the middle of the last century, game was relatively common in the Jebel Marra region. Greater kudu and scimitar-horned oryx were the largest antelope represented, and there was also a small (but now long-gone) lion population. Baboons still live on the higher slopes and dorcas gazelle are sometimes spotted lower down. The closest Jebel Marra gets to a prize mammal are the Burton's and hairy-footed gerbils, both endemic to the area and critically endangered.

Among the birdlife sightings, Nubian buzzards and black vultures are common, with the most widespread species being the African collared dove. The rusty lark is a near-endemic.

Jebel Marra is an extinct volcano, with a huge crater, or *caldera*, formed by the collapse of its cone. At its centre is a large lake, and a smaller secondary crater that is also full of water and that's known as 'the eye of Jebel Marra'. The two lakes (*deriba* in Fur) are ascribed genders, and the local Fur tell stories about the supernatural powers of the smaller, female lake. Some say that any bird flying over it will be sucked down into its bottomless depths or that it is inhabited by spirits, although herders seem happy enough to graze their goats on its shores.

The nearest large town to Jebel Marra is Nyala. You may require a permit from the secuirty police to travel to the plateau; for the forseeable much of the same ethnic mix as Darfur. President Idriss Déby initially replied to a call for assistance from the Sudanese government by sending troops and helicopters to take part in attacks against the SLA and JEM, despite his Zaghawa roots. While Déby relies on the Sudanese for support in his own unstable country, Chad's military and political elite is also Zaghawa and has covertly given support to Darfur's rebels.

In September 2003, Déby managed to convene meetings between the government and SLA in Chad that resulted in a ceasefire, despite a JEM

---

future the Sudanese authorities are likely to be wary of letting foreigners wander around unaccounted for.

The old trekking route to the Jebel Marra crater started at Neretiti, a small town halfway between Nyala and Zalingei. From here it was possible to buy supplies and even arrange a guide (or pack donkey) if needed. The route heads straight for Jebel Marra, with a half-day walk to the village of Queila (called Karonga on some maps), where there is a pretty waterfall in a valley and good potential for camping. The path continues through a canyon up the side of Jebel Marra, passing hot springs along the way. The climb is steep and sometimes indistinct among the rocks. Ahead is the flat-topped peak of Jebel Idwa, Marra's northern twin. At the top, the path follows the rim of Jebel Marra, offering spectacular views of the crater itself and the surrounding area. The descent is tricky and the path completes nearly half a circuit of the rim before a gap allows passage back down. The green crater bottom provides a stark contrast to the rocky walls of the crater. It is possible to camp in the crater, but the lakes are sulphurous and fresh water springs are tricky to find. With an early start, one can reach the crater from Quaila and return – or continue descending the opposite side of Jebel Marra – in one day. The village on the eastern slopes of the mountain, Tarantonga, used to have a weekly market on Saturday, with trucks running to Nyala. Attempting this in the opposite direction, it may be possible to hire a guide in Tarantonga.

For a longer trek, there are plenty of options in the open country. One possible route could be to approach Jebel Marra from further east, starting in Menawashi (on the Nyala-El Fasher road) and spending several days walking in the rolling hills on the lower slopes of the plateau. The village of Gollol, a day's walk south of Jebel Marra, was also popular for its waterfalls.

The 1:250,000 Sudan Survey Maps available in Khartoum are the best available, but given their age they should not be relied upon totally. The central part of the plateau is covered by four sheets, but Sheet ND35 covers most of Jebel Marra itself. A compass is essential, as are waterproofs in the rainy season. Nights are cold throughout the year, so warm clothing and a sleeping bag are also a must. It is best to be as self-sufficient as possible regarding food, so stock up in Nyala as there is little on offer in the villages around Jebel Marra.

boycott and the continuing plunder of the *janjawid*. The tentative peace process broke down within three months amid mutual recriminations. With its attention focused on the prospects of a peace deal in southern Sudan, the West largely held its tongue.

At the start of 2004 the situation in Darfur was seriously deteriorating. Government bombing increased, causing thousands more refugees to flee into Chad. In North Darfur, an estimated 60% of villages were reported burned by joint government/*janjawid* operations, with wells destroyed and orchards cut down. The *janjawid* even started to mount raids into Chad. In February 2004, after sustained fighting, the government proclaimed an end to the war, in the face of all the available evidence, and the SLA and JEM boycotted Bashir's proposed peace conference. Humanitarian access to Darfur was repeatedly blocked.

In April, international pressure led to another attempted peace process, again under the auspices of a confused Chadian government. The ceasefire it produced was repeatedly violated, and of small hope to the million refugees the conflict had produced. It was hoped that the signing of the peace deal between the government and SPLM/A would finally allow attention to switch to Darfur, but the prospects for its inhabitants continued to look bleak. Increasing international pressure led to the sending of African Union monitors, with the Sudanese government reluctantly accepting the deployment of AU troops to observe a repeatedly broken ceasefire. The government has given repeated commitments to disarm the *janjawid*, but with little follow-up action. For their part, the rebel groups have equally frustrated relief efforts, even kidnapping aid workers. In September 2004 the US government declared the actions of the *janjawid* to be genocide. Although other nations were reluctant to follow suit, a UN Security Council resolution was passed urging the Sudanese government to take immediate action to halt attacks on civilians and threatening sanctions, although Chinese interests in Sudanese oil made this threat unlikely to be carried out with great effect. In late 2004, AU-sponsored peace talks in Abuja ground on, with few signs of an imminent breakthrough. With deaths from malnutrition and disease still mounting and international efforts to solve the causes of the conflict largely ineffectual, at the time of going to press Darfur remained Africa's worst humanitarian crisis.

TRAVEL IN DARFUR
With route notes provided by Andi Petic and Grant Hastie of Oasis Overland
It is not currently possible to travel in Darfur. Travel permits are no longer issued from Khartoum and the Chad border has been firmly closed since the second half of 2003. Darfur is likely to remain dangerous for the immediate future. If travel does become possible during the lifetime of this book, please refer to the warning given at the beginning of this chapter and check up-to-date sources of information – news, government advisories and even other travellers – before travelling. The routes below are presented in a west–east direction, as the majority of travellers previously passing through Darfur have

done so from Chad en route to Khartoum as part of a larger overland trip.

Roads in Darfur are extremely poor and often entirely non-existent, making driving through the bush a necessity. The available maps such as the ITMB Sudan map or the Michelin 954 North East Africa sheet should not be relied upon to give accurate road gradings. There are some sealed roads around Nyala, but the majority of roads are just dirt trails, ranging from heavily rutted tracks to gravel and sand. If you have your own vehicle, carry as much fuel and water as possible. Sand mats are absolutely essential as getting stuck in the sand is very common. Public transport is similarly rugged. Trucks are a common way of getting around, as are the tough desert buses used in the north of the country. Travel times are slow and stops are frequent – speeds of over 20km/h are more of an aspiration than the norm.

Travellers are usually required to register with the police on entering any town, irrespective of whether they plan to stay or not, an understandable measure given the chronic security problems. This is often carried out at police checks on the edge of town. There should be no charge for this, except for the security registration in El Geneina required on arrival from Chad.

If you are entering Sudan from Chad there is a Sudanese consulate in Abeché, 100km before the border. Although they do not issue visas, they have regularly been reported by travellers as being friendly, and they can advise on the current status of the border and the security situation in Darfur.

From the Chadian border post of Adré it's a short drive to El Geneina, where there is a large police compound on the edge of town for immigration, customs and registration. After El Geneina the main road heads south to Zalingei and the regional capital Nyala. The direct route to El Fasher is little used due to its poor quality, and even before 2003 was notorious for its bandits. The road to Zalingei is a dirt track, with very broken tarmac appearing between Zalingei and Nyala.

Given its isolation, Nyala has all the facilities of a large town – tarmac roads, banks, markets, a hospital and plenty of motor repair shops for vehicles that have taken a battering on Darfur's backroads. Nyala is also the railhead for a fortnightly service to Khartoum.

There are two options from Nyala. Heading north, there is a decent road to El Fasher with good tar until almost halfway. After El Fasher, sandy and rutted tracks continue to En Nahud, which has a decent market. The other route from Nyala heads southeast to Ed Daein.The track consists of very soft sand and the easiest way to proceed is to follow the railway tracks. From Ed Daein you can either continue alongside the railway to Babanusa (see the Kordofan chapter, page 210) before turning north to En Nahud, or go northeast along the track heading for the same town. Both routes are equally sandy and difficult.

After En Nahud, the tracks continue east, before eventually turning into a good gravel road. Tarmac finally appears soon after this, about 100km west of El Obeid. From here smooth roads lead all the way to Khartoum.

Due to the extremely poor (and often non-existent) roads in Darfur, travel between July and September is incredibly difficult due to the rains. Vehicles frequently get bogged down and make the slowest progress. You can count on

THE FORTY DAYS ROAD

The Darb al-Arba'in, or Forty Days Road, was one of the greatest of desert trade routes. Driven by camels and the profits from the slave trade, it made the Fur Sultanate rich.

Africans kidnapped from Bahr el Ghazal were brought to the markets of Kobbay, just north of El Fasher, where the great caravans would assemble. Most caravans comprised about a thousand slaves, with twice that number of camels, although one source hints at a staggering 24,000 animals. As well as slaves, merchants would take rhino horns, ostrich feathers and gum arabic, and were usually accompanied by brave Muslim pilgrims.

From Kobbay it was over 400km to the wells at El Atrun. With no escape in the desert, slaves walked unshackled, and were fed a paste of millet flour to conserve food and water. Caravans typically set off in the height of summer to avoid the cold pneumonia-inducing nights that would otherwise ravage the human cargo. Many died nonetheless from heat and exhaustion. After El Atrun were the bandit-infested lands en route to Selima Oasis, and finally the Egyptian border at Kharga. To save on taxes, slave children were often hidden in empty water skins. The total journey could take several months; the caravan's name probably derives from the forty or so marching stretches of the journey, which were interspersed with rest and grazing for the camels.

George Browne was the first European to visit Darfur in 1793, which he did by following the caravan on its southern return journey. So many camels perished on this trip that the Arabs had to bury their merchandise to recover it at a later date.

British pressure on Egypt's involvement in the slave trade put an end to the Forty Days Road, and the country's southern borders were patrolled throughout the 1880s to keep the Mahdist threat at bay. When the caravans eventually restarted, the camels that enabled the slave trade were now the valuable commodities themselves. Tens of thousands of camels are still driven from Darfur to Egypt every year, destined for the Cairo meat markets. The caravans now cut close to the Nile near Dongola, but it is thought that up to a third of these animals are smuggled past customs through the desert.

Nothing else now remains of the ancient trade route, yet more than sixty years after the last slave caravan, a British survey in this remote corner of Sudan was still able to record part of the route as being 'one mile wide marked with white camel-bones'.

more or less doubling expected travel times. Even during the driest times of year, a straight transit from the Chad border to the tarmac at El Obeid should take around eight days of non-stop travel. Whatever the conditions, be they political or climatic, Darfur is not an easy place to travel in.

Nyala

The capital of South Darfur state, Nyala is west Sudan's largest town. It is also the base for the African Union monitors and those NGOs working in Darfur. Even before the outbreak of the current crisis, security is Nyala was tight and all visitors were required to register with the police on arrival.

Nyala is a low, sprawling town set back from Wadi Nyala. It has a large market and the best transport connections in the region. Three Sudan Airways flights a week link the town to Khartoum, with a slow train (taking at least four days) running in the same direction twice a month. Road transport links Nyala to El Fasher, Zalingei, El Geneina and east to Babanusa and the tarmac road at El Obeid.

Nyala once had a tourist office, but whether it still exists is anyone's guess.

El Fasher

El Fasher means the courtyard or gathering place of the royal palace, and the town was the seat of the Fur Sultanate from the 18th century until 1916. The palace of the last sultan has been converted into the Ali Dinar Museum, which displays many artefacts from the period. It sits on a hill overlooking the town and its lake. An important market town, El Fasher was a gathering place for traders and camels en route to Kobbay, the starting point of the Forty Days Road. Salt merchants also came here to buy bars of rock salt from the Zaghawa, who transported it by camel from mines in the Tabago Hills, a trade that still carries on, or at least it did until the recent troubles.

SLA raids on El Fasher in April 2003 destroyed several planes of the Sudanese airforce but provoked terrible retaliation from the government and *janjawid*.

El Geneina

This dusty town is Sudan's major border post with Chad and the heart of the Masalit homeland. At the centre of El Geneina is the white palace of the hereditary Masalit sultan, who has prestige but no political power. On the edge of the Sahel, the town is well-wooded and watered, with many orchards. The town's *souq* has always been lively, prospering from the cross-border trade. It has also seen its share of political trouble, with nomad-farmer conflicts and the overspill of fighting from Chad. More recently, El Geneina has become a major centre for Masalit refugees, which numbered around 60,000 by the middle of 2004. Relief workers are the town's only other visitors.

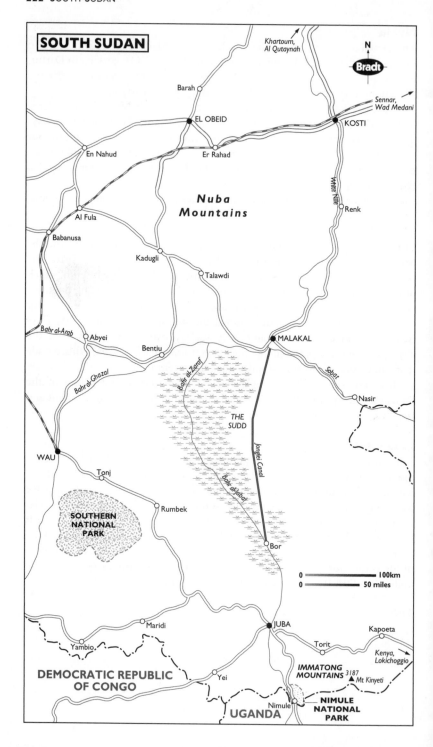

South Sudan

Civil war has raged across South Sudan almost continually since independence in 1956, making it Africa's longest running conflict. The war has gone to the core of Sudan's identity as a nation. More than just a straight fight between North and South, it has encompassed conflicting ideas of central government against regional self-determination, Arab against black, and opposing visions of Sudan as an Islamic or secular state. The resources of South Sudan, from oil and water to rich pasture and livestock, have provided sparks and fuel for the conflict in equal measure.

In 2002 glimmers of hope for an end to this cycle of misery came with the Machakos Protocol and its subsequent ceasefire. This was followed by further deals between the government and SPLM/A rebels on wealth-sharing and regional autonomy. A final comprehensive peace agreement was signed in January 2005, and for the first time in years there was genuine optimism that the decades of suffering for the people of the South might be about to end.

The implications for travel in the region are still being worked out. At the time of going to press, South Sudan was neither accessible nor travel recommended. This chapter necessarily includes very little travel information about the South, but holds out for the prospect that safe access may be realised within the lifetime of the book. I have also included travel information for Kosti in this chapter. While Kosti has always been a fully accessible part of the North (no travel permit is required) it is a major port on the White Nile, so if conditions improve it will be an important departure point south for boats to Malakal and Juba.

THE CIVIL WAR

Understanding South Sudan means understanding the roots and history of the civil war, so this chapter attempts to identify the main causes and events of the conflict as it has been fought since 1983. Many developments in the civil war will be best understood in the context of trends elsewhere in Sudan, for instance the policies of the National Islamic Front government that took power in 1989. In such cases, readers are directed to the general history in the front of the guide.

Historic North-South relations

It seems to be a truism that the relations between the north and south of Sudan have been based on conflict, but this is a construct of the modern era, starting with the Turco-Egyptian conquest of the 1820s. The South was a place of great natural riches, but for the centralised states along the Nile, those resources were often difficult to access and the border between the two remained that of the state and its margins. Before the industrial age, there were often close if competing relations between tribes on either side of the border – the Funj and the Shilluk or the Dinka and the Baggara.

Mohammed Ali changed all that. His Nile steamers swept all before them in their drive south. Arab ivory traders and slavers followed the soldiers. Great swathes of the Dinka lands in Bahr al-Ghazal and the Shilluk Kingdom along the White Nile were decimated, indelibly imprinting on the population a fear of northerners. Few settlements were built, only forts and trading posts. The South, it seemed, existed to be mined for its resources.

When the British took control of Sudan they inherited a state whose borders stretched all the way to the Congo watershed, and they recognised the damage wrought on the South. While Khartoum looked north to Egypt, the decision was made to effectively administer the South as a separate country. Many colonial officers even envisaged joining South Sudan with Uganda and Kenya as part of British East Africa.

Britain's Southern Policy had three strands, all of which would haunt the South at independence. First was the Closed Districts Ordinance, which sought to remove all Arab influence from the South. Arab merchants were restricted and Arabic replaced with English in administration. Second, Indirect Rule proposed handing local government over to tribal chiefs, overseen by District Commissioners. While this worked for hierarchical societies like the Shilluk, it resulted in the British creating tribal chiefs and structures in societies where none had previously existed. Third, educational policy was handed over to missionary societies. Settled pastoral tribes like the Azande and other Equatorians profited from this in a limited way, but the nomadic Dinka and Nuer were largely excluded.

As late as 1948, the colonial authorities still assumed that when independence was eventually granted, the North would necessarily become independent years before the South. When independence did come in 1956, the South was completely unprepared. The process of Sudanization that started in the 1950s saw a sudden influx of Northerners into the South to take up administrative positions, as the Southerners were ill-educated. Old fears soon resurfaced. For their part, the Northerners knew little or nothing about the South, having been barred under the old Southern Policy. Such mutual mistrust was the background to the first civil war. Lasting 17 years from independence, it was the birth cry of the South Sudanese political movement. The Anyanya guerrilla movement eventually fought the government to a standstill. In 1972 the signing of the Addis Ababa Agreement between President Nimeiri and the South Sudanese Liberation Movement finally brought peace and the creation of a loosely federal Sudan.

The years of peace

While there was much rejoicing for the end of a long and dirty war, the Addis Ababa Agreement contained the seeds of its ultimate failure. Many Southerners were bitter about the indefinite postponement of an independent South Sudan that they had advocated and fought for. Although touted as a federal solution, the newly formed Southern Region, with its capital in Juba, lacked several key powers that left it politically weak.

Most importantly, the Southern Region had little control over its economy. Southerners continued to believe that Khartoum was only interested in exploiting the South's vast resources for its own purposes. These suspicions were borne out with the discovery of oil in Bentiu in 1973. Not only did the Southern Assembly have no control over its mineral and oil rights, when the oil was tapped Nimeiri moved to build the necessary refinery on northern territory, and when that plan failed he proposed piping the oil straight through to Port Sudan. In 1974 the Jonglei Canal scheme was steamrollered through despite the protestations of many southerners at the inevitable loss of water access and pasture. Between 1972 and 1977 only a fifth of the South's development budget was allocated by Khartoum. There was little infrastructural investment.

The Anyanya fighters were absorbed into the Sudanese army but continued to be stationed in the South. Many Anyanya resisted this integration and remained in the bush, continuing to carry out low-level guerrilla attacks on government targets. They were loosely organised, dubbing themselves Anyanya 2.

By the end of the 1970s, Sudan's economy was in crisis and Nimeiri became increasingly reliant on the traditional political parties for support. All had varying degrees of Arabic or Islamic policies, which immediately began to affect Khartoum's relationship with Juba. All favoured an Islamic constitution and pressured Nimeiri to withdraw his support for the Addis Ababa Agreement. Attorney General Hassan al-Turabi made plans to redraw the borders of the Southern Region so that the oil fields and rich pastures of Upper Nile became part of the North, although this scheme was ultimately turned down.

Nimeiri couldn't reject the calls for regionalization. Southern politicians like Joseph Lagu had been pressing for decentralising power from Khartoum and Juba to make local government more efficient. Instead, Northern parties decided to cut the South down to size even more. The Southern Assembly was dissolved in 1981. In 1983 Nimeiri moved unilaterally to split the South into three regions of Bahr al-Ghazal, Upper Nile and Equatoria. Each had reduced governing powers to make them more reliant on Khartoum. Anyanya 2 raids became more and more audacious, army defections were commonplace and when a Southern army battalion mutinied in Bor in July 1983, refusing to be redeployed to the North, the stage was set for civil war to flare up again. Nimeiri put coals on the fire by finally announcing that *sharia* law would apply in the South as well as the North.

OPERATION LIFELINE SUDAN

Sudan is at the centre of the world's largest and longest-running humanitarian relief programme. Operation Lifeline Sudan is an umbrella body of five UN agencies with around 40 participating Non-Governmental Organisations. Its main headquarters are in the northwestern Kenyan town of Lokichoggio near the Sudanese border.

Following the government's failure to respond to the 1988 famine it was decided that a new framework was needed to provide relief to Sudan, and so OLS was set up. Previously the UN and other organisations had dealt with humanitarian relief in South Sudan by helping those who had fled to neighbouring countries. The UN had barred its agencies from dealing with the SPLA after extensive lobbying by Khartoum. The USA was successfully convinced that the government controlled 97% of southern Sudan and thus there was no need for any external relief effort. In the resulting famine perhaps 250,000 people died, mainly in SPLM/A-controlled areas.

The framework that OLS worked within was designed to avoid such terrible outcomes. Key to its operations was famine prevention by negotiated access. With the mood in late 1988 favourable to a negotiated settlement to the war, both the government and the SPLM/A signed up to this. Relief flights would only operate with the consent of both parties to maintain the UN's strict neutrality, with access to an area only to be denied if there were major security concerns.

This policy turned out to be open to massive abuse by both sides. Every month OLS could put in a flight request to transport aid, but access to certain

A return to arms

The Sudanese army sent the head of the Omdurman Staff College, John Garang, to quell the nascent rebellion. Garang, a Dinka, had fought briefly for the Anyanya and had been assimilated into the army in 1972. Marked for promotion, he was sent to the USA for military training where he also completed a PhD, writing a critique of the Jonglei Canal for his thesis. He was anything but a safe pair of hands. Garang had been conspiring with other Southern officers for several months to encourage soldiers to defect to Anyanya 2. Instead of restoring order as Nimeiri had hoped, he marched the mutinous battalion into exile to join the rebels.

From Ethiopia Garang announced the formation of the Sudan People's Liberation Movement (SPLM) and Army (SPLA). Its manifesto was thick with the Marxist rhetoric common to many rebel groups of the time and was heavily influenced by Ethiopia's communist dictator Mengistu, who would prove to be the SPLM/A's most enthusiastic backer. The movement declared its aims as national liberation for the whole of Sudan and heavily criticised underdevelopment across the whole country. At its heart was Khartoum's conflation of national identity with Islam and Arabism, and the overthrow of Nimeiri was its first major goal. In the SPLM's 'New Sudan', the South would areas was frequently denied according the aims of the warring parties. The government placed a blanket ban on flights to SPLA-controlled southern Equatoria, but this could at least be reached by road from Uganda and Kenya. More serious was the prevention of humanitarian access to Upper Blue Nile. This oil-rich area was purposefully depopulated by Khartoum to safeguard its output. Civilians were targeted and OLS flights only permitted to neighbouring regions, encouraging people to flee to these areas to receive aid.

The SPLA were no less cynical in their manipulation of OLS. Aid could bring political power and the rebels sought to control their civilian constituency by controlling their access to aid. They frequently purposefully moved whole populations to vulnerable locations to attract more relief, which was then heavily taxed. Most notoriously, in 1992 SPLA-United moved thousands of relatively well-fed people to the 'hunger triangle' around Yuai specifically to attract aid, most of which was appropriated by soldiers. A year later it was thought that up to 80% of food aid to South Sudan was being stolen.

Such manipulation has led to severe criticism of OLS and many have argued that it became complicit in extending the suffering of South Sudan by allowing it to be so manipulated by the warring factions. As the major supplier of relief, abuse was perhaps inevitable, but in the UN's eyes the alternative – total withdrawal – was far worse.

In October 2002, as part of the Machakos Progress, OLS was granted unimpeded access throughout southern Sudan as well as the Nuba Mountains, which were excluded from the original agreement.

be fully autonomous, although many Southerners tacitly accepted this as code for 'independent'.

Just as Joseph Lagu had united the Anyanya in the 1960s, Garang moved quickly to bring the disparate rebel groups under his direct control. Many Anyanya 2 units were absorbed, but those that refused to join were brutally attacked. As army defections continued, the SPLA grew militarily stronger and Garang's leadership more uncompromising. Not all Southerners supported the SPLA, which was seen as primarily a Dinka movement, although it also contained many Nuer. Equatorians in particular were mistrustful, and as the SPLA began to expand its base inside Sudan, it was as often seen as much as an army of occupation as one of liberation. The government tried to exploit such differences by arming local Equatorian tribes such as the Murle, Toposa and Mandari, who had traditionally competed for resources with the Dinka.

When Nimeiri was overthrown in 1985 there was hope for peace, but the army coup leaders were even more entrenched in their attitudes towards the South and repealed the secular constitution. When civilian rule returned the following year, the new prime minister Sadiq al-Mahdi refused to budge on the *sharia* issue.

Sadiq's policy was war by proxy. As well as continuing to arm Southern militias, he gave arms to the drought-stricken Baggara Arabs along the North–South border and encouraged them to mount raids into Dinka territory. These *murahilin* militia depopulated whole areas and the cattle they captured swelled the coffers of Khartoum's merchants. The SPLA targeted civilian populations in return, attacking rival Southern tribes and blockading garrison towns. Food insecurity led to repeated localised famines, which were mostly hidden from the rest of the world. Despite a steadily rising death toll, the Sudanese government claimed that there was no civil war, merely inter-tribal violence.

By the late 1980s the SPLA was militarily ascendant. Arms flowed in from southern African countries and a series of regional capitals began to fall to the rebels. At the turn of the decade the government had lost control of Equatoria, the Ethiopian border regions, swathes of Bahr al-Ghazal and significant areas of Upper Nile. Juba and Wau became government islands in a sea of rebel territory. The remnants of the Anyanya 2, Nuer forces led by William Kong Chuol, were finally absorbed into the SPLA, who even took troops away from the Sudanese fronts to fight the anti-Mengistu rebels in the Ethiopian Civil War.

The Sudanese army pressured Sadiq into compromise. Tentative contacts in early 1989 led to the acceptance of a ceasefire agreement and a proposed suspension of *sharia* in the South. Before this was signed into law, Sadiq was overthrown by an army coup sympathetic to al-Turabi's National Islamic Front. The new government saw the war in purely Islamic terms. The militias were formally integrated under government control as the Popular Defence Forces, and for the first time the Sudanese air force starting bombing civilian areas. On the ground the two forces were evenly balanced and the fighting ground on with little hope of either peace or outright victory.

The SPLA civil war

In May 1991, Mengistu was overthrown in Ethiopia. The SPLA were immediately faced with a pro-Khartoum government in Addis Ababa and the loss of their bases and supply lines. Not only this, but there were over 300,000 Sudanese refugees in SPLA-run camps just inside Ethiopia. Ethiopian forces raided these, and so without warning the SPLA evacuated the entire population into Sudan. The UN was caught completely unawares, but the SPLA aimed to control access and aid to the refugees to maintain political advantage.

At the same time, some factions in the SPLA were growing restive at the progress of the war. Garang ran the SPLA by strict authoritarian rule with more than a hint of a personality cult. The flight of refugees from Ethiopia gave some commanders bargaining chips to deal directly with outside agencies and helped inspire a rebellion against the leader.

In August 1991 Riek Machar, a Nuer commander based in Nasir near the Ethiopian border, and the Shilluk officer Lam Akol, mounted a formal challenge to Garang. Their Nasir Declaration announced the overthrow of Garang and a new pluralist and democratic structure for the SPLA. The newly formed SPLA-United faction called for full Southern independence rather than any federation with the North. Although they had gained the support of the influential Nuer, ex-Anyanya 2 leader William Kong Chuol, Riek and Lam failed to reach out to any major Dinka commanders. Garang was in Kapoeta at the time and reacted with predictable ire at learning of his apparent toppling. Dinka support coalesced around the leader and the mutiny looked increasingly like a Nuer-Shilluk conspiracy.

When the confrontation came it was inevitably bloody. Lam's Shilluk split their support down the middle, isolating Riek and the Nuer. Initial skirmishes were ineffectual, convincing Riek that the only way he could gain wider Southern support was to strike hard at Bor, Garang's home and a Dinka stronghold.

Riek's men moved on Bor, collecting along the way scores of disaffected Nuer villagers eager to pay back the Dinka for their age-old feuds over cattle, and for more recent fighting between the SPLA and Anyanya 2. A Nuer prophet declared victory for this White Army and they arrived in Bor with a terrible fury. Over 2,000 Dinka civilians were killed in what became known as the Bor Massacre, and 100,000 people fled the area. The Nuer returned home triumphant, but Riek had helped engineer a deep split between the peoples. Ironically, the Dinka cattle that were so happily looted turned out to be harbouring rinderpest, which within months had decimated the Nuer herds causing great hardship.

The developments did not go unnoticed in Khartoum. Contacts were struck up between the government and SPLA-United. Khartoum allowed preferential access to Operation Lifeline Sudan to the areas that Riek controlled. In return, Riek later received arms from the government and allowed the army to move through his territory.

Khartoum ascendant

Riek and Lam's split and the loss of the Ethiopian bases put the SPLA on the back foot. Over the next few years the Sudanese army pushed deep into their territory in a series of dry season offensives, reaching as far as the Ugandan border in 1994. With such momentum they weren't inclined to listen to outside attempts to broker peace. Two internationally sponsored conferences in Nigeria, Abuja I and II, failed to make any headway. The SPLA factions could not be reconciled, and Khartoum became convinced that it could end the war on the battlefield rather than around the negotiating table.

The Southerners remained determinedly fractured. The inter-tribal fighting provoked a civil war amongst the Nuer themselves, as those attacked and displaced by the Dinka blamed their fellow tribesmen for their situation. Khartoum bought off commanders with promises of autonomy and then set them against their neighbours. The South became a patchwork of competing militias.

Slowly the SPLA began to recover its position. Weakened in the South it reached out to opposition groups in the North, including the Umma Party and the DUP. In 1995 they signed the Asmara Declaration, recognising Southern self-determination and calling for the overthrow of the National Islamic Front government by any means. New fronts were opened in the Nuba Mountains and Eastern Sudan. Slowly the SPLA began to recapture territory.

OIL AND THE WAR ECONOMY

In 1973 massive oil reserves were discovered around Bentiu in Unity state, just below the historic border between North and South Sudan. Such reserves made Sudan a potentially rich country, but also helped fuel the continuing divisions between the two halves of the country.

Chevron initially planned to build a refinery near Bentiu but this plan was blocked by President Nimeiri, who wanted it built away from the oil fields in northern Sudan. The newly formed Southern Assembly was already smarting about the fact that it did not have the right to control access to the oil found on its territory, and were incensed that Nimeiri planned to divert the proceeds from the industry away from the South and funnel them into his grandiose agricultural schemes in the North. As it turned out, Chevron decided to concentrate on investments elsewhere in the world, and the Bentiu oil fields weren't developed to anywhere near their potential.

The waters were muddied considerably with the resumption of the civil war in 1983. The government was preoccupied with maintaining control of the oil fields. Chevron even followed Khartoum's lead in employing *murahilin* militias to protect its properties on the Kordofan border.

In 1990 Sudan was thrown out of the International Monetary Fund for missing interest payments on its debt, so developing oil production became an even higher priority. Insecurity led to Chevron selling its stake in Sudan in 1992. Three years later a consortium led by the Canadian firm Arakis, with Petronas from Malysia and the Chinese National Petroleum Company, began to develop the oil fields. They were assisted in this by the government's sponsorship of both *murahilin* and the Nuer factions who had broken away from the SPLA. Local commanders were promised shares of the wealth and positions in government in return for maintaining a security cordon around the oil fields. This policy, touted as 'peace from within', led to the Khartoum Peace Agreement in 1997, with SPLA defector Riek Machar its most prominent signatory.

The SPLA split also began to heal itself, with the return of many commanders to Garang, but Riek remained stubbornly outside. He signed a peace deal with President Bashir in 1997, joined the government and was given control over the oil-rich areas of Western Upper Nile, reorganising his troops as the South Sudan Defence Force. This continued the split within the Nuer and provoked further chaos in their heartland. Despite their outward support, Khartoum still chose to sponsor rival groups and keep Riek militarily weak. In 2000 Riek left the government, reconstituted his militia and began to seek a belated reconciliation with Garang.

Overtures of peace

The situation in South Sudan appeared intractable. Neither side was capable of a knock-out blow and the fighting ebbed and flowed according to the season

In 1998 a cash-strapped Arakis sold out to Talisman Energy, one of Canada's largest energy companies. Talisman succeeded in building a long-touted pipeline to Port Sudan. The following year Sudan became an oil exporter and was granted instant readmittance to the IMF. By 2002 oil revenues had reached US$805 million. Other European oil companies rushed to invest in Sudan.

The people of Upper Nile bore much of this cost. Peace from within was anything but. The militias, working with the Sudanese army, repeatedly led assaults on the civilian population in a thinly disguised plan to clear the entire area and produce a sterile buffer zone around the fields. Roads and airfields built by the oil companies were pressed into military use. Flush with new funds, the Sudanese government spent 60% of the new oil money on arms, including helicopter gunships and Mig-29 jet fighters that it then put into service to protect its investment.

Reports by western human rights groups did much to bring the scorched earth policy to the attention of the world. Talisman became the focus of an international campaign to get it to withdraw from Sudan, accusing it of complicity in human rights abuses.

The Swedish company Lundin Petroleum and OMV from Austria pulled out altogether, but Talisman initially held firm and pointed to the development work it was doing, running clinics and digging bore holes for locals, who were in fact Baggara who had displaced the native Dinka population. Talisman finally withdrew from Sudan in 2003 in the face of massive pressure and undeniable evidence of attacks and abuses in the oil region.

Oil money has proved to be a highly contentious issue for Sudan. A deal signed in January 2004 split oil revenues, now at 250,000 barrels a day, equally between the North and South, an agreement central to the prospects of the peace settlement. South Sudan will desperately need that money for reconstruction.

– massive government offensives in the dry season rolled back the SPLA, with the rebels recapturing the ground when the rains came. The one bright spot was the Wunlit Conference of 1999 that finally brought reconciliation between the Dinka and Nuer. The Sudanese army was flush with new supplies paid for by oil exports, and campaigns to pacify the oil areas of Upper Nile intensified. In the middle of all this was a civilian population suffering massively, with each military advance displacing thousands, with the attendant loss of crops and livestock. With food supplies permanently insecure and reliant on outside aid, the spectre of famine was never far away. Further rounds of peace talks, hosted by the Egyptians, Libyans, Eritreans and the regional body the Inter-Governmental Authority on Development (IGAD), had come to nothing. In early 2001 the SPLA signed a memorandum of understanding on self-determination with the Islamic firebrand Hassan al-

Turabi, now out of favour with the government, who reacted by immediately placing Turabi under house arrest.

Fresh moves for peace came from an unexpected direction. The arrival of President George W Bush in the White House did much to invigorate the search for peace. He appointed Senator John Danforth as his peace envoy to Sudan. Bush's links to the US Christian right and the lobbying of the Congressional Black Caucus and human rights groups had provoked renewed American interest in Sudan. The changed political landscape after September 11 also helped Khartoum to seek rapprochement with Washington and an exit from the bloody war.

Danforth's approach was to build confidence between the two sides, and by the start of 2002 he had brokered a six-month renewable ceasefire in the Nuba Mountains and proposed zones of tranquility for humanitarian aid. Fighting in the South still continued, but the two sides agreed to peace talks in Kenya. In July 2002, to the surprise of even themselves, they signed the landmark Machakos Protocols. As part of the comprehensive peace deal, Khartoum agreed to a six-year interim period, after which there would be a referendum on Southern self-determination. *Sharia* law would only apply to the North. The signing was followed by the first face to face meeting between President Bashir and John Garang. Both sides pledged to continue talking and agreed to a renewable ceasefire across the whole of the South.

Machakos and beyond

Peace talks continued throughout 2003 in Kenya, sponsored by IGAD and the so-called Troika of the USA, Great Britain and Norway. Garang and the Sudanese vice-president Ali Osman Taha threw themselves into negotiations. In September 2003 a security agreement was signed announcing a complete cessation of hostilities. Integrated Sudanese army/SPLA units were proposed to be stationed in sensitive areas, with redeployment of independent army and SPLA forces elsewhere. Garang remembered the total absorption of the Anyanya through the Addis Ababa Agreement and was determined to retain a power base. Nevertheless he announced that the road to peace was now 'irreversible'. Three months later a senior SPLM/A delegation was invited to Khartoum for discussions, where they were met by cheering crowds of tens of thousands of South Sudanese on arrival.

In January 2004 the two sides agreed to split oil revenues equally between North and South, with a new non-*sharia* banking system to be set up and run from Juba. Three major sticking points remained – the status of the 'Three Areas' of the Nuba Mountains, the status of Southern Blue Nile and Abyei, and the final shape of the power-sharing government that would oversee the interim period after the peace deal.

The Three Areas straddle the North–South border and are claimed by both sides. The Nuba Mountains have been at the centre of the struggle for regional identity throughout the civil war. Southern Blue Nile is agriculturally rich and the source of much Northern wealth, but it had been an important focus for SPLA fighting since 1984. Abyei is historically part of Kordofan, with a mixed

Ngok Dinka and Arab Messeriyya population, rich pastures and the added complication of newly discovered oil deposits.

Finally, in May 2004 a series of protocols were signed paving the way for a peace deal. Significant autonomy was agreed upon for Nuba Mountains and Southern Blue Nile, while Abyei was given special administration status, to be governed by an executive council and represented in both Khartoum and Juba. Southerners were exempted from *sharia* law in Khartoum. During the interim period, Bashir would remain president, with Garang becoming vice-president as well as head of South Sudan. Seats in the National Assembly would be divided between the government, the SPLM and other Northern parties, with civil service quotas on jobs for Southerners.

In total, six protocols were signed during the tortuous negotiations that had taken place since the Machakos deal of July 2002. Despite delays caused by the Darfur crisis, a comprehensive peace deal that encompassed them was finally signed in January 2005, bringing an end to Africa's longest-running civil war.

SOUTH SUDAN: OPEN FOR TRAVEL?

With the peace process moving slowly but steadily forward, within the lifetime of this guidebook it may be possible to visit South Sudan for the first time in over 20 years. This is an exciting prospect for travellers, but at the same time it must be remembered that this is a region of the country that has been ravaged by a decades-long civil war. Even before this South Sudan was remote and isolated, and the most persistent sign of the developed world is often the Kalashnikov rifle.

The immediate concern should the South begin to open is safety. There is a serious landmine problem in the region, which is also awash with small arms. Aside from the government forces and the SPLA there are numerous semi-independent militias. Continued fighting in the Shilluk Kingdom points to the ease with which local power struggles between rival commanders and ethnic groups can become major conflagrations. At the very least, banditry may exist and security will remain a problem in many areas for the near future. Before even considering a trip is it absolutely essential that you gather up-to-date information on the situation on the ground from reliable news sources and government travel advisories. If you find yourself in any trouble you will most likely be a long way from any help, so it's important to treat your personal safety with the highest priority.

In general, Sudan government and SPLM/A administered areas have had good security since the ceasefire that followed the Machakos Protocols in 2002. The final signing of a peace agreement calls for the redeployment of the majority of the Sudanese army to North Sudan, for the withdrawal of SPLA forces and for mixed army/SPLA units to be stationed in sensitive areas. The exact nature of the administration that will oversee this (along with the timetable) remains unclear.

As things stand at the time of going to press, South Sudan remains divided. The government holds the major towns of Juba, Wau and Malakal, plus Bor on the White Nile and Torit in eastern Equatoria, with over three-quarters of the surrounding region – including Sudan's entire southern border – run by the SLPM/A. Although these areas are generally peaceful, travelling between territories controlled by the two parties is essentially equivalent to crossing an international border. As well as a valid Sudanese visa, a permit from the Sudan Relief and Rehabilitation Commission (the humanitarian arm of the SPLM/A) is required to enter 'New Sudan'. These are issued from SPLM/A offices in Nairobi and Kampala – fees operate on a sliding scale, starting from US$30 for aid workers. Trying to cross between territories without prior permission from both parties is both foolish and potentially dangerous. SPLM/A territory has also used different currencies, accepting US dollars and Ugandan or Kenyan shillings instead of Sudanese dinars, although this is expected to change with a peace settlement.

In the past couple of years, a few hardy and adventurous travellers have succeeded in transiting South Sudan from Central Africa Republic to Uganda, all through SPLM/A territory. Such a trip should not be lightly considered. Along with the obvious potential pitfalls in Sudan, transiting north CAR is not recommended, as it is rife with bandits, mutinous soldiers and diamond smugglers, as wild and lawless a corner as it's possible to imagine. The picture these travellers brought back from South Sudan is a good illustration of what might be expected should it become accessible: no roads, minimal infrastructure, little formal accommodation and not much fuel for the 4WDs essential in such conditions. They did, however, speak of the same warmth and hospitality that can be found throughout the rest of Sudan, as well as of the burning desire for peace.

If the peace deal sticks, the first areas likely to be opened to access by foreigners are likely to be Juba, Wau and Malakal, as these are already served by Sudan Airways flights. Permission to travel overland to these destinations will probably be less forthcoming, as many routes pass through SPLM/A areas. Permits would have to be applied for in Khartoum in the same manner as permits for travelling elsewhere in the country. As the picture of the new administration and the military redeployment becomes clearer, other areas may open up.

Should open travel become a reality, there are two main overland routes through South Sudan, neither particularly easy. The first is along the Nile, travelling by boat from Kosti to Malakal and then on to Juba. This route runs entirely through government territory. For more information on this, see the boxed text *Slow boats going south*, page 240. The alternative, potentially more difficult, route travels southwest from Khartoum to Wau in Bahr al-Ghazal, and then by whatever means are available in a loop down to Juba. Between Wau and Juba is the major SPLM/A town of Rumbek, so access to this route will presumably remain sketchy, pending settlement of southern administration policies. This road is reported as being heavily mined, although clearing and road upgrading work is under progress. The United Nations Joint Logistics Centre regularly publishes detailed assessments of southern Sudan's transport infrastructure on its website (www.unjlc.org), which are highly useful for route planning.

Regarding the southern borders, the first to open to foreign travellers will be between Yei and Koboko in Uganda via the Sudanese border town of Kaya.

Passenger vehicles run from Koboko to Yei (taking around three hours), linking this part of South Sudan to the Ugandan transport network. A second border crossing is at Nimule, between Juba and Gulu, although this road is not used due to mine threats. The Sudan–Kenya border is expected to open at Narus, between Kapoeta and Lokichoggio in Kenya, and this road is under repair at the time of going to press.

What transport may be available away from the river is anyone's guess, although the return of internally displaced people and cross-border trade is certain to spur demand. Commercial vehicles service most destinations in western Equatoria – accessible from Uganda – potentially opening these areas to travellers. The largest fleets of vehicles operating in South Sudan are currently those run by international aid organisations, although it should go without saying that there are they to help the local populace rather than to provide any services to itinerant travellers. Of all the tarmac roads in Sudan, those in the South barely reach double figures, making overland travel highly seasonal. Summer rains – starting as early as April in the far south – can turn hard earth roads into impassable mud tracks, while elsewhere the rising Nile simply floods the plains, isolating great swathes of land.

Even with a final peace settlement, travel in South Sudan will not be for the fainthearted.

Kosti

By the standards of north Sudan, Kosti feels positively verdant. It's a large, good-natured town on the lush banks of the White Nile, and it owes its position to the river trade. Kosti has a busy port and barges regularly sail south to Malakal and occasionally Juba. Before the resumption of civil war in 1983, there was a regular passenger ferry to Juba, and it is hoped that with the beginnings of peace in the South that this route will be open to travellers in the near future.

Kosti is named for a Greek merchant who had a trading post here in the 19th century, but apart from an Orthodox church, there isn't much left of this heritage. In addition to the port, the town has links to the massive Kenana Sugar Company on the opposite side of the river in Rabak. Kenana is a legacy of Nimeiri's ill-fated 'Breadbasket' project of the 1970s and is the largest employer in the region.

The Nile at Kosti is wide and lazy. There is plenty of birdlife here, and fishermen can be seen in their tiny boats casting their nets. The banks and fields along the river to the north of the town are ideal for exploring, with their thick green grass and mango trees.

Just north of Kosti is Aba Island, where the Mahdi first preached, and which is still a stronghold of support for the Mahdist Umma Party today.

Getting there and away

Kosti is situated just off a good tarmac highway and is roughly equidistant between Khartoum and El Obeid. The Souq Es-Shabi serves both destinations and is a ten-minute *boksi* trip west of Kosti. On arriving, take

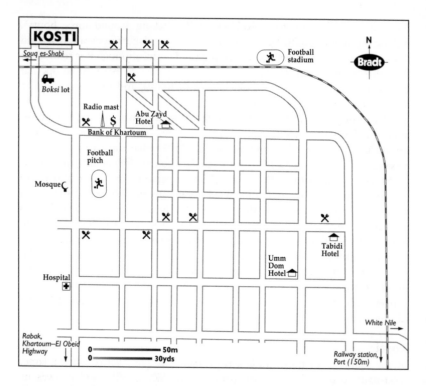

transport heading to Souq Kabir in the centre of town. Minibuses run throughout the day to Khartoum; the five hour trip costs 1,200SD. The same sum will also get you to El Obeid, but the majority of traffic heading there departs in the early morning.

Kosti is on the train line between Khartoum and Nyala. The Nyala service passes through Kosti on the first and third Friday of the month, arriving in Nyala on Sunday. The return service to Khartoum departs Kosti on the following Tuesday, taking about four times as long to get there as a minibus.

For more on heading south from Kosti on the White Nile see the boxed text *Slow Boats Going South* on page 240.

Where to stay and eat

You won't be spoiled for choice when it comes to accommodation in Kosti.

The pick of the bunch is the **Umm Dom Hotel** (tel: 0571 2125), easily picked out on the Nile side of town as one of Kosti's tallest buildings (this is a good job, as it's not well signed otherwise). Rooms with a sink and one or two beds cost 1,800SD. The communal showers and toilets are clean, and there's a restaurant on the roof, with fine views over the river.

Just around the corner is **Tabidi Hotel**, with pennants from local football teams decorating the front office. It's more of a *lokanda*, with basic toilets and shower. Beds cost 1,200SD, but if there's space the manager seems happy for you to have a whole room for 1,700SD, irrespective of occupancy.

Closer to the souq is the **Abu Zayd Hotel**. Another *lokanda*-style place, it feels like it's fallen on hard times. Rooms and toilets are basic and the management didn't seem to want to encourage *khawaja* guests. If you get in, beds are a rock-bottom 300SD each.

The Umm Dom Hotel's rooftop restaurant offers Kosti's tidiest dining experience, but it's best to check in advance when it's open, as it can keep erratic hours. There is a selection of kebabs, chicken and grilled fish on offer, with bread and salad. If you have walked all the way across town to find it closed, console yourself with the really excellent *taamiya* and salad sandwiches from the hole-in-the-wall place across the road by the Tabidi Hotel.

The street leading from the two hotels to the football pitch features several eateries serving the usual Sudanese fare, and there are plenty of stands and cafeterias in the *souq* around the railway line. The *souq* is equally well-stocked with fresh produce. Next to the football pitch itself there are several juice bars, and the tea stalls under the trees there are a relaxing spot to take a drink, or watch an impromptu football match.

Aba Island

A 14km-long strip of land in the middle of the White Nile, Aba Island (or Gezira Aba) is the spiritual home of the Mahdist movement.

Prior to his rise to power, Mohammed Ahmed lived on Aba, where he was devoted to his religious studies. His 1881 declaration that he was the Mahdi sent to renew Islam threatened the Egyptian power in Khartoum, who sent a force to Aba to arrest him. Terribly organised, the Egyptian troops fired on each other and the Mahdi's followers did for the rest. The victory was seen as a divine blessing and was the spark that lit his rebellion.

Aba was the scene of another showdown between the Khartoum and the Mahdists nearly a hundred years later. Fresh from siezing power, Nimeiri moved to crush the Ansar in 1970. Following riots in Omdurman, their leader Iman al-Hadi, a grandson of the Mahdi, had retreated to his power base on Aba. Nimeiri wanted to move on the island but was prevented by massed Ansar demonstrators who later clashed violently with the army. Nimeiri's response was to send in the air force. Some estimates put the number killed in the bombardment and subsequent occupation as high as 10,000, and al-Hadi fled to exile in Ethiopia and was later killed.

The palatial al-Mahdi family house is now used as the Faculty of Law of the Iman al-Mahdi University. It's a collection of buildings next to the radio tower where the minibuses drop you off. The university's students are eager to practise their English and talk about the history of the area. The headquarters of the Umma Party are around the corner, and Ansar flags (three horizontal bands of black, red and green surmounted by a white spear and crescent) are flown everywhere.

On the west side of the island, a 2km walk straight out of town, is **al-Kar Mosque** where the Mahdi himself taught. It's a small unassuming square building, whitewashed with blue windows, and carpeted inside with a simple *mimbar* (pulpit). It looks distinctly modern to my eye, so I wonder if the British tore down the original (as they did with the Mahdi's Tomb). Either way, it's only mildly diverting, and you'll probably find equal pleasure in watching the fishermen on the river bringing in their catch and sorting their nets.

THE WHITE NILE EXPEDITION

In 2004, a rafting expedition followed the White Nile for the first time from its source to the sea. Natalie McComb was one of the crew. For more information see www.thewhitenile.com

I had been in talks with the SPLM/A for ten months to arrange the necessary permits to travel through southern Sudan. They were instrumental in terms of getting information and clearances to get through the South, then under ceasefire due to the peace talks.

We entered southern Sudan at Nimule, where the White Nile changes its name to Bahr al-Jabal. Mt Moyo divides Uganda and Sudan, where the river flows around a massive ox-bow to the east before heading northwest. There are mountains on both sides of the Nile, with thick riverine woodland and papyrus and reeds along the banks.

Nimule is set back from the river on a hill, its few concrete buildings crumbling from neglect and artillery damage. People throng through the centre, pumping water from bore holes and herding long-horned cattle through the brick maker's yards. Nimule is a gathering point for refugees and internally displaced people from northern Uganda as well as south Sudan. Scattered along the hills are mud-brick huts with straw roofs, but on the outskirts of town lie the congested IDP (Internally Displaced People) camps, which house people who receive extremely limited relief and are exposed to unsanitary conditions.

We stayed at an orphanage called the Shekinah Fellowship, for children who have lost their parents, or been abducted by the warring factions for use as child soldiers, 'wives' and porters.

Apart from the huge military presence, progress is being made in conserving the nearby Nimule Game Reserve. Although we didn't actually see any game when we passed through this area, we were brought warthog meat and told that there were many elephants and antelope around. Soldiers hunt for bush meat in order to survive, so with the coming of peace the area should hopefully flourish once more.

After Nimule, the Fola Rapids runs for approximately 100km, almost halfway to Juba, with the cataracts slowly calming as you paddle north. It is bush the entire distance, with no-one living on the river's edge until you reach the first government garrison, 70km south of Juba. Soldiers move through the bush of course, but we didn't see a single soul the entire way.

Juba is the main town in the South controlled by the government. A young Princess Elizabeth once visited the Juba Hotel here before becoming the Queen. It has electricity and water supplies and even a mobile phone network. It is very much a military town, with huge barracks and a curfew at night. An estimated 55,000 refugees live in camps around the town's

Aba is known for its fish, fried and sold in paper to be eaten with bread and lemon. There is a small *souq* in the streets behind the university where you'll find it being sold.

edges; some have been resident for over 20 years. Facilities are better here than anywhere else we visited; there's an airport, hospital and office blocks, as well a beautiful cathedral and some lovely, but dilapidated, colonial-style buildings. In Juba there are some fantastic markets frequented by many tribes from the Dinka, Nuer, Mandari, Bari, Tiposa, Kuku and Kakwa.

Moving north the river widens slightly and the Mandari and Bari peoples graze and water their cattle here in the dry season. When the river floods the plains on either side are underwater for several kilometres in all directions. The tribes here walk around completely naked apart from the beads around the waists and necks. They are often covered in ash, while the smoke from their cow dung fires hangs thick in the air. They have spectacular forehead scarification and the women also have marvellous scars on their bellies. We were welcomed with open arms by them and spent many happy hours being shown around their camps. The digital camera proved a magical delight for these people, who were fascinated by the pictures and dragged out their favourite cows, goats and dogs to be snapped as well!

As we headed north we crossed more front lines – six in total. The towns are mainly under government control, with the areas between held by the SPLM/A. At every place we arrived people couldn't believe the other side had let us through without any trouble. Some of these places are only 60km apart yet most people had no idea or contact with the people from the other regions. There is a huge amount of weaponry in the area – tanks, anti-aircraft guns, Kalashnikovs, and mines and unexploded bombs lying on the ground.

One of the main challenges was to cross the Sudd, the world's biggest wetland. Within the swamps the Monythany people live on the floating papyrus islands, catching fish. We spent nights with them on their tiny patches of land, fending off the mosquitoes.

Snakes and crocodiles also live in the Sudd and at night we could hear hippos and hyenas in the distance. We had to move neck deep through the swamp in places, pushing our rafts through narrow channels, hoping that nothing worse than leeches would decide to take a bite out of us. For eight days we pushed through with nothing to see forward and backwards except for the narrow channel clogged by papyrus. Occasionally massive lakes would open out in front of us – it is a confusing, hot, green, no-man's-land and we easily understand why the early explorers had such trouble finding routes through.

The people of southern Sudan have suffered an enormous amount over decades of fighting and they all want peace more than anything. The memory that will stay strongest in my mind was people calling out to us from the banks 'You are welcome, you are welcome. If you are here, peace is coming'.

Getting there and away

There is no direct transport between Aba and Kosti. Instead you must take a 20-minute minibus from Souq Kabir across the White Nile Bridge to Rabak and change there. Rabak is sprawled out along the main highway to Khartoum, so ask for 'Mogof Gezira Aba' to find the right minibus stand. Aba is a further 20-minute ride from Rabak and linked to the mainland by a causeway; minibuses drop off and leave for the return journey from Aba town by the radio mast in the main square.

Malakal

Located just downstream from where the Sobat River joins the White Nile, Malakal is the largest town in Upper Nile and the real gateway to South Sudan. An important port, the town lies within the Shilluk Kingdom that ruled this stretch of the White Nile from the 15th century until the Egyptians penetrated the area in the 1840s. The Shilluk have retained a semi-autonomous administrative structure through their king or *reth*, who still rules from Pachodo, downstream from Malakal near Fashoda.

The Shilluk Kingdom has continued to be troubled with fighting despite the ceasefire agreement that has formed part of the peace process. In 1997, the Shilluk forces of Lam Akol signed a peace deal with the government. When he returned to the SPLA fold in late 2003 the militias split, creating a power

SLOW BOATS GOING SOUTH?

Kosti is Sudan's northernmost port on the White Nile and so provides one of the major transport links to southern Sudan. From here, boats sail regularly upstream to Malakal and infrequently Juba. This route formed part of the original overland 'Cairo to Cape Town' route through Africa, and it's hoped that with the implementation of the peace deal between the government and the SLPM/A it will soon be possible for foreigners to travel on these boats once again. Check the situation when arranging travel permits. There is a River Transport Corporation security office at Kosti port that may send you back to Khartoum if you don't have the correct paperwork.

When I visited the port there were two of the old Juba ferries tied up at the port, and the soldier on guard was happy to let me clamber about them. They weren't in any state to travel – they had been completely stripped bare and the water hyacinth around them was so thick it was supporting several curious goats. A few other ferries are in dock in Khartoum North, opposite the Blue Nile Sailing Club, although whether they are in any serviceable condition is anyone's guess.

In the meantime, the best option will probably be one of the cargo boats that you'll see being loaded in dock (two boats I saw moored carried field artillery and huge hardwood logs from Equatoria, as good an illustration of historic north-south relations as you're likely to see). These are mostly 50m vacuum in the area. In the resulting fighting between the factions, Shilluk and Nuer militias loyal to Khartoum raided and destroyed villages along the west bank of the Nile, displacing up to 120,000 people, most of whom have relocated around Malakal. The security situation remained unresolved at the time of going to press and may prove to be a major sticking point in the implementation of a final peace agreement.

Malakal itself is a mainly Shilluk and Nuer city and is probably the most developed place in South Sudan – it has a few tarmac roads, a regular electricity and water supply and plenty of new buildings. New mosques are proliferating and tensions between recently incoming Northern migrants and Southerners have been reported.

Malakal can be seasonally reached by road from Kosti between January and April; the White Nile is navigable along this route all year.

Juba

Juba was founded near the site of Gondokoro, the southernmost outpost of Egyptian rule in Sudan and the former capital of Equatoria. As well as being a garrison, Gondokoro was an important staging post on the expeditions of Samuel Baker to find the source of the Nile, and was his base when he was made governor of the region. Cataracts just south of Gondokoro prevented further navigation and marked the effective extent of Egyptian control. The

long flat barges that are often tied together in pairs and pushed by a tugboat.

Conditions are exceedingly basic. There's no formal accommodation, so passengers cram on the deck with their goods and animals. Many people take along rope beds as the passage takes several days. There is little or no shade. A space on the roof of the tug ('first class') costs around 9500SD, or you are crammed in on the deck with barely a square metre to call your own. You'll need to provide yourself with at least a mat to sleep on and some sort of shade. A mosquito net is essential. It may be possible to buy food on the boat but it is best to be as self-sufficient as possible. Kosti's shops are well stocked with fruit, biscuits and tinned goods. All water on the boat is drawn from the Nile, so must be treated to make it potable.

While barges run frequently between Kosti and Malakal (taking around three nights with several stops), onward connections to Juba currently look less viable. Twenty years of neglect has left Juba's port silted up and unusable, meaning that barges have to be laboriously offloaded by hand straight on to the riverbank. As barges travel this route in convoys of 30 vessels or more, it can take two months to offload, reducing turnaround times to a crawl. Factoring in similar supply stops between Malakal and Juba, the total voyage time south is currently two to four months. The barges sail north largely empty taking just one month to reach Kosti – but still keeping traffic on this route down to just two convoys a year.

site was later abandoned for health reasons; malaria and other diseases took a particularly high toll amongst the European missionaries based here. Juba became the regional capital during the Condominium.

The biggest prize in South Sudan, Juba was never captured by the SPLA during the civil war despite continuing blockades and several large-scale assaults. Throughout this time Juba was a depressing, claustrophobic place, but the ceasefire has started to bring the city back to life. New buildings are being built, a phone network is being installed, the shops and markets are full of goods, and the University of Juba (based in Khartoum throughout the war) is being refurbished. Juba's population of over 300,000 is expected to triple in the next few years as Southerners return home.

There are over 50,000 internal refugees in camps and government-run 'peace villages' around Juba. As well as having been displaced by the civil war, many have also fled fighting by the Ugandan Lord's Resistance Army.

Juba has the only bridge across the Nile south of Kosti, isolating the SPLM/A-controlled sections of Equatoria from each other. Roads from Juba as far as the rebel areas are reportedly usable throughout the rainy season. In September 2004 a German contractor was reported to have signed a deal to build a railway to link Juba with the Ugandan town of Gulu. Even with a final peace settlement, don't expect to be booking your ticket soon.

Wau

The city of Wau on the Jur branch of the Bahr al-Ghazal river marks the southern extent of the train line from Khartoum. It is the second largest town in South Sudan after Juba and has a largely Dinka population, who have traditionally grazed their herds on the wide surrounding plains. South of Wau are the great tropical forests of Western Equatoria, and the town has grown from processing its riches – teak, mahogany and an abundance of mangoes.

In more recent years, however, Wau has become better known as a centre of famine. Bahr al-Ghazal was wracked by massive famine in 1988 in which up to a quarter of a million people died as a by-product of the civil war. Exactly ten years later hunger struck again, ushered in by a major SPLA assault on the town. The SPLA commander Kerobino Kuaniyin Bol had defected to the government the previous year, but conspired to switch back to the rebels and aid an attack on the town. The initial attack was successful and the SPLA captured the railway station and airport, but Kerubino's men started looting and were eventually expelled by the Sudanese army. In the aftermath, hundreds of local Dinka were killed in revenge and much of the population driven into the countryside. Humanitarian flight access was denied and thousands faced starvation. The resulting famine did much to turn the Dinka of Bahr al-Ghazal against the SPLA.

The railway that linked Wau to the north is no longer functioning. Wau is not currently accessible by road during the rainy season from May to December, so is highly dependent on its air links with Khartoum.

Appendix 1

LANGUAGE

Sudan's official language is Arabic. English is the common language of South Sudan (and the language of education) and there are moves to upgrade it to official status following the peace deal between the government and SPLM/A. You can often find someone who speaks at least a few words of English, however broken, although it is worth trying to pick up whatever Arabic you can. The Sudanese delight in others trying to speak their language, so however much you think you're mangling the words, your attempts will be appreciated.

Grammatically, Arabic is a tricky language to learn from scratch. There is no universally agreed method of transliterating Arabic into English, so extra care has to be taken with pronunciation. On top of this, there are big differences between written and spoken Arabic. The written language is taken from the Classical Arabic of the Holy Koran. The Arabic written today is Modern Standard Arabic, an updated form of the original and used throughout the Arab world – the differences between the two are akin to the differences between the English of Shakespeare and a modern newspaper. But if the written language, derived from the literal word of God, is unchanging, spoken Arabic has evolved constantly into a variety of dialects. All spoken Arabic is colloquial, so that while Arabs from Morocco and Syria could read each other's newspapers, they would actually have trouble carrying out an intelligible conversation with each other.

These differences may seem academic to the traveller, but Arabic phrasebooks are often derived from Modern Standard Arabic, which is not spoken anywhere. You'll be understood, but you might find it hard to understand what others are telling you. For Sudan, your best bet is to take a phrasebook for Egyptian Arabic (*Lonely Planet* and *Rough Guides* both produce good books) and go with that. Egyptian and Sudanese Arabic are very similar – Egyptian Arabic is also understood throughout the Arab world, due to Egypt's prodigious output of films, television and music.

There are two key differences to bear in mind if you're using an Egyptian Arabic phrasebook: the 'g' in Egypt is pronounced as a soft 'j' in Sudan. Hence a camel is *gamal* in Cairo and *jamal* in Khartoum. Second, the 'q' sound, a hard-to-pronounce glottal stop, is rendered closer to a hard 'g' in Sudan, making things easier to get your tongue around.

A final note – the prefix *al-* is the Arabic equivalent of the definite article. It naturally runs on to the word it is attached to for ease of pronunciation, so as well as *al-* you will also come across words such as *as-Sudan* (Sudan), *at-talata* (Tuesday) and so on.

Pronunciation

All the words in the vocabulary section are spelled as they are pronounced. Some letters to take particular care of are:

aa	Long a from the back of the throat, as in 'car' pronounced slowly
u	Long u, as in 'loose'
q	Hard q half-swallowed. Often transcribed as 'gh' or even 'k'
kh	Guttural, as in Scottish 'loch'

Double consonants are both pronounced. An apostrophe denotes a glottal stop.

Vocabulary
Greetings

Hello (polite)	*salaam alaykum* (literally 'peace be upon you')
Hello (reply)	*wa alaykum salaam* ('and peace be upon you')
Hello (simple)	*ahlan*
How are you?	*keef haalak?* (to a man)
	keef haalik? (to a woman)
Good (reply)	*kwayees*
Good morning	*sabaa al-khayr*
Good evening	*misa al-khayr*
Goodbye	*masalaama*

Basic needs

Yes	*aywa*
No	*la*
Thank you	*shukran*
Thank you very much	*shukran gidan*
You're welcome	*afwan*
Thanks to God	*hamdulilah*
Where is ...?	*feyn...?*
Is there ... ?	*fee... ?*
I want... /I do not want	*ana ayiz.../ana mish ayiz*
There is/is not...	*fee.../... mafee*
How much is...?	*... bikam?*
When?	*emta?*
Is it possible... ?	*... mumkin?*
It is not possible	*mish mumkin*
Go	*mashee*
Where are you going?	*mashee feyn inta?*
I want to go to...	*ana ayiz aruh...*
Let's go!	*yalla!*
What is your name?	*esmak-eh?/esmik-eh?* (to a man/woman)
My name is...	*esmi...*

Useful words

and	*wa*	me/you	*ana/inta*
airport	*matar*	meat	*laahma*
bank	*bank*	minibus	*hafla*
bathroom	*hammaam*	money	*floos*
bed	*sireer*	mosque	*masjid*
bicycle	*biseeklet*	newspaper	*gornaal*
boy	*walad*	passport	*basbor*
bread	*aysh/kisra*	permit	*tasreeh*
bus station	*moghof otobees*	petrol	*benzene*
bus	*otobees*	police	*polees*
camel	*jamal*	post office	*bosta*
car	*sayaara*	postcard	*kart*
chicken	*frakh*	pyramid	*ahram*
coffee	*ghawa*	railway station	*mahata al-guttar*
country	*baalad*	restaurant	*matam*
cow	*ba'ara*	road/street	*tareeh/sharia*
doctor	*doktor*	room	*oda*
donkey	*homaar*	sorry	*malesh*
embassy	*sifaara*	shop	*mahaal*
expensive/cheap	*gaalee/rakeesh*	shower	*dosh*
ferry	*banton*	stamp	*taabee*
fish	*samak*	tea	*shai*
food	*akl*	ticket	*tazkara*
foreigner	*khawaja*	ticket office	*maktab at-tazkara*
friend	*saahib/saaba* (male/female)	toilet	*tawalet*
girl	*bint*	town	*madeena*
good/bad	*kwayees/mish kwayees*	train	*guttar*
hospital	*mostashfa*	village	*qarya*
hot/cold	*sochun/berit*	visa	*veeza*
hotel	*funduq*	visa extension	*tamdeed veeza*
key	*miftah*	water	*moya*
letter	*gowaab*	with/without	*be/bedun*
man	*raajil*	woman	*sit*
market	*souq*		

Numbers

0	*sifr*	9	*tisa*
1	*wahid*	10	*ashara*
2	*itneen*	11	*adaash*
3	*talata*	12	*itnaash*
4	*arbaa*	13	*talataash*
5	*khamsa*	14	*arbataash*
6	*sita*	15	*khamstaash*
7	*saba*	16	*sittaash*
8	*tamania*	17	*sabataash*

18	*tamantaash*	80	*tamaneen*
19	*tisataash*	90	*tisaeen*
20	*ishreen*	100	*miya*
30	*talateen*	1,000	*alf*
40	*arbaeen*	½	*nus*
50	*khamseen*	first	*awwal*
60	*siteen*	second	*taani*
70	*sabaeen*	third	*taalit*

Time

today	*an-naharda*	later	*baadeen*
yesterday	*embareh*	day	*yom*
tomorrow	*bokra*	night	*layl*
now	*delwatee*	hour	*saa'a*

Sunday	*al-ahad*	Thursday	*al-khamis*
Monday	*al-itneen*	Friday	*al-juma*
Tuesday	*at-talata*	Saturday	*al-sabt*
Wednesday	*al-arba*		

| What time is it? | *as-saa'a kam?* |
| Three o'clock | *saa'a talata* |

Countries

America (USA)/American	*amreka/amrekanee*
Australia/Australian	*ostraylya/ostraalee*
Egypt/Egyptian	*al-masr/al-masree*
England/English	*ingliterra/ingleezee*
Ireland/Irish	*irlanda/irlandee*
New Zealand/New Zealander	*nyuzeelanda/nyuzeelandee*
Scotland/Scottish	*eskotlanda/eskotlandee*
Sudan/Sudanese	*as-sudan/as-sudanee*

Appendix

GLOSSARY

adis	Stewed broth of yellow lentils
Ansar	Followers of the Mahdi and latterly, the Umma Party
Anyanya	Southern rebel movement during first civil war, 1956–72
araki	Alcoholic spirit made from dates
Baggara	Generic name for nomadic cattle-raising Arabs
Beja Congress	Main Beja opposition group
bokra	Tomorrow
boksi	Ubiquitous pick-up transport (plural: *bokasi*)
caro	Donkey cart
cataract	Stretch of rapids on a river
Condominium	Period of British rule from 1898-1956
dhikr	Sufi ritual to induce ecstastic state of oneness with Allah
DUP	Democratic Unionist Party led by the al-Mirghani family
dura	Sorghum
emma	Man's scarf, usually worn as a turban
faqi	Holy man or religious teacher
fasuliya	Bean dish akin to baked beans
ful	Stewed fava beans, a Sudanese staple
funduq	Hotel
Funj	Black sultanate ruling from Sennar, 1504-1821
ghaffir	Caretaker
ghawha	Coffee
haboub	Summer dust storm
hafla	Minibus
IGAD	InterGovernmental Authority on Development. Regional body overseeing peace talks between the government and SPLM/A
inshallah	'If God wills it'
jallabiya	Long robe worn by Muslim men
janjawid	Government-backed Arab militia operating in Darfur
jebana	Spiced coffee served in a long-necked pot
JEM	Justice & Equality Movement. Darfur rebel group
karkaday	Drink made from infusion of hibiscus flowers
khamsin	Light wind of fifty days
Khatmiyah	Sufi movement based in Kassala
khawaja	Westerner

kisra	Bread
Kush	Ancient Sudanese realm along Nile, roughly between the Third and Sixth Cataracts
lokanda	Cheap hotel with communal sleeping arrangements
Mahdiya	Period of Mahdist rule from 1885-98
malesh	Expression of regret
merissa	Beer brewed from sorghum
Meroitic	Period of Kushite rule with royal cemteries at Meroe 270–320BC
moghof	Bus/minibus station
moya	water
murahilin	Government-backed Baggara Arab militia
Napatan	Period of Kushite rule with royal cemeteries at Napata, 890–270BC
NDA	National Democratic Alliance, umbrella group of opposition parties, including the SPLM/A, Umma Party, the DUP and Beja Congress
NGO	Non-Governmental Organisation
NIF	National Islamic Front, ruling political party (also called National Congress)
OLS	Operation Lifeline Sudan. UN-run relief body for South Sudan
PDF	Popular Defence Forces, government-funded Arab militia
shai	Tea
sharia	Islamic law derived from the Holy Koran
sibir	Nuba festival, usually at harvest time
SLA	Sudan Liberation Army. Darfur rebel group
Souq es-Shabi	People's market, often synonymous with the main transport terminal
souq	Market
SPLA	Sudan People's Liberation Army. Military wing of the SPLM
SPLA-United	Breakaway rebel faction led by Riek Machar
SPLM	Sudan People's Liberation Movement. Main Southern opposition party
Sudd	Swamp area of the White Nile in South Sudan
Sufi	Follower of mystical path of Islam
taamiya	Fried chickpea balls akin to falafel
tariqa	Sufi order
tobe	All-encompassing robe worn by Muslim women
Turkiyah	Period of Turco-Egyptian rule from 1821-85
Umma	Political party led by al-Mahdi family
wadi	Seasonally dry watercourse
zar	Ritual for exorcising spirit possession
zir	Earthenware water pot

Appendix 3

WHO'S WHO IN SUDANESE HISTORY

Note: European names are listed by surname; all others are listed in full.

Abdullah ibn Mohammed	The Khalifa and ruler of Sudan during the Mahdiya, 1884–98
Ali Abd al-Latif	Founder of White Flag League, 1920s independence movement
Ali Dinar	Last Fur Sultan, ruled 1899–1916
Amara Dunqas	Founder of Funj Kingdom in 1504
Arnekhamani	Kushite king from 235–218BC and builder of Lion Temple at Musawwarat
Badi Abu Duqn (Badi II)	Funj ruler who expanded his kingdom into the Nuba Mountains and the Shilluk Kingdom in the 16th century.
Baker, Samuel	British explorer and the first governor of Equatoria during the Turkiyah
Emin Pasha	German governor of Equatoria at time of Mahdist revolution
Garang, John	Dinka leader of SPLM/A, 1983–present
Gordon, Charles	Governor general of Sudan, 1877–79 and 1884–85, killed during Mahdist capture of Khartoum
Hasan al-Turabi	Islamist leader and spiritual father of 1989 coup, now in opposition
Hicks, William (Hicks Pasha)	Commander of Egyptian army at Battle of Sheikan, 1883
Ibrahim Abboud	Military coup leader and president of Sudan, 1958–64
Ismail al-Azhari	First president of independent Sudan, 1956
Ismail Pasha	Son of Mohammed Ali who led Turco-Egyptian conquest of Sudan in 1821
Khedive Ismail	Ruler of Egypt from 1863–79
Kitchener, Horatio Herbert	British commander, Anglo-Egyptian conquest of 1989
Lagu, Joseph	Leader of Anyanya rebel movement during first civil war (1956–72)
Lam Akol	Shilluk SPLA commander, one-time defector to SPLA-United

Mohammed Ahmed	The Mahdi, leader of Islamic revolution that overthrew the Turkiyah between 1881 and 1885
Mohammed Ali	Egyptian ruler from 1807–48 who oversaw the 1821 conquest of Sudan
Nimeiri, Jaafar	Military coup leader and president of Sudan, 1969–85
Omar al-Bashir	Military coup leader and president of Sudan, 1989–present
Osman Digna	Beja leader during the Mahdiya
Piye (Piankhi)	Kushite king and builder of first pyramids at El Kurru, 747–17BC
Riek Machar	Nuer SPLA commander who founded SPLA-United breakaway faction, previously allied to the government
Sadiq al-Mahdi	Prime minister of Sudan, 1967–7 and 1986–89. Great-grandson of the Mahdi and leader of the Umma Party
Slatin, Rudolf (Slatin Pasha)	Austrian governor of Darfur held captive during the Mahdiya
Suleiman Solongdungo	Founder of Fur Sultanate (Keira Dynasty) in the 17th century
Taharqa	Expansionist Kushite king and prolific builder who briefly saw Kush's borders stretch to Palestine (690–64BC)
Tanwetamani	Nephew of Taharqa who ruled from 664–53BC
Thutmoses III	Egyptian pharaoh from 1504–1450BC who conquered Sudan as far as the Fifth Cataract
Wingate, Reginald	Governor general of Anglo-Egyptian Condominium, 1899–1916
Zubeir Pasha	Powerful slave trader during Turkiyah and ruler of Bahr al-Ghazal

Appendix 4

FURTHER READING

Bookshelves aren't groaning with volumes about Sudan, as many books deal with the country as an adjunct to a separate subject – ancient Egypt for example, or colonialism in Africa. But dig deep and you can find some gems. In Khartoum, the **New Bookshop** off Sharia al-Qasr has a reasonable selection of titles on Sudan, as does the **Acropole Hotel** on occasion.

The internet has made tracking down hard-to-find books fantastically easy. Of the dot-coms, **Amazon** is the most notable bookseller, with **AbeBooks** being excellent for out-of-print and second-hand titles.

The **Africa Book Centre** in London has a wide selection of titles on Sudan and Africa as a whole, and is a delight to browse in or shop online with (38 King Street, Covent Garden, London WC2E 8JT; tel 020 7240 6649; email: orders@africabookcentre.com; web: www.africabookcentre.com)

History and background

Adams, William *Nubia: Corridor to Africa* Princeton University Press 1977. Masterful survey of all things Nubian, from traditional culture to ancient history. Its only problem is that it's too big to put in a rucksack.

Churchill, Winston *The River War* 1899. Some people might be put off by this book's 'Boys' Own' feel, but this history of the Anglo-Egyptian Conquest is a real page-turner and has been in print continuously since publication. Essential reading from someone who was there.

Holt, PM & Daly, MW *A History of the Sudan (Fifth Edition)* Longman, 2000. The most accessible modern history of Sudan, covering the coming of Islam to the rise of the National Islamic Front government. Excellent on the politics but poor on coverage of South Sudan.

Johnson, Douglas *The Root Causes of Sudan's Civil Wars* International African Institute, 2003. A keen untangling of the messy relations between North and South Sudan and a fine history of the civil war since 1955.

Morkot, Robert *The Black Pharaohs: Egypt's Nubian Rulers* Rubicon Press, 2000 The 25th Dynasty of Piye and Taharqa is analysed in this book, one of the best approaches to the ancient Nubian experience in Egypt.

Moorehead, Alan *The Blue Nile* Penguin, 1962. First of two volumes recounting the history of the Nile in the 19th century. It starts with Napoleon's invasion of Egypt, following up with the Turco-Egyptians in Sudan. Great popular history.

Moorehead, Alan *The White Nile* Penguin, 1962. The follow up to The Blue Nile, covering the search for the Nile Source, the Mahdi, Gordon and the Anglo-Egyptian Conquest. Never less than fascinating.

Nicoll, Fergus *Sword of the Prophet* Sutton Publishing, 2004. A modern and well-told account of the rise of the Mahdi and the death of Gordon, with a refreshing emphasis on the Sudanese – rather than British – perspective. Reprinted in paperback as *The Mahdi and the Death of General Gordon*.

Pakenham, Thomas *The Scramble for Africa* Thomas Ball, 1991. Masterly overview of European colonial adventures in Africa during the late 19th century, with Sudan frequently grabbing centre stage. A gripping read and essential for understanding the parcelling up of the continent.

Petterson, Don *Inside Sudan* Westview, 1999. Petterson was US ambassador to Sudan in the 1990s. He gives a blow-by-blow account of relations with the Islamists in government and failed attempts to find peace in the South.

Reader, John *Africa: A Biography of the Continent* Hamish Hamilton, 1997. Possibly the best single-volume history of Africa available, from the geological formation of the continent to the mid-1990s. A chapter on the Nile neatly puts ancient Kush and Egypt into their larger context.

Scroggins, Deborah *Emma's War* Harper Collins 2003. On the surface this book is the tale of the English aid worker who gave everything up to marry SPLA rebel Riek Machar. In the telling, Scroggins gives as neat an account of Sudan and its civil war as you're likely to find anywhere. Highly readable.

Shipman, Pat *The Stolen Woman* Bantam Press, 2004. While many accounts of Victorian exploration are unbearably masculine, this account addresses the balance in the life story of Florence Baker, the equally intrepid wife of Samuel, and their attempts to reach the Nile's source in the mid-1800s. Reprinted in paperback as *To the Heart of the Nile*.

Welsby, Derek *The Kingdom of Kush* British Museum Press, 1996. The best book available on the Napatan and Meroitic kingdoms of Kush, from pyramid-building to encounters with Egypt and Rome. Academic but very accessible.

Welsby, Derek *The Medieval Kingdoms of Nubia* British Museum Press, 2002. Welsby does for Christian Nubia here what he did for Kush before. A huge, essential survey of one of the least known periods of Sudanese history.

Travel writing

Asher, Michael *In Search of the Forty Days Road* Longman, 1984. Fantastic adventure story of one man attempting to follow camel caravans through Kordofan and Darfur in the early 1980s. Sadly out of print and hard to track down but more than worth the effort.

Garland, Alex et al *The Weekenders: Travels in the Heart of Africa* Ebury Press, 2001. A curious collection of writers taken to South Sudan to write a fundraising book for famine relief. Featured writers include *Trainspotting* author Irvine Welsh and the comedian Tony Hawks. A bit of a mixed bag.

Hoagland, Edward *African Calliope* Random House, 1978. Rambling travelogue from the Nimeiri period, mainly covering South Sudan in writing as lush as the surroundings.

Stewart, Stanley, *Old Serpent Nile* Flamingo, 1997. A thoughtful account of a trip up the Nile from the sea to the source in the mid-1980s. Very evocative of Nubia, but

Thesiger, Wilfred *The Life of My Choice* Harper Collins, 1988. Autobiography of the master explorer. Thesiger spent the 1930s working for the Sudan Political Service and produces a wonderfully evocative account of life on camelback in Darfur and by steamer in Upper Nile.

Fiction

Salih, Tayeb *The Season of the Migration to the North* Heinemann, 1969. One of the Arabic world's most important writers, Tayeb Salih writes elegantly simple stories of life along the Nile in northern Sudan. A wonderful taster for anyone planning a trip. Also try *The Wedding of Zein* Heinemann, 1969.

Online resources

www.crisisweb.org Conflict resolution think tank which regularly produces excellent reports on Sudan.

www.darfurinfo.org News and background on the conflict in Darfur.

www.gurtong.com Website of the Gurtong Peace Project, a development and information network run by the Southern Sudanese diaspora.

www.horizonsunlimited.com Motorbike overlanding website, but with an excellent bulletin board useful for anyone taking a vehicle to Sudan.

www.khartoummonitor.com Banned newspaper – if it starts publishing again, read it online.

www.nubamountains.com Excellent website of all things Nuba, from culture to politics.

www.nubasurvival.com Website run by the Nuba advocacy journal *Nuba Vision*

www.nubianet.org Well-designed interactive guide to ancient Nubia.

www.reliefweb.int Good place to keep up with humanitarian developments in Sudan

www.sas.upenn.edu/African_Studies/Country_Specific/Sudan.html African Studies Centre Sudan page, with excellent links to Sudanese resources.

www.splmtoday.com Official website of the SPLM/A.

www.sudan.net General Sudan country portal website.

www.sudanair.com Sudan Airways website.

www.sudan-embassy.co.uk Sudanese embassy in London website.

www.sudanembsassy.org Sudanese embassy in Washington DC website.

www.sudanmfa.com Official website of the Ministry of Foreign Affairs.

www.sudanmirror.com Online newspaper based in Uganda, with a heavy slant on Southern issues.

www.sudantribune.com News website collating Sudanese stories from worldwide media.

www.sunanews.net Website of the government news agency SUNA.

www.sul.stanford.edu/depts/ssrg/africa/sudan.html Stanford University gateway site, with links to further Sudanese websites.

www.unsudanig.org Sudan Information Gateway. Excellent portal site for UN activities in Sudan.

Bradt Travel Guides

Africa Overland	£15.99	Kiev	£7.95
Albania	£13.95	Latvia	£12.95
Amazon	£14.95	Lille	£5.95
Antarctica: A Guide to the Wildlife	£14.95	Lithuania	£13.99
The Arctic: A Guide to Coastal		Ljubljana	£6.99
Wildlife	£14.95	Macedonia	£13.95
Armenia with Nagorno Karabagh	£13.95	Madagascar	£14.95
Azores	£12.95	Madagascar Wildlife	£14.95
Baghdad City Guide	£9.95	Malawi	£12.95
Baltic Capitals: Tallinn, Riga,		Maldives	£12.95
Vilnius, Kaliningrad	£11.95	Mali	£13.95
Bosnia & Herzegovina	£13.95	Mauritius, Rodrigues & Réunion	£12.95
Botswana: Okavango Delta,		Mongolia	£14.95
Chobe, Northern Kalahari	£14.95	Montenegro	£13.99
British Isles: Wildlife of Coastal		Mozambique	£12.95
Waters	£14.95	Namibia	£14.95
Budapest	£7.95	Nigeria	£15.99
Cameroon	£13.95	North Cyprus	£12.95
Canary Islands	£13.95	North Korea	£13.95
Cape Verde Islands	£12.95	Palestine with Jerusalem	£12.95
Cayman Islands	£12.95	Panama	£13.95
Chile	£16.95	Paris, Lille & Brussels: Eurostar Cities	£11.95
Chile & Argentina: Trekking		Peru & Bolivia: Backpacking &	
Guide	£12.95	Trekking	£12.95
China: Yunnan Province	£13.95	Riga	£6.95
Cork	£6.95	River Thames: In the	
Costa Rica	£13.99	Footsteps of the Famous	£10.95
Croatia	£12.95	Rwanda	£13.95
Dubrovnik	£6.95	St Helena, Ascension,	
Eccentric America	£13.95	Tristan da Cunha	£14.95
Eccentric Britain	£13.99	Serbia	£13.99
Eccentric California	£13.99	Seychelles	£14.99
Eccentric Edinburgh	£5.95	Slovenia	£12.99
Eccentric France	£12.95	Southern African Wildlife	£18.95
Eccentric London	£12.95	Spitsbergen	£14.99
Eccentric Oxford	£5.95	Sri Lanka	£12.95
Ecuador: Climbing & Hiking	£13.95	Sudan	£13.95
Eritrea	£12.95	Switzerland: Rail, Road, Lake	£13.99
Estonia	£12.95	Tallinn	£6.95
Ethiopia	£13.95	Tanzania	£14.95
Falkland Islands	£13.95	Tasmania	£12.95
Faroe Islands	£13.95	Tibet	£12.95
Gabon, São Tomé & Príncipe	£13.95	Turkmenistan	£14.99
Galápagos Wildlife	£15.99	Uganda	£13.95
Gambia, The	£12.95	Ukraine	£13.95
Georgia with Armenia	£13.95	USA by Rail	£13.99
Ghana	£13.95	Venezuela	£14.95
Hungary	£14.99	Vilnius	£6.99
Iran	£14.99	Your Child Abroad: A Travel	
Iraq	£14.95	Health Guide	£9.95
Kabul	£9.95	Zambia	£14.95
Kenya	£14.95	Zanzibar	£12.95

WIN £100 CASH!
READER QUESTIONNAIRE

Send in your completed questionnaire for the chance to win £100 cash in our regular draw

All respondents may order a Bradt guide at half the UK retail price – please complete the order form overleaf.

(Entries may be posted or faxed to us, or scanned and emailed.)

We are interested in getting feedback from our readers to help us plan future Bradt guides. Please complete this quick questionnaire and return it to us to enter into our draw.

Have you used any other Bradt guides? If so, which titles? . . . .
. . . .

What other publishers' travel guides do you use regularly? . . . .
. . . .

Where did you buy this guidebook? . . . .

What was the main purpose of your trip to Sudan (or for what other reason did you read our guide)? eg: holiday/business/charity etc. . . . .
. . . .

What other destinations would you like to see covered by a Bradt guide?
. . . .

Would you like to receive our catalogue/newsletters?

YES / NO (If yes, please complete details on reverse)

If yes – by post or email? . . . .

Age (circle relevant category) 16–25   26–45   46–60   60+

Male/Female (delete as appropriate)

Home country . . . .

Please send us any comments about our guide to Sudan or other Bradt Travel Guides. . . . .
. . . .
. . . .
. . . .

Bradt Travel Guides
23 High Street, Chalfont St Peter, Bucks SL9 9QE, UK
Telephone: +44 (0)1753 893444 Fax: +44 (0)1753 892333
Email: info@bradtguides.com
www.bradtguides.com

CLAIM YOUR HALF-PRICE BRADT GUIDE!

Order Form

To order your half-price copy of a Bradt guide, and to enter our prize draw to win £100 (see overleaf), please fill in the order form below, complete the questionnaire overleaf, and send it to Bradt Travel Guides by post, fax or email.

Please send me one copy of the following guide at half the UK retail price

Title	*Retail price*	*Half price*
. . .	. . . .	. . . .	. . . .

Please send the following additional guides at full UK retail price

No	*Title*	*Retail price*	*Total*
. . .	. . . .	. . . .	. . . .
. . .	. . . .	. . . .	. . . .
. . .	. . . .	. . . .	. . . .

Sub total . . . .
Post & packing . . . .
(£1 per book UK; £2 per book Europe; £3 per book rest of world)
Total . . . .

Name . . . .

Address. . . . .

Tel . . . .   Email . . . .

☐ I enclose a cheque for £ . . . . made payable to Bradt Travel Guides Ltd

☐ I would like to pay by credit card. Number: . . . .

   Expiry date: . . . / . . .   3-digit security code (on reverse of card) . . . .

☐ Please add my name to your catalogue mailing list.

Send your order on this form, with the completed questionnaire, to:

Bradt Travel Guides/SUD
23 High Street, Chalfont St Peter, Bucks SL9 9QE
Tel: +44 (0)1753 893444 Fax: +44 (0)1753 892333
Email: info@bradtguides.com
www.bradtguides.com

Index

*Page numbers in bold indicate major entries;
those in italic indicate maps*